# THE *SHOWRUNNERS*

*A SEASON INSIDE*

*THE BILLION-DOLLAR,*

*DEATH-DEFYING,*

*MADCAP WORLD*

*OF TELEVISION'S REAL STARS*

# THE
# SHOWRUNNERS

# DAVID WILD

HarperCollins*Publishers*

HarperCollins books may be purchased for educational, business, or sales
promotional use. For information please write: Special Markets Department,
HarperCollins Publishers, Inc., 10 East 53rd Street, New York, NY 10022.

FIRST EDITION

*Designed by Elliott Beard*

*Text ornament by Ann T. Heilmeier*

ISBN 0-06-019378-6

99 00 01 02 03 04 ❖/HC 10 9 8 7 6 5 4 3 2 1

# CONTENTS

*Photographs follow page 140.*

## ACKNOWLEDGMENTS

During the writing of *The Showrunners*, remarkable news from the St. Petersburg Zoo made both the *Moscow Times* and *USA Today*. According to the reports, a Samsung TV had been installed just outside the cage of a family of orangutans. In a possibly well-meaning attempt to improve the mother and father's parenting skills, videos on the topic were repeatedly played for the previously TV-deprived residents. Unfortunately, this progressive plan backfired when the father, known as Rabu, became so addicted to watching the television—like many partially evolved dads before him—that he started ignoring his wife and his son. As a result, Rabu's TV hours were cut back, no doubt cruelly from the simian point of view of our hairy neophyte tube addict.

In a spirit of post-*glasnost* fellowship, *The Showrunners* is sent off to Russia with love for the all-too-human Rabu and all the TV animals everywhere who have found themselves both charmed and paralyzed by that powerful magic light box in the corner of so many of our individual cages.

This book is dedicated to my own showrunners, Andrew Dylan and Fran, and all in the extended Wild and Turk families, and to our child who's in development as these words are being written.

First and foremost, thanks go to David Hirshey, my mentor/mohel at HarperCollins. I'm also grateful to Michael Soloman, who helped tag-team this beast into submission.

Thanks also to my agent with the mostest—that is, 15 percent—Sarah Lazin, and everybody who helped with research and transcription, including Julie Hall, Dale Hoffer, Leslie Turner, Kris Perera, Lisa San Miguel, and Carlos Peña.

Thanks in perpetuity to Jann Wenner and the entire cast and crew of *Rolling Stone* and most especially to all the showrunners and their staffs who graciously allowed this oversized fly on their walls.

# A SCENE FROM
# THE PRESEASON

He's a pinball wizard.

Of course, Aaron Spelling has one advantage over the rest of us in that nobody else has access to the pinball machine in question. The seventy-four-year-old Spelling—the single most prolific producer in the history of television, with the *Guinness Book of World Records* entry to prove it—is the proud owner of two such personalized machines, both custom-made by order of his wife, Candy, as surprise holiday gifts back in 1994. Sure, a nice tie might have sufficed, but as F. Scott Fitzgerald once suggested, the rich—or at least their gift-giving budgets—*are* different. One of these two-of-a-kind pinball machines can be found at home in Spelling's famously expansive and expensive Holmby Hills estate, regal digs that dwarf even Hugh Hefner's nearby Playboy Mansion and virtually any other private dwelling on planet Earth.

The other pinball machine is here inside Spelling's large, homey office with its multiple couches, its luscious tan shag carpeting, and a uniformed waiter somewhere in attendance. Here in a commercial stretch of Los Angeles known as the Miracle Mile, a casually dressed Spelling is at his desk working the phones on a sizzling early August afternoon, days after he's hit the trades by bringing Luke Perry back to

Fox's *Beverly Hills 90210* and adding Alyssa Milano to the cast of *Charmed*, his new sexy witch-sisters series for the WB, which against all odds finds him reuniting with his onetime *90210* diva Shannen Doherty.

Challenged to play a game of pinball, Spelling rises quickly, puts down his beloved pipe, and turns on the machine without the use of a single quarter—further proof that ownership has its privileges.

*"Happy Hanukkah, honey! I love you, sweetheart. Being married to you is my Emmy."*

The digital voice cooing from the pinball machine's speakers is that of wife Candy Spelling.

*"I love you, Daddy!"*

It's daughter Tori Spelling, twenty-four now and for years Donna Martin—America's most beloved scantily clad virgin—on the Spelling-produced *Beverly Hills 90210*. Donna's still on the show but she lost her famed prime-time cherry in 1997.

*"I love you, Dad,"* adds the deeper voice of Spelling's seventeen-year-old son Randy, whom you might have seen on Spelling's daytime soap *Sunset Beach*, and before that on the short-lived NBC nighttime soap *Malibu Shores*.

Covering the pinball machine are assorted painted images of the Spelling family and assorted TV icons with whom Spelling has been associated, as well as a screen that offers an ever-changing succession of friends and colleagues in bright lights.

Before Spelling puts the first ball into play, still more voices ring out, including his own. The machine offers a tantalizing sound bite from the tycoon's early acting days: Spelling singing—for reasons perhaps best lost to the ages—the *Davy Crockett* theme song in what sounds like some Wild West form of Yiddish.

*"Hey Aaron, you and me and the Hooker,"* William Shatner announces in his familiar, actorly tones.

*"T. J. Hooker,"* Spelling jumps in to explain, referring to the 1982–1987 Spelling-produced eighties CBS cop show starring *Star Trek*'s former Captain Kirk as a hard-nosed sergeant and future *Melrose Place* savior Heather Locklear as his sexy daughter and police trainee.

Other voices come fast and furious. One announces, repeatedly and with considerable passion, *"It's another hit!"* A different female voice asks that timeless Hollywood query, *"Who do I have to screw to get out of this?"* Finally, after one more warm *"Happy Hanukkah, honey"* from Candy, Spelling gets down to business. Sadly, his first ball goes down even faster than *Models Inc.*, a *Melrose Place* spin-off that couldn't outlive the 1994–1995 TV season. Still, Spelling somehow manages to rack up more than 1 million points for his trouble—hey, it's his machine.

"I can do better than *that*," Spelling says softly but emphatically as he hugs the machine's controls tighter. One of the richer men on the planet, Spelling comes across courtly and quietly focused. Such attributes probably served him well growing up as—he recalls—the only Jewish kid in his public school in Dallas. "Till I was thirteen, I thought my name was *Jewbaby*—Jewbaby Spelling," he recalls. "I got my ass kicked *so* much that I had a nervous breakdown when I was like nine years old."

How did Spelling's clan of wandering Jews come to settle deep in the heart of Texas? "You won't believe this story," says Spelling, who knows a thing or two about storytelling and believability. "When my grandfather came over from Russia, they went to Ellis Island and they were talking about, 'Where would you like to go?' Most people went to New York, but the only English word my grandfather knew—*true story*—was 'cowboy.' So they sent him to Texas."

After surviving Dallas and graduating from Southern Methodist University, this Jewish cowboy rode into a kinder, gentler Hollywood in 1954. Appearing in more than fifty TV shows and a dozen movies, the young actor/playwright got his first breaks writing Westerns for early TV shows, like *Dick Powell's Zane Grey Theater*, a CBS anthology show from Spelling's mentor Powell—the onetime movie star who bought Spelling his first suit. Spelling scored his first script sale when he wrote the Wild West–themed "$20 Bride" episode for Jane Wyman's *Fireside Theater* on NBC.

That was more than four decades and a few dozen hits ago, back in a more innocent age when *South Park* was just some land in Colorado. Since then Spelling-produced shows have included *Dynasty,*

*The Colbys, Hart to Hart, Charlie's Angels, Fantasy Island, Starsky and Hutch, The Love Boat, T. J. Hooker, Matt Houston, Vegas, The Mod Squad, The Rookies,* and *Family.* Spelling's early work was done with Dick Powell's Four Star Films; then, after a decade there, Spelling formed a partnership with Danny Thomas, with whom he would bring the world shows including *The Mod Squad*—an influential cool cop show for the rock-and-roll generation.

In TV terms, Spelling owned much of the seventies—forming a partnership with Leonard Goldberg, he would over eight years have a run of shows like *Charlie's Angels, Starsky and Hutch, Fantasy Island,* and *Hart to Hart,* as well as the more acclaimed if lower-rated domestic drama *Family.* During this period, Spelling spread out, producing movies as well, including the comic smash *Mr. Mom;* '*Night, Mother;* and *Soap Dish,* but TV remains his creative playing field of choice.

Spelling's led a singular life in TV—even his first marriage was to Carolyn Jones, most familiar as Morticia Addams on *The Addams Family,* quite arguably the sexiest macabre mom in all tubular history.

All this must have made it all the more painful when, after *Dynasty* ended its eleven-year run in 1988, Spelling was written off as a TV relic. "I remember *Daily Variety* ran a story with a big headline saying 'Spelling's Dynasty Dead' but *Dynasty* wasn't in quotation marks."

Word of Spelling's professional demise was grossly exaggerated. His second coming—or third or fourth, depending on how one counts—kicked off in high school style with the launch of Fox's *Beverly Hills 90210,* which started in October 1990, and spun off the increasingly soapy *Melrose Place* for the same network in 1992. Collaborating with Darren Star—the young creator of both shows—and partner E. Duke Vincent, who concentrates more on matters of physical production and finance ("I hate the business side," Spelling insists), this supposed relic found himself reborn as an unlikely graying king of youth TV during the age of grunge.

Underneath his fatherly—or grandfatherly—manner, Spelling remains a fierce competitor, a man who has trouble getting out of bed for a few mornings after any show gets canceled. Nearly forty years after the first show he ever created and ran—a CBS Western called *Johnny Ringo*—bit the cowboy dust, Spelling is a sixty-minute man who still cares deeply about every ratings duel won and lost. Still standing and fighting, Spelling is one of those who made television what it is today—whatever the hell that may be.

As he prepares for the 1998–1999 season—the last full television season of the twentieth century and one fraught with a record number of real and present dangers—Spelling remains a busy man, with his still steady hand on six network series on the fall schedule: *Beverly Hills 90210*; *Melrose Place*; the spiritually uplifting WB family drama *7th Heaven*; *Charmed;* UPN's relaunching of *Love Boat: The Next Wave;* and ABC's appealingly stylized, Rat-Packy detective show *Buddy Faro.* Furthermore, one of Spelling's vintage shows, *Fantasy Island,* is being remade by film director Barry Sonnenfeld (*Get Shorty, Men in Black*). As his own production studio, Spelling deals with all networks. This season, he's also got *Any Day Now,* an original series for Lifetime, at a time when cable's getting hotter and the networks are going down, at least in the ratings if not for the count.

Spelling's manner may be retiring, but the man is not. Unlike anyone else at his age, he is still very much in the prime-time game he has played so winningly. In a tough town that throws its legends few bones apart from a kindly obit, Spelling is a vital player even if— as one writer who's worked with him observes—his famously prodigious notes can sometimes get "a little dusty." Occasionally he repeats himself, but repeats are important in TV.

"He's a smart man, a guy who is a storyteller, writer, and actor, and he's never forgotten that part of his soul," says one former colleague. "Yes, sometimes he may get a tad cynical. If somebody comes to him and says, 'We'd like a show about sexy nurses,' he'll give it a shot, but Aaron's a hands-on guy in terms of the characters, the storytelling. He *knows* what he's doing."

Within the television industry, the decreasingly select but still small group of men and women entrusted with the daunting and sometimes conflicting responsibilities of running a prime-time series are known as showrunners. They are the transitory gods of the little screen. Of course, Aaron Spelling has been running shows since before many of

today's network executives were born. He's one of the last men standing from the black and white days. He's been on the better-paying side
of the TV screen for virtually the entire time there's *been* TV.

With that sort of experience it can rankle a bit when, as happened
just pre-pinball, a young network executive calls up and second-guesses
Spelling. "Some little *schmuck* at a network who's had a job for *two* minutes is telling me that blue is prettier than green, and an apple tastes
better than an orange," Spelling says, shaking his head in frustration
with this pushy *pisher* who believes he knows better than a guy with
more than 3,500 hours of episodic television under his belt. This is not
to suggest that Spelling knows everything. He tries to treat his assorted
TV collaborators with respect, and he expects the same in return. Certainly that's a reasonable expectation for a man who is now really an
*Über*-showrunner—a man who safely could be called "Mr. Television,"
at least when Milton Berle's not in the room.

Right now Spelling's also a guy fearlessly facing down a pinball
game with his own face on it. When the theme from *The Mod Squad*
comes on during his second ball, his game picks up. Soon he's scored
a hotly sought after Tri-Ball Rerun, which gives him the chance to
try to keep three balls in play simultaneously—a pleasing prospect
for a fellow who's thrived on doing a few things at once. As he plays
the three balls, he still finds time to talk back to the loved ones speaking to him through the machine.

"*I love you, Daddy!*" Tori tells Daddy again with the same dramatic
enthusiasm.

"Thank you, Tori," answers Spelling, keeping his eye on the balls.

"*Hey, Aaron, you and me and the Hooker,*" Shatner declares.

"Oh, shut *up!*" Spelling responds with a mischievous grin. "Put
'im in *one* show and all he does is *talk.*"

"*You're a winner!*" Candy Spelling's voice announces a bit stiffly as
her beloved husband approaches 3 million points.

"Bad reading, Candy," Spelling notes warmly. Perhaps inspired by
all this virtual support, he begins to battle heroically, scoring yet
another Tri-Ball Rerun on the next ball and racking up a final score
of 17 million and change. Spelling has triumphed again.

Ultimately, Spelling succeeds—which is to say he fails less than everybody else—by being the people's choice far more often than the critics' darling, a smart position in a medium as inherently populist as television. He has displayed an innate understanding that audiences don't necessarily want shows with good taste; they want shows that *taste* good.

"If I have any talent at all, it's *knowing* the audience," Spelling explains as he sits back in a favorite chair and lights up his pipe. "It's no secret that I don't fly, so when we travel we either go by car or go by train. And every time we travel by train and people come over for an autograph, I'll go, 'What do you watch?' Invariably, you hear words like 'I just want to *enjoy* it. I just want to *relax*. It's a rough day at the office. I'm worried about my family. I'm worried about my job.'"

Hardly someone forced to be frugal, Spelling even does some free market testing closer to home. "When those tour buses stop in front of my house I go out and talk to them because first of all, they *built* that fuckin' house," he says slowly and meaningfully. "They literally *built* that house and again I'll ask those questions. Invariably they'll say, 'Oh, *90210*,' and they'll name all your shows. And I'll say, 'No, no, no, what *other* shows do you watch? What are you *not* getting?'" He would clearly like to be the one who gives it to them.

One secret of Spelling's success may be almost absurdly simple—in a town full of people seeking to judiciously split the difference between high art and good business, he remains unambivalent about the profitable and in his mind ultimately noble job of simply pleasing those people on the other side of that screen. Sure, he's taken the high road—the groundbreaking AIDS drama *And the Band Played On* or the new *Any Day Now*, which looks at civil rights—but he's chosen his battles carefully and taken the trashier, more mindless path when need be. As befits a man whose home features a private bowling alley, Spelling's unafraid of throwing one straight down the middle—or, if you prefer, more toward the gutter.

Whatever you think about some of Spelling's lesser shows—and thinking may not be the correct verb—he's endured because he viscerally understands he's in what *Network*'s mad TV genius Howard Beale

*DAVID WILD*

called "the boredom-killing business." In a world increasingly shaded in gray, Spelling's happy to kill some boredom with shows that serve up reassuring black and white truths and a generous side order of sex.

"You know, there used to be a very nice word and when you use it now it's a *dirty* word, a beneath-you word, and that's *entertainment*," Spelling says. "Is there anything *wrong* with entertainment? I'll be honest with you, that'll be on my epitaph. It'll say, 'He did *Charlie's Angels*, *Love Boat*, and *Dynasty*, and he's the father of Tori and Randy.' *That's* what I'll be remembered for. They never mention *Family*, they never mention *7th Heaven*—the fact that a Jewish kid from a very religious family is doing a show about a Methodist minister. How about *And the Band Played On*? All about AIDS and the thing I'm most proud of. You can take all the shitty reviews in the world if you can make that."

Just then Spelling's assistant enters and hands the boss a note with a name and a phone line on it—it's Luke Perry returning Spelling's earlier call from the *90210* set.

"I just called to see how you're doing," Spelling tells his homecoming hero, who's returned to the *90210* zip code after leaving during the 1995–1996 season. Since then Perry's tested the film waters and recently had a buzzed-about *Jerry McGuire*–ish pilot about a sports agent that failed to get picked up. Now Perry's agreed to come back to the old neighborhood, convenient timing since the show's other long-standing heartthrob, Jason Priestley, will be leaving midseason and the Fox series is facing off with the WB's younger youth hit *Dawson's Creek*.

"Just read the outline of Episode Eight," Spelling tells Perry. "And I think you're going to *love* it."

The pair spend a few minutes philosophically debating how much Perry's eternally brooding character, Dylan McKay, should reveal of where he'd been and what he'd been doing there when he returns. In discussing Dylan's psyche, it's as if the pair are chatting about an old friend, and considering what Dylan's meant for each of their careers, that's exactly what they *are* doing.

Others in the field may fear darkness, but Aaron Spelling sees enough light ahead to be optimistic about the state of television as the twentieth-first century approaches, even if he doesn't fully comprehend that state. "I don't understand the hierarchy at ABC, for instance—I don't know who's running things," he says. "Who do you call? We have a deal now with ABC and I *still* don't know who to call. I'm glad we have this deal, but if I had a deal to put somebody's show on the air, I think I would call and at least to say, 'How you feeling? Any writers you want to bring in? Any ideas?'" Once ABC was said to stand for Aaron's Broadcast Company. Spelling relates a surprisingly nonmoldy gag apparently once told by Milton Berle—if LBJ *really* wanted to end that war in Vietnam, all he had to do was put it on ABC, then it would *definitely* be over in thirteen weeks.

Spelling's secretary returns with another pressing call—this time it's Viacom chairman Sumner Redstone. Viacom tried to sell its 80 percent stake in Spelling's company a few years back, but potential buyers were put off by a price tag in the rather ritzy $1 billion neighborhood. Rather than share some obvious mogul banter, the two have a brief, warm chat that finds Spelling at one point urging Redstone to "do something for *yourself* for a change." Who knew masters of the entertainment universe spoke to each other so sensitively?

As the tycoons chat, there's time to explore Spelling's office. Behind a framed old *Melrose Place* cast photo across the room, you'll find a 1985 letter from President Ronald Reagan on White House stationery congratulating Spelling for being named Man of the Year by the Beverly Hills Charitable Foundation and B'nai B'rith Lodge. "Just about everybody that watches TV—and that means just about everybody—knows your work," Reagan wrote. "You help America relax and enjoy itself."

Before Spelling gets back to the business of helping America relax, he's asked if he believes he and Reagan have a little something in common, both being Great Communicators and all.

"Leaving politics aside, I've known him all my life," Spelling answers eventually. "He was a good friend of Dick Powell. I also did something called *Burke's Law* and he was the first guest star we put in it—that was back in the black and white days. Nancy was in it too and he's always been *so* nice to me. I feel so bad for what he and

Nancy are going through." Perhaps being polite, Spelling doesn't mention the fact that Jane Wyman—another of his early boosters—was the *first* Mrs. Reagan. "He *was* a great communicator," says Spelling of Reagan. "I don't know enough about politics to say if it was good or bad, but *nobody* could do a speech like him. And hey, he didn't have any interns running around the Oval Office."

Interns in the Oval Office? Now *there's* an idea for a TV series.

# THE *SHOWRUNNERS*

# Pride Goeth Before the Fall

Television is not the truth, television is a goddamn amusement park.

Howard Beale in Paddy Chayefsky's script for *Network*, 1976

*A* half-century into its history, network television has increasingly become a place where pandering, compromise, and failure have become constants, a scary high-profile stratosphere where most TV pilots are doomed to crash and burn. Television has become a world of ridiculous bidding wars, shaky commitments, unending research, and creative magical mystery tours that cost millions of dollars but usually end up going places we've all been before *ad nauseam*. It's a treacherous landscape where once-invincible networks try to slay, or at least slow, a slippery multiheaded monster called cable. It's a field in which much of the "creative community" tries to Xerox whatever worked the previous season. It's a place with a language all its own, where you'll hear all about "arenas," "pilot season," "entities," "ownership issues," "overall deals," "syndication," and, yes, "showrunners."

"Showrunner" is a term primarily used within cozy TV industry circles. For the uninitiated and possibly uncorrupted, showrunners are the TV equivalent of head coaches. They are generally writers/producers—though some do not write—who are perceived by network or production studios as being capable of steering a weekly sitcom or drama. Showrunners can be individuals or come in pairs or even trios. They are charged with supervising the writers' rooms and dealing with the sometimes irrational demands of their casts, as well as those of the networks, the production studios, the agents, and ultimately a fickle and unpredictable viewing public. They come as close to being *auteurs* as one can in television. The buck stops with them, at least until the bucks stop completely.

Showrunners, it could be argued, are the *real* stars of television— the ones whose names you might not know, the ones who don't get overexposed or typecast but who, with a single hit, can be set for life. Who are these people and what on earth do they want? To achieve great art? Enduring fame? The proverbial "fuck you" money? Do they imagine they can hit the unholy trinity? How do these influential individuals live and—in Nielsen terms—die?

Despite the fact that the industry trades *Daily Variety* and the *Hollywood Reporter* seem to proclaim a new multimillion-dollar deal every day, most insiders agree there are very few showrunners who can get the job done consistently, as people like David E. Kelley (*Ally McBeal, Chicago Hope, The Practice*) and the team of Kevin Bright, Marta Kauffman, and David Crane (*Friends, Veronica's Closet*) have managed to do in recent years. The consensus is that there's been a brain drain among TV talent in recent years as some relatively untested—or "unseasoned"—writer/producers are prematurely bumped up to the status of showrunners, many only to fall flat on their wealthy young faces.

Generally, you'll find showrunners listed in the credits as executive producers, though like most words in Hollywood, that title has a multitude of meanings. In truth, the seemingly conflicting, even contradictory responsibilities of the showrunner are enormous. There are different types of showrunners—including writers/creators who get shows started in the first place and more custodial showrunners who come in and keep the franchises going. Showrunners brought in to oversee near-death shows are sometimes referred to as morticians. All these supposed "creative types"—generally up from the rumpled ranks of writers—suddenly find themselves thrust into the position of serving as CEOs of multimillion-dollar corporations that can rise or fall on the basis of a single poorly rated episode.

Being a showrunner in television today means being simultaneously in the catbird seat and the hot seat. Shed no tears for the modern showrunners—they're well paid for their flopsweat. Deals for the top talent in the field have been going through the roof during the nineties even as the network ratings slump. Success is rewarded handsomely and failure pays pretty well too. And why not, since the top showrunners are deities of sorts. It's not for nothing that they are sometimes called Creators.

These people with keys to the cathode-ray kingdom are mainly men and predominantly white. "If I could find a bunch of black female TV writers, I'd be a *very* happy guy," offers one top TV agent. There are many Jews in the field. One network executive of the faith offers this compelling theory to explain why: "Jewish boys at thirteen have a bar mitzvah and learn that if you put on a show, people pay you all sorts of attention and give you *all* kinds of money," he says. "They get the message."

As a rule, showrunners tend to look a little more like the people who watch TV than the pretty people on it, with notable exceptions like David E. Kelley, who is leading-man handsome and married to Michelle Pfeiffer.

Writing for TV is increasingly a young person's game—anyone whose perception of TV writers dates back to *The Dick Van Dyke Show* should understand that few people in fin de siècle writing rooms look much like Morey Amsterdam or Rose Marie anymore. This could be a result of ageism, burnout, or the tendency of some TV types to drop off the face of the known broadcast world into film and other nefarious activities.

During the nineties, showrunners have become fiscal superstars in their own right. One need only look at the *Forbes* annual list of the highest-paid entertainers. The fall 1998 issue's list begins with Jerry Seinfeld at $225 million, with his former showrunning partner Larry David breathing down his neck at $200 million. Others on the list include Mike Judge and Greg Daniels, who created *King of the Hill*, followed closely by Chris Carter of *The X-Files* and *Millennium*; Bonnie and Terry Turner, whose shows include *3rd Rock from the Sun*; the *Friends* team of Bright, Kauffman, and Crane at $40.5 million; and Bruce Helford, the cocreator of *The Drew Carey Show* at $38 million. (This puts Helford—who could walk through any mall in America without causing a riot—a million up on Leonardo DiCaprio, who was forced to make ends meet in 1998 on $37 million.)

Sources intimately familiar with the real numbers earned by top showrunners suggest that some that of these figures are easily misunderstood and in a sense exaggerated. Many of the lucrative "overall deals" consist of not just salary but also guarantees—in essence, advances on future earnings of shows. As the 1998–1999 season gets under way, the low-end salary of showrunners is $1 million a year, and the higher end is $4 to 5 million.

Today's higher-end overall deals are best rationalized as a way of buying exclusivity, of ensuring that in a heat-seeking business the creator of your hit shows doesn't create a franchise for your enemy at a competing network or production studio. Those lower on the food chain must settle for a "show deal"—just getting extremely well paid for the work that they do on a particular show. As the 1998–1999 season gets under way, the price tag for talent below the first tier is beginning to come down. Everybody working does well and has agents to assure he or she will continue to do better and better. It's a cozy atmosphere where your agent might have helped your network boss score his or her job. Few players have any incentive to inject a semblance of fiscal reality into the TV business prematurely. Nobody—and nobody's agent—wants to leave any money on the table. (If they could, nine out of ten agents would negotiate for the table too.)

Showrunners make the money they do because if a television show is intellectual property, it can be property in the best of neighborhoods. NBC is said to have made $500 million in 1997, with a full 40 percent of that total flowing from a single series—*Seinfeld*. Assuming a massively popular show like *Friends* lasts six seasons, it will likely earn something on the order of a billion dollars in its first cycle, with about a third of that potentially flowing to the showrunners.

This is not, however, money for nothing.

Roger Director—a onetime *Moonlighting* showrunner and novel-ist—has served in the trenches and seen the casualties.

"Being a showrunner is like being a bomb disposal expert," he says. "Not only are you keeping this multimillion-dollar venture up and run-ning smoothly, but during the course of every day you're walking through a field of live land mines that Princess Diana wouldn't have visited. Every day there's some kind of overwhelmingly thorny prob-lem holding up shooting. Every day there's some knot in the middle of a script that you're developing that an actor or someone else has decided doesn't work and has to be rewritten by tomorrow. Every day you're dealing with another situation involving casting, scheduling, rearranging postproduction to meet an airdate that is on the face of it next to impossible. There are three of those situations most days in the midst of running a company of a hundred some-odd people, attached to a studio and a network and pleasing *everybody*."

In other words, showrunning's a dangerous job but some lucky bastard's got to do it, even if most bombs end up going off anyway.

At the outset, the 1998–1999 television season promises to be simul-taneously typical and utterly unique. The TV industry is entering a brave, and frankly frightening, new world—one without the ongo-ing reassuring presence of *Seinfeld* but with a spectrum of new threats to the already shaky status quo. The economics of television are changing at a furious pace, with traditional networks trying to beat off the encroaching twin threats of cable and indifference. A new generation of viewers has grown up with little or no sense of what the Big Three networks—ABC, CBS, and NBC—once meant to a relatively passive viewership. Once, most viewers were delighted to have any sort of readily available home entertainment options.

Today, with the addition of Fox, and more recently the WB and UPN, the TV landscape has evolved from the Big Three to the Pretty Big Six.

As the new season gets under way, the very notion of a network is changing. Starting at noon on August 31, 1998, there's the do-gooderish specter of a seventh broadcast network. Lowell "Bud" Paxson—a born-again Christian and creator of the Home Shopping Network—teamed up with chairman and former CBS chief Jeff Sagansky on a mission called Pax TV, a moral safe haven offering up reruns of *Dr. Quinn, Medicine Woman; Diagnosis Murder; Eight Is Enough;* and *Highway to Heaven*, as well as original programming like *Flipper: The New Adventures*.

Putting aside any potential high-minded threat presented by Pax TV, each of the better-known networks has its sundry broadcasting crosses to bear as it enters the 1998–1999 season.

NBC—which has enjoyed a four-season run at the top of the heap—must try to fill the gaping programming hole left by the loss of the somewhat diminished but still eminently must-see–worthy *Seinfeld*, and figure out a way to pay for the rapidly escalating costs of keeping its other long-standing shows on the air, including a record $13-million-per-episode license fee to keep *ER* open.

With the help of its new costly contract with the NFL, CBS will once again challenge NBC and seek to attract a younger and more male audience that has not been brought to the table—or couch—by *Touched by an Angel* or the geriatric thriller *Diagnosis Murder*. Even under the aegis of the respected Les Moonves, this is a tall order for a network on which the fine family show *Everybody Loves Raymond* seems youthful by the theory of relativity.

ABC will attempt to steer its drifting ship in the right direction after years of ratings erosion have seen the network lose 33 percent of its prime-time audience since only 1995, despite a few bright spots like *The Drew Carey Show* and the developing hits *Dharma & Greg* and *Spin City*.

Coming off the surprise smash *Ally McBeal*, Fox is taking the risk of moving its animated hit *King of the Hill* away from the safety of the network's powerful Sunday night lineup, alongside *The X-Files* and *The Simpsons*, and into the Tuesday night network fire. The network must also try to ensure continued life for long-in-the-tooth youth shows like *Beverly Hills 90210* and its more grown-up *Melrose Place*, as well as demonstrate that it can make functional sitcoms with actual, non-animated humans.

Of the more recent upstarts, the WB is seeking to further the advances made first with *Buffy the Vampire Slayer* and one of 1997–1998's pleasant ratings surprises, *Dawson's Creek*. The network's new series *Felicity* is easily the most talked-about 1998–1999 show of the preseason, and the less buzzed-over *Charmed* at least demonstrated the ingenuity to cast former *90210* siren Shannen Doherty as a witch.

On UPN (home to *Moesha*, *Star Trek: Voyager*, and precious little else of note), the most talked-about show is *The Secret Diary of Desmond Pfeiffer*—a strange Hail Mary pass of a sitcom set among the Lincoln White House staff—but the early buzz is not exactly humming.

Another black hole for the networks in 1998 has been the failure of the star system; in the past few seasons, network brass watched in horror as traditional star vehicles publicly flopped with supposedly tested TV talent like Ted Danson (*Ink*), Tony Danza (*The Tony Danza Show*), and Tom Selleck (*The Closer*), demonstrating that you really *can't* go home. Not that one needs big stars to spend big. The troubled UPN is said to have ponied up a record $10 million for a special effects–heavy, two-hour action pilot, *Seven Days*, with no name actors in a effort to create some sort of pulpy new franchise for itself.

As if this competition were not ugly enough, the networks have more than one another to fear. Worryingly, during this month, total cable viewership beat the combined NBC, CBS, ABC, and Fox numbers for the first time ever—though the networks continue to get the bulk of the ad dollars. Cable's current poster children, the minimally animated pack of hard-cussing tykes on Comedy Central's *South Park*, have graduated to a full-blown pop culture phenomenon just as network TV encounters what the *Wall Street Journal* calls "its worst slump in fifty years"—which is to say its entire history.

The simultaneous rise of cable means that whatever battles the networks face will have to be fought on more than seventy different fronts, many with much smaller but more clear-cut constituencies, such as Nickelodeon or the Food Network. Then there are additional high-tech threats like satellite dishes and the Internet. The biggest potential problem for the networks at century's end comes down to this undeniable fact—most of us have now learned how to change the channel. With a simple finger motion, viewers have staged a bloodless coup and taken remote control.

Michael J. Fox—the star and executive producer of ABC's *Spin City*, one of the few star-driven shows to survive in recent years— says that he and his colleagues "try to focus on how well we do our job, because if you think about other things—how every single demographic can conceivably be siphoned off in any half-hour period by the other nets or cable—you can go *nuts*. At any given moment somebody's special interest is being represented elsewhere. I mean, you have the fuckin' Thumbtack Network now!"

All this nay-saying aside, one should not assume the big dogs at the bigger networks are sending their résumés to the Thumbtack Network's personnel department.

"Our business is still the best game in town," CBS president Leslie Moonves says as the fall approaches. "There's nothing else out there that has the reach the networks do, that can promote the big event the way we can."

The Pretty Big Six probably aren't quite ready for embalming fluid just yet. In fact, as the new season begins, the networks demonstrate one fascinating new strategy for survival: No longer are the broadcast networks going to be happy just *showing* us crap. No, now they insist on the privilege of *owning* the crap too.

As costs—including those runaway star and showrunner salaries— have skyrocketed, license fees paid by the networks no longer come close to covering the expenses of producing a series. So syndication has become the enduring payday at the end of the rainbow. Getting there requires that a show somehow stick around long enough to create a sufficient number of episodes—one hundred as a rule.

There are other, less savory solutions. For example, in May 1998, shortly before the death of Phil Hartman, NBC surprised many by renewing his acclaimed series *NewsRadio* despite a less-than-stellar ratings history. Less well-known, but much discussed within the industry, was the fact that NBC demanded, and received, a piece of the ownership action to help the show over its syndication hurdle—a move that sure sounds like a legal but potentially dangerous sort of sitcom shakedown.

In the *Los Angeles Times* in August, Don Ohlmeyer, president of NBC West Coast, summed up the current network atmosphere with refreshing candor: "We would all take a hit from Attila the Hun."

All this worries someone like Tony Jonas, president of Warner Bros. Television, who calls it "very inappropriate for networks—by way of pressure or force—to insist on a coproduction to have a show even get on the air. 'Shakedown' is probably too strong a word, but they should not have the right to insist on ownership just to provide real estate on the airwaves."

As in any other sort of real estate, everything in TV comes down to location, location, location.

For the purposes of perspective, look back at the shows that premiered in the fall of the 1995–1996 season. Here are the not-so-dear-departed TV prime-time series that someone in a position of power figured had potential to still be around today, when they could be about to take their rightful or wrongful place in the syndication winners' circle:

*Dweebs, Almost Perfect, Space: Above And Beyond, Cleghorn!, Too Something, Misery Loves Company, The Client, Minor Adjustments, First Time Out, Pinky & The Brain, Ned & Stacey, Partners, Nowhere Man, Live Shot, Courthouse, New York News, Bonnie Hunt, The Monroes, The Jeff Foxworthy Show, Maybe This Time, Can't Hurry Love, Simon, Kirk, Charlie Grace, Hudson Street, The Naked Truth, The Pursuit of Happiness, Murder One, The Preston Episodes, Deadly Games, Central Park West, The Single Guy, The Crew, American Gothic, Home Court, Bless This House,* and *Strange Luck.*

Here, then, are all the new fall shows from the 1995–1996 season that have survived to make the 1998–1999 fall schedule: *The Drew Carey Show, JAG,* and *Caroline in the City.*

*DAVID WILD*

Fall schedules bring to mind old war movies when the troops heading off to battle are told, "Look at the man to your left. Now look at the man to your right. One of you won't be coming back alive." In TV, however, it's more likely there will be two or possibly three casualties.

Change is arguably the only constant in TV; it is what executives can generate to create the useful illusion that they actually know what they're doing. The writer William Goldman once noted of the film industry that "nobody knows anything." The same applies to the smaller screen except there are more nobodies.

The season's earliest casualty was Fox's *Hollyweird*, which sought to pair *Scream* director Wes Craven with onetime Hardy Boy Shaun Cassidy, who in more recent years established himself as an up-and-coming showrunner with the stylish if short-lived *American Gothic*. By mid-August, it was dropped from the fall lineup.

During the off-season, the general view of TV pundits was that 1998–1999 would be a season of discontent. One man in a position to take in the big picture—*TV Guide* editor-in-chief Steve Reddicliffe—emerged with a sunnier point of view.

"I think the buzz—and it started in midsummer—is that this was going to be a *dreadful* TV season ahead, especially in terms of new shows," Reddicliffe says in August. "That seems to be the chant, but I think that perception is wrong. There may not be a breakout show like an *Ally McBeal* or a *South Park* or a *Dawson's Creek* in this particular bunch, but what there is in many cases is very well made, very well cast, and fairly delightful."

For Reddicliffe, the rise of *South Park* isn't so much the first sign of the death of the networks as it is "yet another sign that the playing field is more level than it's ever been. I also think it's another indication that things are going to change quickly now. We're in an era in the TV business where it's going to seem like you're on a Tilt-a-Whirl."

Prepare to feel nauseated and jump on.

*Friends*—NBC's wildly popular and highly accomplished Thursday night fixture—is an exception to most TV rules, not least of all because it is good.

Like *Veronica's Closet*, with which it shares Thursday nights, *Friends* comes from the showrunning team of Kevin Bright, Marta Kauffman, and David Crane. Having two separate shows in NBC's Thursday night lineup was a remarkable feat for the trio. For the 1998–1999 season they're going for three. The addition is *Jesse*—a new sitcom created by former *Friends* scribe Ira Ungerleider and starring former *Married with Children* star Christina Applegate as a single mom in Buffalo. The considerable clout of Bright Kauffman Crane helped land *Jesse* in a cozy eight-thirty hammock between *Friends* and *Frasier*.

Such a workload necessitates getting an early start, and so while some showrunners are still clinging desperately to the last seconds of summer hiatus, Kevin Bright spent last night with his two partners, Marta Kauffman and David Crane, filming their first postpilot episode of *Jesse* until three in the morning.

"It's funny, when we finished last night I said to Marta and David, 'Well, the great news is one down, sixty-seven to go.'" Bright recalls. "It sort of hit us all. *Sixty-seven shows!* It is daunting but it's also our source of pleasure as long as we can have a life to go with it."

"It's sort of like what I assume people feel like before they climb a mountain—before you even start you're exhausted just looking at it," Kauffman explains later.

When the 1998–1999 NBC schedule was announced in New York back in May, pleasure wasn't the first reaction for Kauffman. As Bright recalls, "The place she went to immediately was the terror of 'How are we going to do *three* shows?' I said what we really should be thinking about right now while we can is that we've accomplished something incredible, something that as far as I know of has never been accomplished before—one production company having three shows on the biggest night of network television at one time. This is what we set out to do as a company. This is what we dreamed about."

The Bright Kauffman Crane dream might be an impossible one if there weren't three of them to make it all come true.

"The reason we work so well as a partnership is we bring different skills to it," Bright says of their power trio. "We don't come to being showrunners from the same place." Bright's background was more in the area of production, direction, and business, while Kauffman and Crane got their start as writers. "There are things they don't want to be bothered with and there are things that I don't want to be involved in," Bright says. "So we all fill the gaps for one another."

On this clear August day, Bright's up in Bright Kauffman Crane's deluxe Burbank office, which literally looks down on the Warner Bros. Studios lot, home of the company they're helping make very, *very* rich. *Friends* and *Veronica's Closet* shoot on two of the soundstages below, while the *Jesse* stage is just a short walk away. Back when *Friends* started in 1994, their offices were housed in a modest space on the Warner Bros. lot. Now they're veritable TV overlords with the killer view to match.

The son of vaudeville comedian Jackie Bright, Kevin Bright has turned his own office space into an impressive if slightly frightening pop culture museum. There are bottles of Dan Haggerty Cajun Barbecue Sauce, James Darren's Mama's Favorite Pasta Sauce, and Muhammad Ali's Scruff Champ Black shoe polish. There are also dolls of Debbie Boone, Andy Gibb, Brooke Shields (autographed during the *Friends* guest spot that helped her get *Suddenly Susan*), and Vanna White, as well as the Captain and Tenille, and both Parker Stevenson and Shaun Cassidy—the last of whom has made that rare transition from action figure to showrunner.

Now with *Friends*, Bright and his partners find themselves at ground zero of a genuine pop culture phenomenon, though one shockingly without the requisite dolls. "There were *Friends* dolls for about five minutes," Bright explains, "but the cast wasn't comfortable with it."

Bright first partnered with Marta Kauffman and David Crane on *Dream On*, an acclaimed HBO comedy starring Brian Benben that ran from 1990 to 1996. That show became known for its inventive use of old TV and film clips, its sly look at adult romantic and professional misbehavior, and an occasional glimpse of the female breast.

Kauffman and Crane were already close friends, having met during their student days at Brandeis. "We were in a play together," Crane explains. "It was my freshman year, Marta's sophomore year. I barely knew her—we were in this play with a huge cast. It was Tennessee Williams's *Camino Real*—I played a street urchin and she was a whore."

"Revealing, isn't it?" adds Kauffman, who reports that Crane was a particularly adorable urchin. And what sort of whore was she? "I was *great*," she recalls with a laugh. "I was cheap."

After college, the pair started to make their names in the New York theater world with contributions to the off-Broadway musicals *A . . . My Name Is Alice* and their successful show *Personals*.

Kauffman and Crane had come out to Los Angeles in 1989 and were working for Norman Lear when they got a call saying a pilot they'd written was actually being shot. "Up to that point we thought, 'Oh, you write pilots but nobody ever makes them,'" Crane remembers. "In the course of that, we met Kevin. I don't know that it was instant chemistry as much as he seemed like a nice guy and he really seemed to know what he was doing. That was enough for us."

Bright graduated from Boston's Emerson College—something of a comedy hotbed—in 1976 and soon went to work producing variety shows for the likes of George Burns, Johnny Cash, and David Copperfield, whom he failed to make disappear. His rise to showrunning found him serving as a supervising producer of the Fox sketch show *In Living Color* and executive producer of *The Ron Reagan Show*.

*Dream On*—briefly rerun in a nipple-free form by Fox in 1995—was enough of a critical success to create significant network interest in the Bright Kauffman Crane team. Still, a 1992–1993 series they did with Norman Lear called *The Powers That Be* ran only one season on NBC despite a gifted supporting cast that included future TV stars Peter MacNichol (*Ally McBeal*) and David Hyde Pierce (*Frasier*). Their

*DAVID WILD*

1993 domestic comedy *Family Album* proved to be even less memorable, closing after just six episodes on CBS.

Having explored early mid-life crisis on *Dream On*, the trio next set out to mine the comedic possibilities of an even earlier, less tied-down time in life. Beginning in the fall of 1994, *Friends* gave them their shot. It also gave them one hell of a time slot—eight-thirty on NBC's Thursday night lineup, sandwiched safely between *Mad About You* and *Seinfeld*.

Bright, Kauffman, and Crane were by no means confident they'd created must-see TV. "We didn't know *Friends* would be a hit—we had no idea," Bright admits. "If anything, the vibe we got from the press and the marketplace was, 'Do you think people are going to want to tune in to see these six slackers sitting around in their apartment from week to week? Who *cares* about these people?" Then there were the concerns from the network like, 'I don't know if people in middle America will relate to a coffeehouse' and 'What's in it for the older audience?' NBC was pushing for the cop on the beat or the postman who comes into the coffeehouse and sort of gives sage advice to the friends." (This someone-for-everyone network mind-set may finally explain Ernest Borgnine's strangely omnipresent doorman on NBC's *The Single Guy*.)

Most hit shows build gradually. There was nothing gradual about the rise of *Friends*, and the showrunning trio found themselves with a runaway hit. Perhaps as an inevitable result, show business physics kicked in—for every cultural action there must be an opposite and equal reaction. The media would play a schizophrenic trick with *Friends*. Because the cast—Courteney Cox, Jennifer Aniston, Lisa Kudrow, David Schwimmer, Matthew Perry, and Matt LeBlanc— were uniformly photogenic, they were exposed on virtually every magazine cover. Almost simultaneously, the same media started taking the show to task for being overexposed.

"In the beginning it was like getting involved in a new relationship, especially with the media," recalls Bright. "You *really* like this person. They're fresh, they're exciting—God, the relationship is great, the sex is hot, and you're really enjoying yourself. Then all of a sudden you start seeing each other a *lot*, maybe you move in. Then the nature of the relationship changes. It feels like, '*Enough* of that. Now I need something new and fresh in my life.' We felt like the jilted lover. Everybody was heaping on the praise, and seemingly wanting more. Then all of a sudden it was, 'You know what? You went one step too far.' That one step seemed to be the Diet Coke commercial the cast did."

Even though Bright Kauffman Crane were hardly TV neophytes, this was new territory. "I think we were inexperienced in terms of handling something like this," he admits. "Unless you've done it, you're *not* prepared for it. So when Warner Bros. was coming to us saying, 'Hey, we've got this idea, a *Friends* cookbook!' You think, this is all good." A reasonable sentiment from an otherwise sane fellow whose office features not one but two Sweathog figurines.

The *Friends* camp was soon to find otherwise. There was a veritable flood of *Friends*, a poppy wave of *Titanic* proportions. The *Friends* theme, "I'll Be There for You" by The Rembrandts, became a radio and video fixture, and the song was also featured on a successful *Friends* soundtrack album. There were mugs, T-shirts, and books.

So it was that *Friends* was for a time nearly swamped by its own massive popularity. "I think it affected us because, even between the actors and us, it was overwhelming," Bright admits. "There's that point where you start believing your own press and you think it's always going to be great. What we learned is you have to rise to another level. I think the second season was everyone kind of getting over what happened in the first."

The cast pushed hard to profit more from their rapidly recognized work. Tensions were high in the summer of 1996 when the cast's demands for $100,000 a week became a topic of mainstream discussion. "We've always had a good relationship with this cast," Bright says. "It's never been them and us, it's been all of us. But there came that point where it became *such* a phenomenon that the cast felt like their share of credit for making that phenomenon happen wasn't compensated properly in their salaries. They looked around the TV landscape and saw what other people made."

Reluctantly Bright confesses, "There was a family squabble. It wasn't like anyone really started it. It's one of those things like someone getting pissed off that the wedding gift wasn't as much as it should have been. You don't know what you did wrong and they think you're the one to be mad at. It was very tense at the beginning of that second season. But once all that contract stuff was settled what we realized was that it was about the success and the sort of poison it pours into the mix. And when that poison becomes public, then it just takes off from there and you can't stop it."

Eventually, it did stop, and by the last season, Bright says, "*everything* was clicking."

The goal for *Friends* during the 1998–1999 season, Bright explains, is to reinvigorate the audience and make good on what was flirted with in the last episode of the past season—the Chandler-Monica relationship that will be played out by Matthew Perry and Courteney Cox. "I think it's going to be a great asset," he says. "I think people have been wanting to see somebody else get together besides Ross (David Schwimmer) and Rachel (Jennifer Aniston). Now it's finally happening."

If the goal of *Friends* is maintaining the show's considerable heat, *Veronica's Closet*—which stars Kirstie Alley as a Victoria's Secret–like catalog queen—has more pressing work to be done in its sophomore season. "With *Veronica* the goal is to make the show stand on its own," Bright says. "We're not idiots and nobody has to tell us that we benefited greatly from the time slot we were in last year. Unlike *Friends*, *Veronica* didn't jell together in as organic a way." Having spent too much time early on dealing with Veronica's relationship with her philandering ex-husband, the show will now focus more on what it's increasingly becoming—a workplace ensemble show, with Ron Silver added to the cast.

NBC has been up front about wanting an upgrade for *Veronica's Closet*. All parties agree on what *does* work about the show. "I think the network *really* believes in Kirstie, and if anything has broken out from the show it's the audience's love affair with her," says Bright. "It's hard because you look at *Friends* or *Frasier*—those are exceptions, *very* few shows come out of the gate in a first season and create impact. *Cheers* didn't do it, *Seinfeld* didn't do it. I think if we weren't in that spot maybe there wouldn't have been so much criticism. Also, it was a great pilot but where we went from there was tough to follow. We started to get a handle on it halfway through last season and I really look forward to this season."

For *Jesse*—as for any new show—the agenda is first survival. In renewing *Friends*, NBC had guaranteed that any sitcom Bright Kauffman Crane developed for it next would get either a Tuesday or a Thursday slot, and in the end *Jesse* beat out the Nathan Lane sitcom *Encore! Encore!* for the prime Thursday slot.

"The goal for *Jesse* is to get a show off on the right foot," Bright says. "While the audience loves Christina Applegate from her work on *Married with Children*, I think the audience sees her in a certain light. They may think, 'Okay, it's *The Kelly Bundy Show*.'" Bright Kauffman Crane are hoping what's going to hook people into *Jesse* is the realization of how good a comedic actress Applegate is. "Then you try to put together the best writing, the best production, the best actors, and hope that it all clicks," Bright explains. "With any new show it's a learning experience as you go. You look at your pilot and see where it really works—that's where you want to go to for stories," says Bright. "You also have to keep an open mind."

That means listening to network and studio notes—even though some showrunners might secretly prefer it if the only notes they received were the ones saying, "Thank you."

"You can't fight the criticism and think that you're right," Bright says. "That's not to say that sometimes they're not wrong. You have to listen and extract."

In television, as in other fields of human endeavor, ideas are like assholes: Everyone has one. Yet even assholes can have a good ideas.

Good ideas—and a consistent ability to bring them to small-screen fruition—have made Bright Kauffman Crane fantastically rich. So too are showrunners who *didn't* create *Friends*. Bright sees the rash of seemingly outrageous deals with relatively unproven talent as part of "a bit of panic" from the studios and networks that has taken hold over the past five years.

"It's almost like defensive chess," Bright explains. "The strategy becomes not so much '*I'm* in love with that guy,' but 'I don't want *them* to have him in case they get a hit,' What that mentality has done for the marketplace is *everybody*'s a multimillion-dollar player regardless of experience. There are people who've never run shows before getting those kind of deals. It may feel like we were an overnight sensation, but the fact of the matter is in different ways we'd all been plugging at it for twenty-odd years before we hit *Friends*. So, yeah, you have a little bit of resentment where you feel like you've paid your dues and earned something. Then you look across the way and you see someone being rewarded for *failing*, and failing upward."

At this moment in television history you'd think Bright Kauffman Crane could get a Kato Kaelin vehicle on some network's schedule were they so inclined, but even for them things aren't ever that simple. This pilot season, the trio had an untitled show idea they believed in created by Alexa Junge, one of the writers from *Friends*. "We pitched it at every network in town and every network was not interested. They didn't like the content."

What content would that be?

"It involved a sexually active gay man, a woman who was HIV positive, another woman who's white with a black son through arti-ficial insemination," Bright explains matter-of-factly. "The idea was a bunch of social outcasts all sort of grouped together, and the goal was to make them like everyone else." Bright remembers ABC was *very* interested in the show, but wondered: Does she *have* to be HIV, do you *have* to get into that? Can't he be *kinduva* a gay guy?

Bright, Kauffman, and Crane—who are straight, straight, and gay, respectively—have already pushed programming boundaries a bit with *Dream On* and now with *Friends*, particularly by making Ross's first wife's homosexuality a prime-time reality and not merely the subject of the occasional sitcom snicker. Some boundaries remain, however, and this season the hardest-working trio in show business will have to be content merely with the small job of over-seeing three different shows on what has been—at least until now—America's night of television.

One's straight. One's gay. Together they're the best of friends . . . and funny as hell!

Yes, it sounds like a sitcom, but in fact, the above situation is also true of David Kohan, thirty-four, and Max Mutchnick, thirty-two, the very real showrunners who created *Will & Grace*, NBC's new sitcom with a mildly controversial twist. Think *When Harry Met Sally* with a Harry who might be more interested in Barry. Sitting inside their shared office in Bungalow 8 at CBS Radford Studios in Studio City—yards away from Gunsmoke Avenue and just a short golf cart trip from Gilligan's Island Way—Kohan and Mutchnick are already hard at work on their yet-to-air show.

This pair of former Beverly Hills High buddies had worked as a writing team on *The Dennis Miller Show, Dream On, Hearts Afire,* and *The Single Guy* before becoming showrunners for the first time in 1995 with the NBC sitcom *Boston Common.* They are both Hollywood kids, hyperverbal, sophisticated, and ambitious. Kohan's father is famed television writer "Buzz" Kohan, perhaps best-known for his work on *The Carol Burnett Show;* his mother, Rhea Kohan, is a novelist. Mutchnick grew up hanging around the Paramount lot, where his mom worked as a marketing executive; his late father was a graphic designer.

TV writing seemed accessible. "I'd liken it to all these lawyers' kids becoming lawyers," says Kohan. "There's a comfort factor we have," Mutchnick adds.

After graduating from college in 1986—Mutchnick from Emerson College, Kohan from the less hilarious Wesleyan—they teamed up as writing partners. Like any good sitcom characters worth their comic salt, these glib fellows banter amusingly, often completing each other's sentences.

Discussing how they went from being writers to being showrunners, Mutchnick jumps in first: "That was a very unique thing to happen. We were coproducers on *The Single Guy* . . . "

"*That's* off the record!" Kohan adds.

"*I* wanted to make that joke," Mutchnick screams, ironically playing the straight man.

In truth the pair knew Anthony Clark—a standup comic who'd become a hot property—and expressed an interest in writing a pilot for him. Castle Rock executive Glenn Padnick, who'd been trying to find writers to match with Clark's sensibility, let the youthful pair take a shot.

In between their *Single Guy* labors, the partners began to put together a pilot, and, Mutchnick says, "Things started to snowball. All of a sudden they realized, 'Hey, these guys are like twelve and thirteen years old,' and that we both had to be bar mitzvahed before they'd let us run our own show. We were over in an office with Jamie Tarses—then an executive at NBC—saying, 'Just give us an opportunity to do this. If we fuck it up, take it away from us. If we can make it through the pilot without any bumps in the road, I think it's fair to say that we can run a series.' Which it's *not*. It was *ridiculous* to ask to run a series at that point, but we pretended to know what we were doing."

Only thirty and twenty-eight respectively at the time, Kohan and Mutchnick soon learned that showrunning requires much more than writing.

"It's two jobs—*completely*," says Mutchnick. "The first half of the day is spent running a large business with 125 people coming in and out of the machine. It's everything from the floor to the network to office managing—dealing with bullshit squabbles in the office."

"We *cook* for these people," Kohan adds in mock outrage.

That's the first job. Then as much—if not more—time has to be spent writing these scripts. Unlike some showrunning partners who divide and conquer, Kohan and Mutchnick tend to do almost everything together.

"We both do both," says Kohan. "We're not good at being apart from one another."

"We do everything together," Mutchnick explains with a grin. "*Almost*."

Eric McCormack—who plays *Will & Grace*'s Will—confirms this. "They really do everything together," he says. "In fact they even dress alike, which gets *really* annoying."

"I think they probably *are* Will and Grace more than they even realize," says McCormack. "I try to think if I were a writing partner with my oldest friend and with him every day, our friendship would have fallen apart years ago. There are days when Max comes in and says, 'My writing partner isn't talking to me.' They must have it out the way Will and Grace do in every episode because it's pretty intense to be together as much as they are."

Whoever it's based on, *Will & Grace* has much going for it: strong writing, a winning cast, the involvement of arguably the most accomplished sitcom director working, James Burrows—a multi-Emmy winner known for his work on shows like *Taxi*, *Cheers*, and *Frasier*—and a little built-in gender-bending controversy. More problematically, *Will & Grace* also has a Monday night time slot that pits it against ABC's *Monday Night Football* and Fox's *Ally McBeal*, a difficult show/phenomenon for any new series to go up against.

"We're going after the football people," says Mutchnick of their strategy. "We think the people who are watching football have the homoerotic instinct anyway. We just put a line in a script about Ally. It's an episode about how Will and Grace have these two bathrooms side by side. Grace wants to break down the wall and have a communal bathroom, and she's like, 'I think it will be very elegant, very sort of ahead of the curve, very *Ally McBeal*.' And Will says, 'Grace, she's a fictional character, we're *real*.'"

A few weeks later, on the *Will & Grace* soundstage on the CBS Radford Studios lot, that episode is being filmed. The *Ally McBeal* line is gone, but "The Head Case" offers bathroom humor of a high level. The studio audience seems locked into the story of Will and Grace—a credit to the two young men huddled together, wearing their grown-up suits and looking like they're very much ready for their prime-time bar mitzvah.

As a new season begins, a lot of series are under pressure, but no other show on the 1998–1999 schedule bears quite the heartbreaking burden of *NewsRadio*, the often brilliant ensemble comedy created by Paul Simms, the Harvard-educated *Wunderkind* who moved from that school's famed *Lampoon* to magazine work to David Letterman's writing staff to *Larry Sanders* to running his own sitcom.

While never a substantial commercial hit, *NewsRadio* had made its own wise-ass mark and somehow survived since premiering in March 1995. Then in May 1998, shortly after NBC surprised many by renewing the sitcom, Phil Hartman was murdered by his wife, Bryn, who then took her own life, a tragedy that would become tabloid fodder for months to come. In early July, word came that Hartman's old friend and fellow former *Saturday Night Live* star Jon Lovitz would join the *NewsRadio* cast. Still, there was the difficult matter of how a sitcom could deal with the gaping hole left by the absence of Hartman, an issue that had to be addressed before the show could move on to any sort of future. How *NewsRadio* would pull off this painful feat remained a mystery, with Simms maintaining a dignified silence.

Simms is not generally known for biting his tongue. In fact, Simms made a splash in April 1997 with his comments in a *Rolling Stone* interview we did during which he referred to NBC executives he felt were killing his show as "cocksuckers" and tastefully described the network's supposedly must-see Thursday night schedule as "a big double-decker shit sandwich." In the happy-talk world of network TV, Simms's words were considered so controversial that they became a topic of other articles—including a piece in the *New York Times* that, ironically, credited his verbal assault with helping save the show from cancellation. The interview even inspired an episode of *NewsRadio* in which the station's news director Dave Nelson (Dave Foley) has to apologize to virtually everybody he knows for attacking them in an article.

It is a slightly older, more restrained Simms sitting, playing his beloved Fender Bass in his dark office at Renmar Studios, a small Hollywood production facility now home to both *NewsRadio* and *OverSeas*, a new midseason series Simms is developing for NBC. The man in charge of this eccentric empire sits behind a Taco Bell–littered desk, the top of which is a huge slab of unfinished wood that he repeatedly pokes at with a pocket knife. On a nearby bookshelf *Les Misérables* is stacked next to *Howard Stern A–Z*, Erasmus's *Praise of Folly* next to an Allman Brothers songbook. To hear associates tell it, it's remarkable to see Simms at all while the sun is out, since his vaguely vampire-ish late night schedule—prime writing time eleven P.M. to *whenever*—is fairly legendary among sitcom writers.

*NewsRadio* started as Simms's comic examination of the workplaces he has toiled in; *OverSeas*—about young people working for a Peace Corps–like group—has its roots in Simms's earlier life. His parents were schoolteachers, and when he was three they moved to Pakistan, where they taught at the American school for four years. When he was seven the family moved to Saudi Arabia, where the Simmses taught the children of oil company executives.

After ninth grade, Simms was sent to prep school in the somewhat less repressed city of Santa Barbara, California. Still, he wasn't your typical all-American TV child weaned on the electronic teat.

"In Pakistan, there was virtually *no* television," Simms remembers. "In Saudi Arabia, there was a little bit more. The oil companies sort of had one TV station and it was only on from like four in the afternoon till eleven at night and they'd show old movies they bought or old TV shows. I remember we were excited when we got *Happy Days* three or four years after it had been big. No movies either, really—there was one theater with old movies that were chopped up and edited to take out anything that would offend the Islamic sensibility."

At prep school, Simms caught the bug for at least one particular TV show and borrowed a miniature television set from a friend to watch David Letterman secretly in his dorm room. At college, he wrote for *The Harvard Lampoon,* which was already becoming a veritable farm team for the best and brightest on their way to the sitcom big leagues. From Simms's small *Lampoon* class came Conan O'Brien; Bill Oakey and Josh Weinstein, who would run *The Simpsons*; David X. Cohen, another *Simpsons* veteran who's creating Fox's 1998–1999 midseason replacement *Futurama* with *Simpsons* creator Matt Groening; and Michael Borkow, who's worked at *Friends* with Bright Kauffman Crane.

Simms graduated in 1988 and worked for a year and a half at *Spy*, the satirical magazine that took on cultural targets large and small, and usually left them a tad smaller. He liked the job and assumed, correctly, that he had to try journalism first because, he says, "I would never go from TV money back to journalism money. There's no going back." Having experienced journalism in all its low-paying glory, Simms made the leap to writing for *Late Night* in 1990, toward the end of Letterman's tenure at NBC.

"It was a dream job having watched that show and having a job I thought was *so* far beyond anything I could ever achieve in my life," Simms says. "There are people in this field whose parents were in the business. I'd never even known anybody who wrote for television. TV was something created by remarkable people in some far-off place. The only downside was after a year and a half there I did sort of feel like I was doing the same thing over and over again and I wanted to try something new."

"Something new" for Simms meant working for a sitcom, but the only two shows he wanted to write for were *The Simpsons* and *Seinfeld*. Simms's contacts at *The Simpsons* said they had an opening and he should send his stuff. "I was *so* excited but they didn't hire me," Simms recalls. "They hired a young man by the name of Conan O'Brien instead. Where did *he* ever end up?"

In the early nineties, *Seinfeld*, though not yet the powerhouse it would become, was already a highly desirable gig. "Everybody's saying nobody gets hired at *Seinfeld*," Simms says. "You had to know [series cocreator] Larry [David] or Jerry," Simms recalls. "I sorta knew Jerry from a *Spy* TV show he hosted so I finally called him and told him I wanted to work for him. He asked if I had a sample script. I said, 'Yeah, I'm almost finished with it. I should have it in two weeks.' Then I sat

down and started to write it." Simms got positive feedback from Seinfeld but it was the end of the season and it wasn't clear if *Seinfeld* had a
future. (It did.)

Simms's agent sent him a stack of pilot scripts. He was unim-
pressed: "I *hated* them—they were all crap, except I was a big fan of *It's
Garry Shandling's Show* and I really liked the pilot for *Larry Sanders*. So
I asked my agent to send the *Seinfeld* script over there, wrote up some
story ideas, and we talked on the phone. Garry offered me the job. I
was kind of torn because I sort of wanted to wait and see what happened with *Seinfeld* but it was also exciting to go to a show that was just
starting, which I could have some role in shaping."

Simms rose quickly by what he makes sound like a process of
comic elimination.

"Garry had written the pilot with Dennis Klein, and then he fired
Dennis," Simms remembers. "By the time I got there he was on its
second showrunner, Fred Barron. Fred was there during the preproduction when we were writing the first scripts and then—I believe
the second day of shooting—Fred was gone. Then it was two guys,
Dick Blasucci and Howard Gewirtz, who sorta saw it through the
rest of that season. Then Chris Thompson was at the beginning of
the second season and then on the first day of shooting Chris
Thompson was gone. That's when I started moving into the role—
maybe halfway through the second season. I don't know—you can
look at the court papers and see what's in Garry's deposition."

The deposition in question involves an ugly flurry of suits involving
Shandling and longtime manager Brad Grey. Back in January, Shandling officially alleged a conflict of interest by which Grey used his
position as Shandling's manager to make TV deals that benefited Grey
but not Shandling. As a result, Shandling sought 50 percent of the prof-
its of Brillstein-Grey Entertainment (which produces, among other
shows, *NewsRadio*), or $100 million, fighting words in a town where
"producing" and "managing" have become strangely synonymous.
Grey responded in March with a $10 million countersuit accusing
Shandling of behavior that cost their partnership financially.

Simms finally left *Larry Sanders*, under "*very* unfavorable circumstances. I don't want to talk about that—it's all going to be in the court case."

Whatever the court decides, Simms was happy to leave behind the backstage drama at the acclaimed backstage comedy. "By my third year there I'd had enough," says Simms. "I'd said I would stick it out through the end of the third season. Halfway through the third season, I quit and then Garry persuaded me to come back and I did and then I got to the end of the season and I wanted out."

Not that Simms isn't proud to have worked on *Larry Sanders*. "I'm *really* proud but I do have to say after the third season there it started occurring to me that I wanted to do something that my parents would understand—a show that would not *only* make my friends laugh."

Simms started to ponder what he'd do with a series of his own. "It started abstractly," he says. "I wanted to do something not revolutionary but different than what was on TV then. Everyone was ripping off *Seinfeld* or *Friends*. For the last six years I've been working my ass off, sleeping at the office. I wanted to do a show about your life at the office. The very last thing I thought of was that it was a radio station. I realized I wanted a big open space 'cause I always liked that on *Taxi*. I didn't want it to be a behind-the-scenes look at anything—I wanted it to be *any* office."

The ultra-clever *NewsRadio* connected with critics from the start, but had a harder time in the ratings, dwelling in a sort of network purgatory. "It's been a huge struggle," says Simms. "It was not a huge struggle to get this show on the air, but subsequently NBC overestimated how established the show was and that's when they started moving it around. This show has *always* been on the borderline. Every time they announced a new schedule it's been down to the last minute."

Many were surprised to see *NewsRadio* make NBC's 1998–1999 schedule, including Simms. Headstrong but far from foolish, Simms is playing the odds. He still recalls hearing from the network it was "99 percent sure" that *NewsRadio* would be a Thursday night show, but as Brad Grey has told him, "It's always the other one percent that gets you."

As if there wasn't enough trouble in TV land, Simms suggests that even syndication is no longer the fiscal nirvana it once was. "That's changing because there are so many more channels, but there are also so many more sitcoms now. You make your money back, and you make a good amount of money, but it's not the huge jackpot payoff it used to be. That's going to affect the business. It used to be production companies could say that ten flops are worth it to get one hit; it's getting to be more like it's worth four or five flops to get one hit."

As *NewsRadio* heads off into the still-green pastures of syndication, Simms is taking a step back from running the show, handing off day-to-day responsibility to another *Harvard Lampoon* alumnus, Josh Lieb, though he insists his decision wasn't related to the Hartman tragedy. "No, no, that was, you know . . . I don't want to talk about that," he says, growing quiet. "That was something that was in the works already. If anything the Phil thing sort of got me back more involved with *NewsRadio* this season than I was going to be, just to make sure we could survive this."

Was he always confident they could?

"No, not at all," he says before grimacing and adding again, "I don't want to talk about it."

Back in 1997, Simms stated his disinterest in developing other shows in no uncertain, possibly sacrilegious terms.

"Yeah, this is the best I can do," he told me in *Rolling Stone*. "Pretend you're God and you say, 'If you do a show about a single father who's dating a lot and has two teenage sons, and it doesn't have to be funny, and it'll be a huge hit.' I'd say, 'Fuck you, God.'"

So now that he's developing *OverSeas,* what happened?

"Do I want to build an empire of *shit* now?" Simms asks. "Last time I mouthed off to you, that's how I felt. For a long time I put everything I have into *NewsRadio* and I don't particularly have a desire to try and create a bunch of bad shows. Then I owed NBC another pilot as part of my deal and I thought, What is *not* on TV now? What could I do that would stand out and yet still be a traditional sitcom? Now of course every show is about people working in an office, so I didn't want to do another one of those."

Simms wrote the *OverSeas* pilot toward the end of the 1997–1998 season, then did a second draft he liked more than the first. Remarkably, he admits the network's notes proved helpful in that process.

"The way I always think about it is when a network person gives you a note you like or don't like, their opinion probably represents, at worst, that of the common person watching," says Simms. "Writers are always going, 'What do *they* know about writing?' Well, that's not the point—the people watching are *also* not writers."

Simms started the casting process, then put everything on hold and decided to shoot the *OverSeas* pilot later in 1998. The pilot script concerns a group of young people in a Peace Corps–like organization in the middle of a jungle of a fictional country somewhere between Pakistan and India and Kashmir. "They're there to build a bridge across a river with no modern resources," Simms explains. "It's about the clash of cultures, about the isolation of being away from home and about a bunch of people working on something bigger than themselves." Sounds like *Lampoon* boy wants to save the world or at least remind everyone that they are part of a larger one.

These days, Simms is getting plenty of experience with things bigger than himself, like NBC, with whom he's now struck a lucrative overall deal despite his memorably harsh words. "Money doesn't change anything," Simms reports. "Money just gives you the freedom to be a *total* asshole."

Simms's death-defying goal for *NewsRadio* in 1998–1999 is "just to prove that it can survive. In some sense, we've always sort of felt like underdogs with hurdles put in our way, and we've derived some pride from overcoming them. This hurdle is the one that actually made everyone stop and think maybe this is the one we *can't* recover from. I guess that's the goal." He also wouldn't mind terribly if cast member Andy Dick—who went into rehab in April—was able to stay on the relatively straight and reasonably narrow.

The goal for *OverSeas*, according to Simms, is more modest. "Get on the air," Simms says with a shrug. "Stay on the air."

"Awesome, dude. *Sweet.*"

That's Trey Parker's immediate reaction to the strange but true notion that his show *South Park* may be hastening the destruction of network TV as we know it.

The truth, however, is that Parker and his scatological partner in crime, Matt Stone, don't even want to commit the dirty deed of slaughtering the televised status quo.

"We don't want to *quite* kill it," Stone clarifies. "We want to get some of their money, *then* kill it."

As they speak, Parker and Stone are sitting on the floor of The Pagoda, their shared faux Japanese teahouse of an office in beachy Marina Del Rey. From the outside, ground zero of *South Park*—cheerily dubbed Casa Bonita—is a fairly conventional industrial building. Inside, Parker and Stone's own space has lost its Zen-like calm and now resembles a Japanese frat house during final exams. Papers, pictures, and CDs lie scattered everywhere. Parker sits cross-legged just a few feet from the crumpled sleeping bag where he has spent the last few nights while cramming to finish the episode to air tonight.

It's only fitting that Parker and Stone would work in this tsunami-struck place. With its hard-cussing kids in a surreally familiar universe, *South Park* has become the fucked-up capital of shaky taste. The most watched show in Comedy Central history—which Stone once compared to "an after-school special that's been chopped up and put in a blender"—broke new ground by embracing the fact that kids say and do far worse than the darndest things.

"There's this whole thing out there about how kids are so innocent and pure," Parker told me in a 1997 *Rolling Stone* cover story about *South Park*. "That's bullshit, man. Kids are malicious little fuckers. They totally jump on every bandwagon and rip on the weak guy at any chance. . . . They are total fucking bastards, but for some

*D A V I D   W I L D*

reason everyone has kids and forgets about what they were like when they were kids."

Proving that Parker and Stone were on to something, children of all ages anxiously jumped on the South Park bandwagon, almost overnight changing the fortunes of Comedy Central. Debuting in August 1997, *South Park* exploded—upping ad rates by a factor of six. In its first year on the air, the show helped Comedy Central ratings climb over 30 percent. It's estimated that merchandise will soon have brought in $100 million in sales.

If *South Park*—with such seminal episodes as "Cartman Gets an Anal Probe," "Big Gay Al's Big Gay Boat Ride" (with George Clooney giving voice to Sparky the Gay Dog) and "Mr. Hankey, the Christmas Poo"—reveals that the network emperors have no clothes, that's fine with Parker and Stone. Both still under thirty, they reflect a generation with no particular fealty to the old networks and their traditional product.

"We went through a lot of people in town telling us *South Park* wouldn't work because it's not a network show," Parker recalls. "We were all surprised how it did and definitely happy because we *hate* sitcoms. We watched Comedy Central all the time because it had *Monty Python*, and *Absolutely Fabulous,* and *Kids in the Hall,* and we were like, Let everyone else watch this network crap."

Sitcoms, for Parker and his friends, were "something your parents watched," he says.

"I'd rather watch the *news*," Stone adds with contempt.

During the early heights of *South Park* mania, Trey Parker reports Jerry Seinfeld was interested in doing a cameo on the show but his people were offended when he was offered the tiny role of Turkey No. 2. Parker and Stone confess to being as shocked as anyone to find themselves in such a position of power.

"We always thought we would have this little under-the-radar weird cult show, kind of like *Mystery Science Theater* was in the beginning," says Stone. "That's about where we see our sensibility appealing."

Parker and Stone—and their shared sensibility—first came together in film class back at the University of Colorado at Boulder in the early nineties. They helped each other with their student films, including Parker's *Giant Beaver of Southern Sri Lanka*. In the end Stone would graduate, while Parker would get booted out for missing too many classes. Before he left he started directing his first feature, a darkly hilarious $125,000 production titled *Cannibal: The Musical*.

In 1994 the pair moved to Los Angeles, where they struggled to make a living. *South Park* evolved out of *The Spirit of Christmas*, an obscenity-laced five-minute video Christmas card commissioned by Brian Graden, then a Fox executive and now at MTV. Studded with lowbrow sacrilege, the hellaciously amusing clip featured a vicious fight between Jesus and Santa Claus. Graden gave the duo $1,200 for the project, knowing full well they would pocket some. The crudely animated *Spirit* became an underground sensation in Hollywood—with admirers like George Clooney circulating it to friends. Parker and Stone went from almost literally starving to being in hot demand. Silly offers started flying, with Parker even being approached about directing *Barney: The Movie* because, he was told, *The Spirit of Christmas* demonstrated he knew how to do "funny stuff with kids."

To its eternal corporate credit and fiscal benefit, Comedy Central fought to make the cussing *South Park* kiddies into TV stars. Almost instantly new mass media mantras like "Don't kick the baby!" "I'm not fat, I'm big-boned!" and the deathless cry of "Ohmigod! They killed Kenny!" were crashing the lexicon. As a result, the network was instantly upgraded—Comedy Central chief Doug Herzog has called *South Park* "the Michael Jordan of cable"—and the show did indeed put the network right up there with the cable aristocracy of WWF wrestling (which Parker and Stone praise as "wild performance art") and *Rugrats*. While *South Park* has led to lots of outside opportunities—writing a prequel to *Dumb & Dumber*, starring in the box-office failure *BASEketball*, and mounting a *South Park* feature film—Parker and Stone spend the majority of their time making *South Park* a weekly reality.

This afternoon at Casa Bonita things are calm—normally sixty people work here; another forty are in a nearby facility toiling away on the *South Park* movie. "It's nice to be employing a hundred people," says Parker, "especially since more than half of them are our friends." Last week, however, things didn't seem quite so pleasant during the crunchiest of crunch times. It didn't help matters that Stone and Parker had to waste time putting down what they term an animator revolt. "They meet people who work on like *The Simpsons* and *King of the Hill*," Parker says, "and they get ideas."

*South Park*, they stress, works by its own rules, inasmuch as it works at all. The show isn't like conventional animation—a wildly painstaking, time-consuming, and expensive process. The *South Park* system allows for some real brushes with brinksmanship. Tonight's episode, says Stone, "walked out the door here about five yesterday afternoon, went to color correct, and was on a plane to the East Coast at about ten P.M. last night." The episode—in which the boys go on a strange trip to a planetarium—*just* made it on air.

The showrunners' job is different on *South Park*. "We're not over-seeing and Band-Aid-ing stuff, we're right in the middle of it," Stone explains. Indeed, they do much of the writing and many of the voices, and they help edit the thing. Nor can they rely on actors to handle the lion's share of the publicity duties. "Not only did we have to do the show, we have to be stars," says Parker. "Talking so much about doing it *and* doing it."

Success has a funny, counterrevolutionary way of corrupting would-be iconoclasts, turning them into the cheeseballs they devour on their show each week. A few days ago, these lovable TV terrorists found themselves in a compromising position when they attended the 1998 Creative Arts Emmy Awards—held before the main Emmys—because *South Park* was nominated.

"It was weird," Parker explains, "because we were there with a bunch of, like, *Mister Ed* guys and Shirley from *Laverne and Shirley*."

"Chicks from *Petticoat Junction*," Stone adds helpfully. "We were, like, are we has-beens *already*? It's only been like a year."

Stone and Parker attended the event only because they wanted to hang out with their fellow animation nominees Matt Groening (*The Simpsons*) and Mike Judge (*King of the Hill*). "Neither of them came so we just felt like stupid fat girls at the party," Stone says.

In the end, *South Park* didn't win—all the better for their endangered rebel credentials as makers of scatology for fun and profit.

"Our fans don't *want* us to win," Parker says. "But it's funny you'd even put a show like *South Park* in a category with *The Simpsons*. This show is *never* going to reach that level and isn't meant to reach that level. It's meant to be a cheap dirty little secret."

Mike Judge—who had been through it all with *Beavis & Butthead*—has warned them that people would love them because they had come from nothing; then, when they hit the jackpot, accusations of selling out would fly.

"You've already gone off the diving board, there's no way you can help but hit the pool," Stone says. "No choice other than quitting our jobs, moving back to Colorado, and starting a farm would stop us from becoming sellouts."

Parker and Stone have commented on the absurdity of their own popularity with Terrance and Phillip, stars of *South Park*'s show-within-a-show. "We completely bastardized it all and said a big 'fuck you' to everyone. People *hated* it and we love it. What we did was create a cult within the cult, because you can't really call *South Park* a cult anymore."

Now it's a major religion with the successful product line to prove it.

"Critics can say what they want," says Parker, "but we *know* we pushed something to another level—for better or worse. No matter what happens if the show dies tomorrow, we *know* we've had an influence."

Who else could have made a popular TV star of the groundbreaking and jaw-dropping Mr. Hankey, almost certainly television's first talking turd? "The shit is out there now," Parker says with a slightly crazy look in his eyes. Both partners feel satisfaction, not just because kids purchasing "I Believe in Mr. Hankey" T-shirts in malls everywhere are making them richer, but also because, tasteless or not, nobody can say *South Park* is another tired TV cliché.

Parker and Stone don't feel like part of the dreaded television community. "We feel like the outcasts of the community, which is good," explains Parker. "That's how we *want* to feel. We now know enough people in that business to know that what we do here is *nothing* like it's supposed to be. We've invented an entirely new system and it barely works."

"The whole idea is you throw dynamite at the whole system, but unfortunately everyone *loved* the dynamite and wanted more," says Parker, whose corporate identity is Carlos, International Terrorist. "How long can we keep throwing dynamite at 'em?"

There's the rub. Even when the revolution *is* televised, it can't stay a revolution long.

# Ready, Aim, Misfire

**Television—a medium. So called because
it is neither rare nor well done.**

**Ernie Kovacs**

*T*he vast majority of network sitcoms and dramas premiere during September, a bewitching and bewitched month of last-minute promotion and early reckonings. Late summer hype and media punditry give way suddenly and often painfully to moments of initial Nielsen truth, brutal or otherwise. This is the month when confidence turns overnight into tentative celebration, muted concern, or outright panic. Think of the debut of a new TV show as a blind date, a multimillion-dollar blind date. Now consider how most blind dates end. Win, lose, or draw, the pressure is on for virtually everybody in the TV business, and with good reason. "There's thirty-six new shows right now," a major TV executive says matter-of-factly, "By the end of the year, thirty will be dead or dying."

*Cupid* is but one of the many life-or-death candidates, and Scott Winant is the man charged with fighting for its right to life. If you were watching TV during the eighties and nineties, chances are you've already felt Winant's pain. An accomplished director and producer, Winant was a key player in *thirtysomething* and *My So-Called Life*. On *thirtysomething*—which ran from 1987 to 1991—Winant was one of the stylistic architects of the show, working closely under its creators Marshall Herskovitz and Ed Zwick. *My So-Called Life*, meanwhile, was a gripping coming-of-age tale that made Claire Danes a star but lasted only nineteen episodes on ABC from August 1994 until January 1995. Under the Herskovitz and Zwick banner, Winant ran the show with his then partner Winnie Holtzman, a gifted writer and another *thirtysomething* alumni.

Now Winant is running *Cupid*, an unusually smart new ABC dramedy that tells the tale of Trevor (played by *Ellen*'s Jeremy Piven), a mental patient who may or may not also be the titular god of love, and his psychiatrist Claire (Paula Marshall, best known as the reporter who wrongly outed Jerry and George on *Seinfeld*), who may or may not become his love interest. The show is an "anthological drama" that will follow Trevor and Claire's progress and that of other weekly love pilgrims.

Today, at the exact hour the Starr Report is hitting the Internet, Winant is on the phone getting an unpleasant report of his own. He's at the *Cupid* office in Santa Monica inside a former medical plaza that now also houses WB's *Dawson's Creek* and UPN's *Mercy Point*, a new *ER*-in-outer-space drama for which the critical prognosis is not encouraging.

*Cupid* is set not in space but in Chicago and actually films in the Windy City, an interesting fact considering that Winant and the show's writers are here toiling halfway across the country in a different time zone. As a result, there are two clocks on the office wall outside Winant's office—L.A. and Chicago time—and below them is a table with useful Chicago maps and reference books. There is also a bulletin board displaying architectural plans and photos of various *Cupid* locations.

In these early days of what he hopes will be a long so-called life for *Cupid*, Winant is discovering that initial fears about the difficulties of having a long-distance relationship with his own show were not unfounded. "Dailies" don't actually arrive until the next afternoon, meaning they are in effect "yester-dailies."

The current episode in production—"Meat Market"—is in its fourth day of production and looks to be going $80,000 over the budget (an average episode of *Cupid* costs $1.2 million). Furthermore, Jeremy Piven is on the phone from Chicago for Winant to passionately express some feelings on the topic.

"Jeremy's concerned for monetary reasons we're not going to a location that would service the story best," Winant explains after hanging up with the actor who's also a *Cupid* producer. "He's *very* concerned—as I am—that we don't 'television-up' the show. Every day you have to struggle with that. We consider Jeremy a collaborator and he's out there and I'm here. I want him to understand that he's going to be heard." Winant's appreciative that Piven signed on for *Cupid* duty when a sitcom or other opportunities would have meant far less work for him. "This is *hard*," Winant says, "and Jeremy's finding that out."

Still, there's a budget to be kept to—or as close to as possible. That's the reason Winant and Rob Thomas—*Cupid*'s thirty-three-year-old creator and one of its writers—make their way to the writers' room for a conference call. Already there is Kelly McCarthy, with whom Winant works closely on all production matters. The call is connected with members of the Chicago production team including the production producer, the episode's director and assistant director, the production designer, and the location manager.

Against the wall is a board with titles for all thirteen *Cupid* episodes of the show's initial order—with titles like "Heaven," "End of Eros," and "Pick Up Schticks"—and a list of checkpoints signifying their status. Categories include "outline," "network script approval," "studio script approval," and the optimistic "Emmy." A board below offering interesting titles like "The Great Spank-a-thon," "Ass Bitch," "Gossamer Nipple," "Blame It on the Cosa Nostra," and one that reads "a) Examination of Man's Duality b) Ajax Eats a Ho-Ho." Rob Thomas explains these are old show ideas left over from *Duckman*, a previous gig of *Cupid*'s executive producers Ron Osborne and Jeff Reno, who are also *Moonlighting* vets. Once the call is connected, Winant starts off with compliments—"Everything's looking fantastic," he tells one Chicago collaborator. "You are the genius you said you were."

**DAVID   WILD**

Pleasantries shared, he sets the agenda: "We have some major problems on this episode. So the goal in the next twenty minutes is to solve them." Seconds later, he's told the price tag of those problems has risen. "We believe the whole enchilada now comes to $116,000 over," a voice from Chicago informs Winant.

"Okay, I'm *not* upset," Winant responds in a manner that suggests he is, but that he means to keep things breezy enough to remain productive.

The long-distance troubleshooting begins in earnest. It quickly becomes clear that the problems come down largely to "days out"—the dangerously expensive and uncertain reality of venturing into the real world for location shoots. Winant searches for solutions. "What about the walk-and-talk with the pimp?" he asks. "Couldn't we just do that right outside the stages?"

Again and again the conversation comes back down to what can be "justified"—in both fiscal and storytelling terms. For the latter, Winant turns to Rob Thomas and asks, "Can you justify that?" When Thomas can't live with something, Winant moves on to another notion.

"How much have we saved?" Winant keeps asking after offering various cost-cutting scenarios—at times he sounds like he's putting items back at grocery store, which, in a TV sense, he is.

Back in Winant's office, he and Thomas sit back for a minute. Above them are portraits of various jazz greats like Miles Davis, Dexter Gordon, Thelonious Monk, and Billie Holiday, as well as Claire Danes, who, like Holiday before her, has a way of suffering beautifully. The cast of *thirtysomething* stares out from a photo across the room. "This is great because you get one showrunner who's worn out, and one guy who's fresh and naive and doesn't know what he's in for," says Winant.

"And yet *also* worn out," adds Thomas.

Winant's first job was as a page at CBS, a gig he got through his mother, who was in casting at the network. Ethel Winant—still active—was in fact the first woman executive of a network, and is a legendary producer and casting director whose TV credits include *Playhouse 90*, *The Twilight Zone*, *The Waltons*, *The Mary Tyler Moore Show,* and *The Bob Newhart Show*. His father, H. N. Winant, was also in the business as an actor. Even with such a show biz pedigree, Winant admits, "I was an *infamous* page." He refers vaguely to past on-lot bike borrowings.

From there, Winant became a production assistant before heading off to film school at USC. After graduation in 1978, his first job was as a film editor on a new show called *That's Incredible!*—an early lesson about the unknowability of public tastes: "You're sitting there cutting this shit about guys putting bicycle spokes through their neck and the Loch Ness Monster, and you're just going, 'Yeah, like *anybody's* going to watch *this*.' And of course, it goes on to be a *huge* hit."

He went on to work in development for veteran producer Bruce Lansbury, whose credits included *The Wild Wild West*. Winant calls his early mentor "just a classy guy. With showrunners, there's a lot of yelling and screaming that goes on in this business. Bruce influenced people to do their best work without having to threaten them and act like an idiot."

Through Lansbury, Winant worked on a project with Ed Zwick, who went on to become a big success in his own right directing *About Last Night* and making a few Emmy-winning TV movies. When word of *thirtysomething* started to spread, Winant wanted to approach Zwick and Herskovitz about producing, but backed off at first because a friend was going for the job. When that friend chose instead to sign on for a *Psycho* TV series—a frighteningly bad choice—Winant pitched himself as the line producer.

"I didn't know *anything* about producing a TV show, and the great thing about Ed and Marshall was they didn't care," Winant says. "They just knew that we were of like mind. They had showrunners pushed on them left and right from the studio, and they choose me. The first day on *thirtysomething*—I'm driving on the lot, I'm the producer of a TV series, and the guard remembers me from being a page. I was a pretty big screw-up as a page. He said, 'Winant, I don't want *any* trouble out of you.'"

Winant learned from his *thirtysomething* collaborators. "Ed and Marshall were willing to support and fight for their point of view," he says. He learned this lesson on a show that was a success in a groundbreaking way. "Ratings-wise it would be a huge hit today but more importantly what *thirtysomething* did was wake up the networks to demographics—we didn't need to get the biggest numbers because we were getting those college-educated professionals with disposable income advertisers loved."

When Zwick and Herskovitz eventually decided to stop the show, ABC beseeched Winant to stay with *thirtysomething* and keep Hope—and the rest of the show's tortured gang—alive. "If I would have come back they said they'd pick up the show," he recalls. "They threw more money at me than I had ever known, but I was completely wiped out. I turned it down, mostly because I wanted to respect Ed and Marshall's point of view. It was always their show."

Like so many before him, Winant went off to start a feature film career. When things bogged down, he and his partner at the time, Winnie Holtzman, decided to go back into television. The result was *My So-Called Life*.

Despite its short network life span, Winant refuses to see *My So-Called Life* as any sort of failure. "I see *My So-Called Life* as *nothing* but a success," he says proudly. "I got to work with Claire Danes, and that's a high mark for me professionally. It was her first leading role, and that's a privilege—that pilot is my favorite work until *Cupid*."

Next Winant directed the film *'Til There Was You*, a romantic comedy with a cast including Jean Tripplehorn, *The Practice*'s Dylan McDermott, and Jennifer Aniston of *Friends*, but the project proved troubled. "Everybody says TV goes too quickly—and that's true," says Winant, "but you do your best and then a few weeks later you get to see it. In movies, you spend two years just *talking* about whether you're just going to make the thing."

Winant and Holtzman returned to television and made an acclaimed pilot for NBC called *The L Word* that was crossed off the network at the last minute. "*TV Guide* said it was the best new pilot of the TV season except they didn't actually put it on the air," Winant recalls, shaking his head. "The decision-making of the network, you *don't* want to try and figure it out," he says. "In the process of figuring out what goes on the schedule, something tested well and everything changed. I'm not a huge believer in testing, I think you can *learn* from it but I don't think you can follow it absolutely. Otherwise, why isn't everything on television a hit?"

Because Winant has a reputation for making quality shows, opportunity continues to knock. For *Cupid*, he was asked to come on board a show created by Rob Thomas, a young Texan writer who spent last season on the breakthrough WB youth drama *Dawson's Creek*. Thomas first moved to Los Angeles in 1994 to work for a television project called Channel One, which he describes as "an awful CNN for high school kids beamed directly into classrooms." He had left a far more satisfying life in Texas, teaching school and playing in a local band called Hey Zeus. Looking for a way out, Thomas started writing his first young adult book, *Rats Saw God,* and finished it within ten months. He quit his day job the day he got an agent, and moved back to Texas to live cheaply and write books.

When the book was published, Thomas sent a copy to then cochairman of Sony, Jeff Sagansky—currently running Pax TV—because his niece had been hired at Channel One and Thomas had received the letter of recommendation from Sagansky. In a cover letter, he asked Sagansky to forward his book to any TV shows involving teenage characters. "It was a long shot," Thomas admits, "but it was my only contact."

That long shot paid off when, six months later, Sagansky called out of the blue and asked if Thomas would be interested in writing for a second season of *My So-Called Life*. Unfortunately, there turned out to be no second season. Still, the lines of communication were open and Thomas sent Sagansky the copy of a film script he'd been hired to write. Impressed again, Sagansky explained he felt the time was ripe for an anthological romantic series and invited Thomas to fly to New York in November 1996 to pitch some ideas.

The two men each had an idea involving Cupid. "The basic difference was that Jeff's *Cupid* was Cupid down from Mount Olympus. Mine was a deranged guy who *functions* as a Cupid," Thomas recalls. "His did feel like *Touched by a Cupid*. I didn't know if that jibed with my writing style. He said, 'He *is* Cupid but write it with your sensi-

*D A V I D   W I L D*

bility,' I thought, How can I stomach this idea and not write something sentimental and stupid? So I started thinking of Dennis Leary as *Cupid*. If I kept writing with him in mind, it helped me like the show."

In the meantime, Sagansky passed Thomas's script on to the producers of *Dawson's Creek*, where Thomas later became the first staff writer hired by Kevin Williamson. "The nice thing about writing for that show is they'd let you be smart and funny, and very few teenager shows let you be those two things," Thomas says. "There's a soapy element to it that I was less interested in. In my mind, it's not *My So-Called Life* but it's not *90210* either. There were some personality conflicts but that's a side issue. It was good for me."

Good is an understatement. Being associated with a hot show is a win-win, and the heat has a way of spreading. "All the writers on staff have been offered every teen movie this year," Thomas admits. Such projects didn't jibe with Thomas's sensibility, and he was more interested in developing *Cupid* for Peter Guber's Mandalay Television and Columbia TriStar, especially when Mandalay asked Thomas what he would think of working with a guy from *thirtysomething* and *My So-Called Life*.

An admirer of both shows, Thomas grew even more excited when Winant immediately cracked the *Cupid* code. "Scott was the one who said, 'Let's play it down the middle. Let's play it like *Miracle on 34th Street*—we'll never know if he's Cupid or he isn't. The show fell into place for me. It's all the benefits of having a fantastical concept while being able to write it as a grounded show. At that point I could write it because *I* understood it."

Winant wanted on because, he says, "I read some of Rob's stuff. When I see writing like this, I'm not a fool. I know that's what it's all about. If I do anything well, I have a high respect for writers and can see what they see and execute their vision. I am driven entirely by material and by actors. Everything I did on *Cupid* was on the page. I basically protected Rob from the simplistic, linear approach that the studio or network might have taken with this show. I have the courage to give Rob the courage to go for it."

Toward that end, a functioning *Cupid* team needed to be put together. Because he was "a writer with exactly one year of television experience, the studio and network didn't trust me to run the writing staff," Thomas says. "The other executive producers were brought in, and so far so good. They've been great about letting this continue to be my original vision of the show." Still, Thomas admits, "it's odd when you're put in a situation where you're interviewing and hiring your boss. From now on, I'm sure in television I won't have to be baby-sat."

"It's about guarantees," Winant explains. "Everybody's trying to build in guarantees. I'm confident that Rob could have run the show—especially because what he doesn't know, I know. But Ron and Jeff are excellent collaborators and bring something to the party."

The multimillion-dollar question now is how long the *Cupid* party will last, especially at ten P.M. on Saturdays for ABC, a time slot from hell that will find this subtle piece of work doing ratings battle opposite the more obvious macho likes of Chuck Norris's *Walker, Texas Ranger*.

For the time being, Winant isn't focusing on the fact that the show is on a tough night at the shakiest of the Big Three. "I feel extremely comfortable at ABC and truthfully this show probably only could have been put on ABC," he says. "I like these guys and—look, I don't want to comment on their position right now, but possibly they may be a little more open-minded. Since I don't tend to do conventional formats, I've always found a receptive ear at ABC."

At this point in the season, the pair remain heartened about *Cupid*'s chances.

"I think our odds are better than even for staying on for the entire season and being picked up," says Winant.

"I'm *naively* optimistic," Thomas adds with a grin. "*He* should actually know better."

As in life off-screen, there are few sure things in television. There's death, taxes, commercials, and, of course, midseason replacements, those hungry hellhounds hot on the heels of every scheduled show. Networks realize in advance that some of their best guesses are going to be wrong, and thus, midseason replacements—backup shows in the bullpen for when a starter falters. These can be shows that just dodge cancellation, shows that missed the deadline for fall placement, and wild cards waiting for desperation to build. Once midseason replacements had a second-rate reputation, but that's been eased by notable midseason breakthroughs like *Just Shoot Me!*

It's a prospective midseason replacement that brings Norm Macdonald—*Saturday Night Live*'s former sardonic anchorman—to Air Canada's Maple Leaf Lounge at Los Angeles International Airport today. Macdonald is waiting for a plane to wing him back to Vancouver, where he's in the midst of shooting a movie. Macdonald flew in this morning so he could take a meeting with ABC about the new sitcom he's supposed to be developing for Warner Bros. TV in collaboration with Bruce Helford, the showrunner behind *The Drew Carey Show*.

Macdonald—wearing a multicolored workout suit he also wore to the meeting—takes a second to check out a bombing on CNN. "What's going on?" Macdonald asks the room in his deadpan way. "A *war* or something?"

Earlier this year, Macdonald found himself in a war of his own when he was ousted from his seat as the host of *SNL*'s "Weekend Update" at the urging of NBC's West Coast president Don Ohlmeyer, who later made headlines by ordering that ads for *Dirty Work*, Macdonald's first starring film vehicle, not air on the network. Eventually, the network relented, but Macdonald's film—directed by former *Full House* star Bob Saget—fizzled at the box office anyway. Yet somehow in the curious science of show business, getting fired and having a bomb movie only seemed to make Macdonald a bigger star.

"Yeah, I got demoted at *SNL* and then I got sort of hot." Macdonald says. "Then the movie didn't happen, and then I got *really* hot." Like America's embattled President, the worse trouble Macdonald steps in, the more his personal approval rating soars.

Macdonald's persona on and off screen is that of a brilliant, slightly zonked-out truth-teller. Asked how his big ABC meeting today went, he says simply, "It went all right. Like there was this other dude Bruce who thought up the idea. I just sat there."

Considering this is going to be his show, didn't he do any hard- or at least soft-selling?

"They wanted me to, but I didn't," Macdonald says. "So I just kind of made some stupid jokes."

Macdonald and Helford met under intense TV circumstances—working at the famously action-packed *Roseanne*, the show where Helford became a showrunner for the first time. Macdonald was one of the standup comics Helford was to whip into shape as a sitcom writer.

That was before showrunning became quite so lucrative. "These guys are all like multimillionaires now—it's *crazy*," Macdonald says. "Like the guys on *Seinfeld*, if they were there for like two years, they will give them *anything*. Some of them never do anything and nobody seems to care because they've already given them *so* much money they don't want to say it was a *mistake* or something. Bruce, they gave huge money to, but he created *The Drew Carey Show*, so he was worth it."

Macdonald was at *Roseanne* for a year and a half, during which Helford was fired. "Bruce got fired for working too hard," is how Macdonald reports it. "He did like fourteen-hour days and stuff and she [Roseanne] didn't think that was necessary. She used to fire guys just to keep people scared."

One can't help wondering why Macdonald's doing a sitcom at all. To hear him, it was something profitable to do after *Dirty Work* put him in what he calls "movie jail."

"As soon as the contract ended with *SNL*, I was going to do all these movies," Macdonald recalls. "Then when the movie came out, I thought maybe I'll never be able to do a movie again. I trust Bruce that he can do a sitcom, and I get to stay in Los Angeles for a while, make some money, and then get back to making movies."

Macdonald says his worst professional experience was playing a supporting character—an anti–woman's lib construction worker—in a failed sitcom pilot. However, even better TV series don't move Macdonald.

"I loved Roseanne as a standup," says Macdonald. "When I got the job, they gave me like forty tapes of the show to watch. So I had to go in this room. I watched like two or three, you know. I kind of got sleepy—I just don't watch sitcoms. Like I don't even *know* anyone who watches them. I never had any drive to do a sitcom because I never had an idea that low-concept, you know. The ideas that work are like—'It's a family!' or 'The guy works in a bank.' I mean, there's no idea. They always want something that will last like seven years or some *ungodly* amount of time to see the same characters every week. I don't know what I'm doing. Bruce will figure this out."

Exactly how much of a sitcom concept has developed to this point?

"None," Macdonald says.

*None?*

"No, Bruce just talked about some characters he thought would be funny," says Macdonald. "Like I told him it would be good if you could just surround me with good sitcom actors because I can't act. So if I could get good comic actors around me, I could just hang like Seinfeld, stand there while everyone is being crazily funny. I'd love to get Laurie Metcalf—that's what I'm really pushing for, because she was on *Roseanne* and she's fuckin' *hilarious,* man."

What about the ugly necessities of a sitcom—say a career for his character? Perhaps Norm could be a standup like Jerry on *Seinfeld?*

"No, no, no, I'm going to have some job like in the *real* world, and then I'll just be one of those guys in the real world who does an inordinate amount of jokes. Like Hawkeye on *M\*A\*S\*H.*"

Here's how Macdonald explains the process of getting his sitcom under way: "You go and meet with these guys and they go, 'Hey, man, you would be *great* on our network. Everybody likes you.' Then they go, 'You've got to meet with some writers' and they go, 'Have you got any ideas for the show?' You go, 'No, *I'm* not a writer. *You're* the writer.'"

Macdonald's asked who turned up at his big meeting today.

"There was this girl Jamie Tarses, then some other guy Stu Bloomberg," says Macdonald, naming his new network bosses

In total, Macdonald reports, there were eight or so people in the room for the half-hour meeting today, Macdonald and Helford, along with executives from ABC and Warner Bros. "All these meetings are like small talk," he says. "You go in there and they go, 'Hey, what's happening? We love you.' And you go, 'It's pretty hot out.' Then it degenerates into talking about Sammy Sosa or something. Then it's over, and they're all happy. This happens over and over. Meetings where you're just talking to people about . . . *nothing*. Nothing at all."

A few days later, on the set of *The Drew Carey Show*, it's like some twisted rock-and-roll fantasy camp. Slash, Joey Ramone, Joe Walsh, Matthew Sweet, Lisa Loeb, and Roy Clark are just some of the musical guests coming to the Warner Bros. lot to film parts for an episode titled "In Ramada Da Vida" that finds Drew becoming a hotel lounge rock star. Everyone on the mostly easygoing *Drew Carey* set appears to be having a blast, with the possible exception of the small goateed man in his forties who looks too busy running around making sure everything gets done to wallow in this rock-and-roll heaven.

Later, while the *Drew Carey* writers' room carries on without him, Helford sits down for a few minutes in his nearby office. Behind him is framed front page of *Daily Variety* with a story about Helford's recent massive deal with Warner Bros. under a headline proclaiming "Helford of a Deal." It's one of the few adornments in this unimpressive space in a building also housing the Olsen twins' new vehicle, *Two of a Kind*. "I guess the word is that I'm the single highest-paid writer in television for an individual, not a team," says the unpretentious Helford with a shrug. "So all day long it was like "That's a *Helford* of a shirt you got on there, Bruce!"

For all his money, the aura in the *Drew Carey* office remains exceedingly working-class. "There's *nothing* glamorous about this show," Helford says with a trace of pride.

In the once proud tradition of *Roseanne*, *Drew Carey* is TV's working-class hit show, but Carey and Helford sure as hell ain't working-class anymore. Helford—Drew Carey's partner and cocreator on the show—once ran *Roseanne* and has the awards and psychic scars to show for it.

Helford grew up a child of TV, lower-middle-class in Chicago. His father was in the pet business and had a traveling bird show called Bird-o-Rama in the fifties. "It traveled around the country for Hartz Mountain because they knew if they sold more parakeets, they'd sell more birdseed," he remembers. The Helford family kept a TV on the dining room table. "We didn't need to talk," he remembers. "We *knew* we loved each other."

Growing up, Helford didn't dream of showrunning, but becoming a professional poet didn't pan out. Later he set his sights on acting, which precipitated his move West. "After my second divorce and finishing college I called my buddy in Chicago," he recalls. "We always wanted to go to California, loved surf music, so we thought let's go to California. So I came out here in 1978 and just *starved*. I was in the pet business most of my life, so I worked at pet shops." He did some freelance work for *Vanity Fair* and *National Lampoon* but says he wasn't good enough to make a living being a print writer.

Helford gave TV writing a shot. "I wrote a spec script for *Family Ties* and they bought it, which is kind of unusual," recalls Helford, who had a writing partner initially. "They bought it and aired it. I was in the business." In 1986 he signed on for a sitcom called *Mr. Sunshine* starring Jeffrey Tambor—the future Hank Kingsley on *Larry Sanders*—as a blind college professor. The show was created by David Lloyd—a famous sitcom great and reluctant showrunner—and staffed with other esteemed comedy vets. With all that talent, how long did this *Sunshine* last? "Thirteen episodes," Helford says matter-of-factly. "It made people uncomfortable but Jeffrey was great and the Braille Institute *loved* it."

Somehow that demographic wasn't enough to save *Mr. Sunshine*.

"They couldn't find any advertisers for a show about a blind guy," Helford recalls. "I suggested Ray-Bans."

After *Mr. Sunshine*, Helford—blind to TV genre—went from the sitcom to a one-hour drama called *The Bronx Zoo* and did two seasons on that show with Ed Asner as a high school principal. "Most times your agents want you to be easily identifiable as a sitcom guy or a drama guy and they usually don't want you to be an hour guy because there's no money in one hour, no syndication, or very rarely. I just wanted to do something different and I *loved* one hour, but I missed show night and live audiences. So I went back to sitcoms for the last two seasons of *Family Ties*."

Once the Keaton family closed up shop, Helford jumped to *Anything but Love* as co–executive producer, a level just under showrunning. "I was there for the last season when we got the plug pulled," Helford remembers. Asked why that romantic sitcom starring Richard Lewis and Jamie Lee Curtis as staffers of a Chicago magazine failed, Helford explains, "The first six episodes were bad and very widely seen because it ran after *Roseanne*. Then they brought in Peter Noah, who turned it around to a really great show, but my theory is once the audience has seen six bad episodes or so, you can't regain confidence. It would have been better if it had never been seen."

Around this same time, Helford worked on a few failed pilots, including a *Family Ties* spin-off called *The Art of Being Nick*, built around Scott Valentine's junk sculptor character Nick who dated Justine Bateman's Mallory. "The pilot tested very badly," Helford recalls. "They aired the pilot after *Cosby* once and it got a forty share but they still felt it was just based on Cosby's strength. It's probably the highest-rated failed pilot in the history of the business." Helford believes he gave *Seinfeld*'s Julia Louie Dreyfuss her first sitcom job for that pilot—among those he turned down was Sharon Stone.

Closer to Helford's heart was another early nineties pilot called *Knights of the Kitchen Table*. "It was about four best friends at three stages in their lives—when they're twelve, twenty-five, and fifty," he recalls. In the *Knights* cast was the omnipresent George Clooney. "It was probably the best pilot I've ever done," Helford says. "The young girl was becoming a lesbian—even at eleven she was realizing it. We shot the pilot for CBS and Jeff Sagansky sat me down and said, 'This is maybe the best pilot I've ever seen but there's no *way* I can put it on the air.'"

Helford recalls being offered to run *The Wonder Years*, after the departure of creators Carol Black and Neal Marlens, but he declined, saying, "I like that show. I don't want to ruin it." Helford—who like Aaron Spelling refuses to fly—had a different reaction when he got a call from his agent in 1992 about attempting to take the reins of *Roseanne* while overseas in Paris after arriving on the *QE2*. "Literally the next day I went and caught the ship I just came in on," Helford remembers. "It almost ruined my marriage."

When he got the *Roseanne* gig, there would be more tension. Helford ran *Roseanne* as head writer and executive producer for 1992–1993, twenty-six long, exhausting, but creatively satisfying episodes. "By show twenty-one, she and I had our big blowup as she did with *everybody*," Helford says. "So I backed off and trained my replacement. ABC and Carsey Werner begged me not to leave, but she and I just could *not* see eye to eye. I think it was one of the best seasons—we won the Peabody and a Humanitas, we swept the Golden Globes. But as is her wont, Roseanne gets to a point where she didn't want anybody to get more important than her on the show, or too familiar."

The damage, Helford feels, was residue from bad blood with Matt Williams, who created the series but left in the middle of the first season. "She had learned to hate and mistrust producers from the get-go because in all honesty, she wasn't led through the process properly. I love Matt Williams, he's a great guy, but I think to a certain extent he created part of that. Roseanne felt that someone would come in and take over. For her to maintain power, she had to treat *everyone* like shit."

Helford admits to being a slave driver in his first year showrunning: "Yes, on *Roseanne* I worked *incredibly* long hours. But it wasn't because of her, it was because I wouldn't settle. That's the other thing that I think makes TV lousy—the attitude of 'That's good enough, it's TV.' So we would stay until two or three in the morning or dawn regularly. We'd work weekends. People were *crying* at the end of the season—they were emotionally broken. But every one of those people on that show—every producer—went on to get a multimillion-dollar deal or run their own show."

Getting booted from *Roseanne* was considered a badge of courage and Helford left red-hot, but the heat dissipated quickly with NBC's *Someone Like Me*, a short-lived 1994 vehicle for kid star Gaby Hoffman that was his sitcom Waterloo. He had made a deal with Disney despite concerns that working for the Mouse was an odd fit for a writer who prides himself on writing "really edgy stuff." As he remembers, "Dean Valentine [now head of UPN] was there at the time. I said, 'Dean, are you *sure* you're going to let me do what I do?' He said, 'That's what we need here at Disney, that's *exactly* what we're looking for.' I said, 'Okay, but I look around and I see *Blossom* and *Home Improvement*.' Soon Helford was asked to fill the *Blossom* time slot.

He met with Hoffman and her mother—onetime Andy Warhol "superstar" Diva—and explained that he wanted to do a show about *real* twelve-year-olds. "There's still not one kid who resembles real life on TV," Helford says. "Maybe *South Park*. So I wrote a pilot and it never aired on NBC. Warren Littlefield said it was too dangerous to air on network television. If you saw it now it's like *nothing*. So I got into this *huge* fight with NBC and Disney about what the show was and they ultimately pushed me off the show. I wanted to quit the business—it was ugly, awful, backstabbing."

Helford stresses he's all for input. "I've always said tell me your problems, I'm the only guy that can fix it," he explains. "I'm one of the most collaborative guys in the business. I don't lock out the network. I don't say, 'You're a bunch of schmucks.' They're smart people, they're my partners, and it's their ballpark I'm playing in. I'm not a fool who says, 'Fuck you, go away.' They're the client, I'm trying to please them, that's the relationship. But when they try to make the fixes themselves, that's *not* what they do for a living, that's why they hired *me*."

Just then a savior arrived in the form of a phone call from then Warner Bros. TV chief—and current CBS chief—Les Moonves. "Les said, 'If I can get you out of Disney, do you want to come to Warner Bros.?' I said, 'I'm in Saigon, I'm on the roof, and you've got a helicopter.'"

Helford soon got two shows on the air—the Dice-less Andrew Clay domestic comedy *Bless This House* and *The Drew Carey Show*. Helford loved the former show, but discovered audiences simply weren't going to forgive Andrew Dice Clay his piggish past. "When they tested it, and people were *forced* to watch it, they loved it," Helford. In a sense, it was a blessing *Bless This House* collapsed, since unlike some showrunners who pick favorites when overseeing multiple shows, Helford says, "I actually ran two shows full on. I didn't sleep. I'd have a car come pick me up in the morning in Santa Monica and sleep on the way to work and then start working again." On *Roseanne*, he'd learned to get by on two or three hours a night.

*The Drew Carey Show*—coming out amid the 1995 fall schedule of *Friends* clones—faced long odds against success, longer than some of ABC's other new shows like *Hudson Street* with Tony Danza. "*Everything* was going against us," Helford recalls. "The network wasn't sure Drew was a leading man. There was lots of concern about not enough pretty people on the show and we had a terrible lead-in—we were put behind *Ellen* when *Ellen* was dropping like a stone. So the thing I'm proud about with this show is we built this on our own with no help, we stuck [it] out in the middle of a night that was *dying*, but I believe audiences will find a good show."

This time a nonpsychotic partnership begat a good show. "When we first started out, I said to Drew, 'Look, I'm *not* going the Roseanne route,'" Helford remembers. "'You're my full partner on this show, to the betterment or the detriment of the show. Your face is on that screen, mine isn't. You have as much responsibility for this show as a corunner.' One great thing about Drew is he's a really methodical, hardworking person. He wrote for me on *Someone Like Me*, and learned how to write first. This show got easier because I had a guy on the floor, a lead actor able to help the actors; he knew what story we were going for. There wasn't this big schism between the actors and producer, like you're some enemy."

Even without those in-house tensions, there was plenty outside to overcome. He was told the show was being kept behind *Ellen* and would be expected to develop a female audience. Helford gave Drew a girlfriend, Katie, and played up that angle. He built up Kathy Kinney's part because "women *really* liked her. She's the voice they *wish* they could have in the office," says Helford. "I knew the show was going to make it at the end of the second season; our numbers kept building and building based on *nothing* but the quality of the show. I think the show could have been way bigger and still could get much bigger, if they put a night around us, but except for us and *Dharma & Greg* everything else on ABC is moving downward. They're hoping to rebuild this season." Helford shares an old joke he heard from the late Brandon Tartikoff about the difference between ABC and the *Titanic*—"the *Titanic* had entertainment."

Because of ABC's limited promotional power, Helford's become a modern-day P. T. Barnum for his show—staging attention-grabbing events like splashy musical production numbers to garner the show some free publicity. Whatever he's done it's working—*The Drew Carey Show* ended the 1997–1998 season in the top fifteen, with an average of 16.7 millions viewers weekly.

With *Drew Carey* heading into its third season in solid shape, Helford's now focusing on the sitcom for Norm Macdonald as "my sole development," though he may use his "umbrella" to develop other projects for which he'll be less hands-on. Certainly with a deal like his, Helford has to do *something*.

"Television is a *really* bad art," Helford offers. "It's like someone going into a museum and saying, 'You know we have a lot of blank walls, let's make some paintings to fill them up,'" Helford observes. "*That's* what TV is—space trying to be filled."

Fortunately for Helford, the museums—make that networks—keep paying better. "You don't get these deals for too many years," Helford admits. "You get them for a couple of years while you're hot. The odds of creating more than one success are *really* small—people like James Brooks or Steve Bochco are so amazing for doing it more than once."

Though he admits, "Norm is quirk defined," Helford's admired Macdonald ever since Norm was one of the raggedy standups Helford was told by Tom Arnold to whip into functioning sitcom writers for *Roseanne*. The two talked about doing a project together before, but Macdonald was still caught up in his *Saturday Night Live* contract.

DAVID WILD

When that situation resolved itself, Macdonald's manager Ray Reo at Brillstein-Grey called and discussions began. From Helford's point of view, he wants to work with Macdonald because "I can write for his voice. I had his voice in my head."

Having Norm Macdonald in your head might seem a scary prospect for some "non-bizzers," but it is an exciting one for this tireless showrunner. Though he's reluctant to give out too many details early, Helford has more to say about the show than Macdonald. His plan is for Norm to play a social worker in New York. "His bizarre take on the world is he has to work with the most insane people around," Helford says. "This is a perfect thing for Norm because you get your social satire along with a sitcom."

The way Helford sells the premise, it sounds like it can't miss. Yet, as with everything else to do even remotely with television, that too could change.

Something big is being born on Stage 24.

Behind the guarded gates of Warner Bros. Studios in Burbank, the miracle of network life is taking place inside the *Friends* soundstage. It's Thursday, September 3, 1998, day 499 of the show's production and the last afternoon of rehearsals for Episode 100 of *Friends*. The episode—which will be the third of the 1998–1999 season to air—is called "The One Hundredth." As any friend of *Friends* knows, all the show's episodes since the series pilot have titles that start with "The One with . . ."—as in "The One with the Lesbian Wedding" or "The One with George Stephanopoulos."

In "The One Hundredth"—aka "The One with the Triplets"— Phoebe (played by Lisa Kudrow) gives birth to the triplets she's been carrying during summer hiatus for her half-brother and his significant other. "The One Hundredth" looks to be a typically smart but eminently accessible confection—heartwarming but not sickeningly so. Phoebe experiences the painful miracle of childbirth, Rachel sets up herself and Monica with some cute male nurses, Joey passes a kidney stone with Ross's help, while Monica and Chandler endeavor to keep their affair secret. Then there's the bizarre obstetrician who's an out-of-the-closet Fonzie fanatic—a Dada-esque twist that must especially amuse happy David Schwimmer, who briefly starred alongside Henry Winkler on a horrific sitcom called *Monty*, an experience so unsatisfying it nearly made him pass on *Friends*.

The episode is to be filmed tomorrow night before a studio audience and assorted VIPs in attendance to celebrate the fact that Bright Kauffman Crane have brought their billion-dollar baby to syndication term. Day 499 of any human activity could sound like a hostage situation worthy of coverage on *Nightline*, and at their worst, TV shows can take on hostage crisis–like qualities. Typically, before they're even allowed to audition for a pilot, actors must sign contracts that obligate them for five or six years. Winding up on the high-profile *Friends* looks like the most cozy, glitzy, and well-compensated prison sentence imaginable. This season the cast members are each getting $100,000 per episode—next season they're to get a raise to $120,000.

Today Kevin Bright—who's directing this episode—and about forty other *Friends* cast and crew members are on the floor; other cast members are upstairs in their dressing rooms. Central Perk, the familiar coffeehouse and hangout that may well have boosted the world's caffeine consumption, and the other usual sets have been dismantled to make room for the hospital where "The One Hundredth" will take place. A few dozen extras and members of Team B (stand-ins for the show's on-air A Team) sit spread out in the bleachers where the studio audience of five hundred will be tomorrow night. Some sleep; some flirt; one young man studies up on the Zone diet. Even in the bleachers, a sort of sitcom caste system seems to have developed with the members of Team B—who have the general body types if not looks of the better-known Friends—mostly sticking together.

TV soundstages are curious places, with an odd atmosphere all their own. They have their own militia (usually a few armed security men at the entrances), and their own cuisine (ever-changing assortments of munchable comfort food). These are the unreal worlds that gradually become more real, unless the ratings slip and they become former homes of dead civilizations. Imagine an overgrown high school theater club working in a windowless airplane hangar. In truth, spending days on a TV soundstage could pass for show biz torture, if it weren't also such a pop culture thrill. Mostly these TV city-states remain fairly isolated. During its first season, the *Friends* stage was next door to the *ER* stage, which allowed for considerable intershow bonding and intramural basketball. Today no one from *Friends*'s new neighbors *Brimstone*—a dark Fox drama starring *thirtysomething*'s Peter Horton—stops by to borrow a cup of sugar or extras.

Throughout the day, "The One Hundredth" is blocked, and rehearsed. Each scene is carefully choreographed and marked with tape on the floor for the cameras. Primarily a four-camera shoot, *Friends* seems infinitely more complicated to direct than a home viewer might imagine. Sitcoms used to be shot in three-camera format (an innovation first used by Desi Arnaz) until famed director Jim Burrows pioneered the use of four on *Taxi*. It's become the new standard, though Bright will use more when necessary, including a Steadicam to capture another point of view on the birth of Phoebe's triplets.

Every angle, every nuance of phrasing, every choice of prop is pondered here. David Crane—as is his tendency—spends most of the day back with the writers across the street, but Bright and Marta Kauffman watch intensely, often looking not directly at the actors only few steps in front of them, but at a nearby TV screen, their chosen creative canvas.

Fine distinctions seem to be getting finer. Regarding Kudrow's breathing during the birth, Bright explains, "She should be huffing and puffing," to which Kauffman replies, "She should be *panting*." Listening to Kauffman and Bright and sometimes Crane discuss hundreds of small issues on the set is like some old *Seinfeld* episode—dissecting every tiny matter becomes an art form. These three appear to have a vaguely telepathic understanding of each other's tastes, born of experience.

Unlike some showrunning teams, Bright Kauffman Crane don't try to do everything together. "They don't feel the need to travel in packs," says *Friends* supervising producer Todd Stevens, who's been with the power trio since the beginning of *Friends*. "If there's safety in numbers, there's not always time for that safety."

The cast has been here all day. The morning's earliest call time—when an actor is requested to arrive on set—was for Jennifer Aniston at 7:30 A.M., the latest for Matt LeBlanc at 8:44 A.M. Still, unlike the showrunners, the actors often appear to hurry up and wait today. The impossibly skinny Aniston—currently all over the magazines partly because she has been linked with Brad Pitt—stands around looking casually stunning in jeans and a floral top, chewing on some of the plentiful snack foods.

"Where's my nurse?" asks Bright aloud, in search not of medical help but rather of a real-life RN who will appear in Scene M, which he's anxious to run through.

Today is the fourth day of a five-day process. Generally for *Friends* day one is table read—an initial read-through usually done by the cast while sitting at a table. Day two is a rehearsal and run-through, following which the writers often spend a late night fixing whatever might be broken. Day three is for more rehearsal, and a run-through for the NBC and Warner Bros. executives. Day four offers yet more rehearsing and camera blocking. Day five is for refreshing the camera moves and the actors. Then in the late afternoon, the audience is brought in and the show in filmed, a process that can and often does last into the early morning hours.

Experienced in all its wearying glory, the making of a sitcom seems a bit like sculpture, artists playing with the material, molding it again and again, stripping away whatever offends. *Friends* has always ended up offending much less than the sitcom norm, offering measurable traces of genuine wit and heart. During the first season, Bright Kauffman Crane found themselves after every episode celebrating "another one that didn't suck." And in television, where "sucking" is a natural act, this represents a rare triumph of the comic will.

In pursuit of that enduring, "nonsucking" status, Bright seems most focused on the technical challenge of getting this ambitious episode done, and done right. He's the one who will oversee the editing, and he knows better than anyone else what he wants. He's almost comically hands-on—even jumping on Phoebe's birthing table to demonstrate precisely how he wants Kudrow to move.

Marta Kauffman trades off ideas, answers all major script issues when Crane is absent, and interfaces with the cast in a way that appears warm and direct. She provides another highly audible service on the *Friends* stage. When something's funny—hardly an infrequent occurrence—she issues forth a laugh best described as hearty, infectious, and, well, friendly. In addition to being a gifted writer, she's one hell of an audience.

David Crane seems to have his heart in working with the writers. It is he who appears to be the leading advocate of the written word and—along with Kauffman—the comic court of last appeal.

Some writers shun the group approach of the writers' room—but not Crane. "It's kind of like sex, whatever works for you," he explains. "If you like a lot of people there, more power to you. If you have fun with just you and another person, or if you like to do it alone, fine. My feeling is you've hired a bunch of these really talented writers—they're funny, smart people. Utilize them. I understand the pejorative of 'Wow, everything's homogenized when it's gang-written.' I don't think that's the case. Frankly I think that helps give a show consistency, so that week after week you're turning out the same show. And so long as everyone sets the bar high, I think it's fine. Sometimes I think there's an arrogance on the part of showrunners who believe they have all the answers. Not so."

The writers are especially busy today since tomorrow morning the cast will do an early table read for Episode 101 because Monday is a holiday.

To document and promote the hell out of this historic episode, each cast member takes a turn being interviewed by an NBC camera crew. They're asked a series of questions—including who arrives first in the morning, who gets the first parking space, and whether they possess a key to the stage. As the afternoon drags on, the cast take drastic measures to keep themselves amused and awake, first crashing each other's interviews, then resorting to interrupting each other's insights with the gaseous sound of a noisy Play-Doh–like product that, when properly massaged, makes an all-too-familiar, frightening farting sound.

"Jenny, what's the name of that stuff?" Matthew Perry inquires with mock seriousness.

"Fudge Sludge," Aniston explains matter-of-factly.

Fudge Sludge isn't the only thing getting massaged inside these walls—a professional masseuse makes the rounds to provide instant stress relief. Snacks are omnipresent—late in the afternoon soybeans are served from a bowl, and supplies of Bit-o-Honey and Bazookas are always dangerously close. The impossibly skinny Cox grazes regularly. There are other forward-thinking benefits—a dressing room had been converted into a nursery since the *Friends* family has experienced a few real-life additions. Throughout the day, babies and dogs make on-set guest appearances.

Still, Bright Kauffman Crane have much work to do even though *Veronica's Closet* and *Jesse* are both on hiatus weeks and the Labor Day holiday beckons, part of what Bright calls their "overabundance of good fortune." At eight P.M., when millions of Americans are home watching a *Friends* rerun, work is proceeding onstage, and it doesn't stop until about ten.

The next morning, on day 500, there is some good TV seasonal cheer. "Happy Hundredth, everybody! Merry Christmas!" says Courteney Cox, greeting some of her *Friends* coworkers.

Yet it's not all glad tidings.

"Where's *Matt*?" an under-the-gun Bright asks of LeBlanc, whom he wants on stage. "Tell him I need him *right* now."

Bright's focus becomes even more intense now that it's show day. He inspects the tiny props being used as Joey's kidney stones, and suggests using rice instead. "You do those things because otherwise you slap yourself later," says Bright. Syndication—like God—is in the details.

The showrunners request assorted line changes from the cast with directions like "bigger," "more," "less," "more seductive," "more defensive," and "even *more* deflated." One might expect a little attitude from the cast, but more typical is Aniston, who responds to one suggestion from Bright with a cheery "Yes, sir" and a brief neck rub. The actors themselves make suggestions—Perry's particularly full of ideas—but not all of these ideas are workable, and it's up to the showrunners to distinguish.

Later in the afternoon there's a break while everyone prepares for the long night ahead. Finally, around five, just as the audiences are shepherded into the bleachers, a giant cake is brought out proclaiming "100th Episode." A banner announcing "Congratulations! *Friends* 100th Episode" is unfurled. There are celebratory floral arrangements and several individual cakes in the shape of letters spelling "Friends."

In these days of cross-promotional synergy, this evening's celebratory toast and cake-cutting will also become a *Today Show* tie-in for NBC. This entertainment news event draws camera crews from CNN and *Access Hollywood,* which will bank stories to run in time to promote the episode's October 8 airing. NBC Entertainment president Warren Littlefield arrives, as does Warner Bros. president Tony Jonas—key players with overlapping but conflicting interests in a politically correct *Friends* photo-op.

In the bleachers, warm-up comic Jim Bentley starts his duties keeping the audience excited. To absolutely no one's surprise, the crowd doesn't cheer nearly as loudly for the showrunners as for the cast members during preshow curtain calls. Then again, the showrunners make more money, have better parking spaces, and never get mobbed on the street.

Bright Kauffman Crane reappear more formally dressed and have no trouble hugging for the cameras. Toasts are made. "Contrary to popular opinion, it doesn't feel bad to hit one hundred," Bright tells the crowd. Unsurprisingly, Crane salutes the show's writers, while Kauffman hails the cast ("You are the friends, and you are *our* friends"). Unfortunately, there are a few technical problems during the toasting ceremony, including accidental Jimi Hendrix–like mike feedback, a screw-up that irks the perfectionist Bright. "The show is better than this, I *promise*," he tells the audience.

Finally, at 5:55 P.M., take one of Scene A rolls, and Bright calls, "Action" for the first time of the night. The cast—who have appeared varying shades of rusty today—immediately seem polished. Whatever was tentative becomes confident and sharp.

Things move quickly at first, until Scene B, during which things slow dramatically and hilariously. In the script, Phoebe responds to news that her doctor is not coming to deliver her children by telling the friends, "Easy for you to say! I don't see three children coming out of your vagina!"—a sort of dialogue never heard on *Father Knows Best* or *Leave It to Beaver*. Tonight other versions of the line are attempted—substituting "ho-ho" for "vagina," for instance. As things bog down, the cast confers; then Kudrow, with some visible reluctance, throws in the phrase "dick ditch." Later Schwimmer explains that the entire cast has bet Kudrow she wouldn't try it. "She got some *serious* money for saying that," Schwimmer says admiringly.

Not everyone pays up. "I feel bad asking for money from my cast-mates over that," Kudrow explains later. "LeBlanc actually threw it out because the writers were trying to come up with something other than 'vagina.' While they went off to figure out something, LeBlanc said, 'How about dick ditch?' We laughed so hard because that was the most *horrible* thing we ever heard. Somebody said, 'I will pay you $200 to say that.' And I said, 'Yeah, well, I'll say it.' Matthew Perry was like, 'No, no, don't really, though. You really will? Oh my god, I don't think I could. You really gonna?' I was like, 'Yeah,' I don't understand what the fear is. Why not, it's the one hundredth episode, what's going to happen—I'm going to get fired?"

Even during filming, work goes on. Crane tries out a new joke on Kauffman, who laughs loudly, then rushes over to LeBlanc with it. A minute later, the line is on film. "To me if you just heard a joke die, how do you go on?" asks Crane. At 10 P.M., Bright, Kauffman, and Crane are still discussing how to stage a particular bedpan joke. By this time the happiest sound is the cry of "Moving On" whenever a scene's deemed finished. A few audience members file out, even though the *Friends* birthday cake is being brought up to the stands. At eleven P.M.—as Scene YY is shot—the DJ plays the Ramones' "I Wanna Be Sedated."

Around midnight, it's finally a wrap, and the *Friends* private post-show festivities get under way. The cast and crew gather in the hospital waiting room set, and familiar friends of *Friends* appear, including Cox's boyfriend David Arquette and Paul Reubens, aka Pee Wee Herman.

"One more order," Bright announces. "Everybody onstage grab your champagne, please!"

Bright Kauffman Crane gather the troops and hug the cast and crew members as "That's What Friends Are For" plays over the stage's sound system. Looking around this huge room of *Friends*, Kauffman looks moved, if exhausted, as she makes the inevitable yet fitting final toast. "Here's to another hundred that don't *suck!*"

"Before we begin I'd like to say how honored I am to be taking over this spot," Frasier Crane declares in the opening of the September 24 season premiere of *Frasier*. "Obviously I have some rather big shoes to fill. My predecessor here was much beloved, but I have never been one to shrink from a challenge."

In the storyline, prime time's most beloved shrink was actually auditioning for a new TV job, but Kelsey Grammer and his *Frasier* colleagues managed to make a graceful nod to their blessing of a challenge in inheriting the holy *Seinfeld* time slot.

That blessing looked more mixed in the fresh light of ratings when the hallowed NBC Thursday night lineup encounters an 18 percent viewership decline from the previous year's *Seinfeld* premiere numbers. Twenty-eight million viewers watch *Frasier* that Thursday rather than the 38 million who'd watched *Seinfeld* in the fall of 1997. *Friends*—

beaten out along with *Mad About You*, *Just Shoot Me!*, and *3rd Rock from the Sun* by *Frasier* for the *Seinfeld* slot—performs better, bringing in 32 million, many of them no doubt anxious to find out the latest on Ross's cliffhanger wedding and Monica and Chandler's surprise hop into the sack. *ER* falls from 43 to 32 million viewers, *Veronica's Closet*, gets 10 million less hangers. *Jesse* starts off strongly, holding its own far better than *Union Square* did in 1997 and instantly becoming the most watched new series of the season.

Two days later, *Cupid*'s arrival is greeted by a less than hearty critical reception. "Modestly lovable" could be read as burying a show with too faint praise, but "interminably long and talky" is plain old burying. Both phrases pop up in Howard Rosenberg's *Los Angeles Times* review of the show when it debuts on September 26, while on the other coast, the *New York Times* offers a noncommittal comment calling *Cupid* "wistful."

All this seems forgotten later that evening when a hundred or so *Cupid* fellow travelers gather at creator Rob Thomas's small house in the Hollywood foothills for a little premiere party. Near Thomas's bar there's a *Cupid* promo poster with a photo of Jeremy Piven and the words:

**Ginseng. Spanish Fly. Barry White.**
**All Rolled into One.**
***Cupid***
**A Unique New Drama**
**ABC Saturdays.**

On Thomas's refrigerator, there is a picture of the show's leading lady, Paula Marshall, signed, "Why am I in Chicago and you're here in the Jacuzzi?" The party crowd—a mix of show staff, network and studio types including Mandalay Television owner Peter Guber and president Scott Sanders—is mostly young, attractive, and clearly excited, though most have seen the pilot before. As the show's *Fantasy Island* lead-in ends with a tired Clinton gag, the partygoers grow quiet, take seats, and watch with great interest as this moment of TV truth arrives. The *Cupid* pilot unfolds; everyone cheers heartily before the commercial breaks for Tylenol or Taco Bell and the other products *Cupid*'s advertisers are looking to push.

Thomas doesn't allow himself to get too overwhelmed by this encouragingly vocal response from a bunch of the ringers. "I think it's a *slightly* partisan crowd," he explains with a sly grin. Listening carefully, Thomas notices that the smaller crowd in the kitchen has become more vocal than the living room gang. "Apparently, the show's better in the other room," he announces.

When *Cupid* ends at eleven, the news breaks in with word that Mark McGwire has hit home runs number sixty-seven and sixty-eight. The next morning it will be clear that *Cupid* hasn't hit so solidly in its first Nielsen at-bat. Monday morning's *Daily Variety* will refer to the show as one of the weekend's "biggest ratings disappointments"—enough to make a showrunner yearn for the days of "modestly lovable." *Cupid* finishes the week in seventy-fourth place. Ninety-nine episodes before heavenly syndication, *Cupid* is already suffering the slings and arrows of outrageous Nielsen fortune.

## OCTOBER

# A Chill in the Smog

E stands for exulting in the success of others, especially your competitors and those who consider themselves your enemies.

Deepak Chopra,
*Creating Affluence: The A-to-Z Steps to Success*

Once upon a time, Phil Rosenthal ran P. J. Bernstein, a deli restaurant on Third Avenue and Seventieth Street on Manhattan's East Side. These days he's running another tasty operation, *Everybody Loves Raymond*.

"It was very similar to what I do now," the menschy Rosenthal says of his bygone days pushing Dr. Browns Cream Soda and pastrami. Right now, before heading off to a *Raymond* rehearsal, he is in his roomy office on the Warner Bros. lot, a space formerly occupied by animation great Chuck Jones near Warner Bros. Studio's Laramie Street faux Western Town, where films such as *High Noon* and *Blazing Saddles* were shot.

Resolutely down-to-earth with a voice that suggests a younger, noncantankerous Jackie Mason, Rosenthal is a nice Jewish boy in his thirties, a *hamisha* hotshot who could convince you that producing a great TV show isn't that dissimilar from making a great sandwich.

Food actually turns out to be a serious matter in the world of *Everybody Loves Raymond*. The name of Rosenthal's production company is Where's Lunch? and he proudly explains that it has "the only changing logo in television—a different plate of food each week." Arguably the most beloved person on the *Raymond* set isn't one of the mere on-screen stars but John Lee, provider of the show's craft services.

"Food is the writers' main preoccupation," Rosenthal explains. "You're stuck in the room, in the veal pen all day—where is the light coming in? The light is the *menus*. On the set, we have John, who's not from television but from huge movies. He did *Terminator II*. If he can make Arnold Schwarzenegger happy, he's gonna make our little sitcom *very* happy."

The writers' room is down the main hallway from Rosenthal's office. On the way there, you pass interoffice memos including one which reads:

> Yes, *Frasier* will always beat us in the ratings, but with your help we can find other ways to humiliate them. No, it's not Lew Schneider's Ex-Lax idea, it's . . . 1998 Prime Time Softball.

Tragically, *Raymond* is having a fairly dismal season on the softball diamond, while *Desmond Pfeiffer* tops the Prime Time League's Western Division. In every other way, *Raymond*'s emerging as one of the season's few clear-cut ratings winners—despite the fact that it overlaps one half-hour with the country's litigious, lightweight heartthrob Ally McBeal, whose weight has becomes a topic of national concern despite her prodigious onscreen chowing during Fox's World Series coverage.

Once the Queens-born Rosenthal dreamed he'd end up on the other side of the camera. He studied acting at Hofstra University on Long Island with the goal of being a comic character actor. "I was pretty good at it but what I could not take was the audition process—I just didn't have the stomach for it," he recalls, sitting in front of a *Broadway Danny Rose* poster. Summer stock gave Rosenthal formative training. "Every week we put on a huge musical: *The Music Man*, next week *South Pacific*, the next week *My Fair Lady*—this is the same thing," he says. Of course, the money's a little different from summer stock. "Little bit, little bit," Rosenthal answers, "though in summer stock everyone slept together and so far that hasn't happened here."

After graduating from Hofstra in 1981, he took odd jobs in New York City to subsidize his acting, including the deli gig and a stint as a Metropolitan Museum of Art security guard. Eventually, like so many young men before him, Rosenthal was told to go West.

"An agent saw me in a play off-off Broadway and said to come out here and I would *never* stop working," Rosenthal remembers. "I came here and I never *started* working. Nothing. *Nothing.*" He met with a casting director; still nothing. Tired of waiting for the phone to ring, Rosenthal paired up with Oliver Goldstick—a playwright he had first met in New York—to try and write sitcom scripts. Together they wrote a *Roseanne* about Rosenthal's time as a museum guard and a spec script *Murphy Brown*. "Within two weeks we had an agent at William Morris," Rosenthal says, still sounding surprised.

His first writing job with a series was on *A Family for Joey*, a sitcom created by *Love American Style*'s Arnold Margolin, starring Robert Mitchum as a homeless man who pretends he's the grandfather of a group of kids. "Yeah, you hear Mitchum, and right away you think *sitcoms*," Rosenthal says with a grin. The show premiered midseason for NBC in March 1990 and was dead by August. It wasn't a particularly good show, but Rosenthal says, "They tell me what you learn on your first show you can learn on any show. You just want to learn how it works; it doesn't matter if it's good or bad, it'd be *better* if it was good. I learned the workings of television. I learned what *not* to do, and Robert Mitchum was a thrill to know. He was very accessible and funny and his attitude was like, 'I'm a plumber—I come in, I do my job, I get paid and go home.'"

From there Rosenthal and Goldstick attended the troubled birth of *Baby Talk*, a 1991 ABC series based on the 1989 wisecracking baby flick *Look Who's Talking*. "You know who played the Travolta part in that one?" Rosenthal asks. "George Clooney. The executive producer was a great man, Ed Weinberger. I wanted to work with him on whatever—it happened to be *Baby Talk*."

*DAVID WILD*

Next Rosenthal and Goldstick followed Weinberger to *A Man in the Family*, an ABC sitcom starring Ray Sharkey. The experience was "a little unpleasant." Why? "He wasn't a nice person," says Rosenthal of the actor, who later died of AIDS. "It's terrible what happened to him but it wasn't a comedy feeling on that set."

Happier times were had making *Down the Shore*, a Fox series that debuted in the summer of 1992, about a bunch of young New Yorkers hanging out in a beach house. "That was a *great* experience," Rosenthal says. "One of my best friends from high school, Alan Kirshenbaum, created the show about him and his friends—one of whom happened to be me. It was honestly a precursor to *Friends*, the only problem was we didn't have the *Friends*. We had very good people, but they didn't catch on."

When *Shore* sank, Rosenthal and Goldstick went over to the already established *Coach,* which Kirshenbaum was running under creator Barry Kemp. "It was like a comedy factory; you had to meet production deadlines," Rosenthal says. "I learned how to work ahead. Then you don't have to work as hard—you can eat more and work less. *That's* the key of good showrunning."

After the second season assisting *Coach*, Rosenthal and Goldstick amicably split as writing partners. Partners, he explains, are the bargain of the business. "They pay you like you're one entity, but you're *not* one writer," Rosenthal says. "We're in the room *spritzing* and giving jokes—not whispering to each other and saying, 'Here's *our* idea.' We split up because it was enough already, plus *Coach* wasn't Oliver's sensibility. It wasn't mine either but I thought, 'I'm going to stay one year and establish myself on my own in comfortable surroundings.'"

During his third season at *Coach*, Rosenthal was asked to take a meeting with a comic named Ray Romano, whom he had caught on a Letterman spot a few months earlier. The pair met at Art's, a popular deli in the Valley, in November 1995. Romano was impressed on many levels.

"For the amount of food he eats, it's the flatness of his ass that's amazing," Romano says of his surprisingly trim boss. "I challenge any star of show and showrunner in a total girth and width of ass contest. Between me and him we are the flattest-assed combo."

Before such corporeal glory, however, they were just two guys on a sort of sitcomical blind date—a potential star looking for a potential showrunner. Romano had already lost one TV role—after a single day of rehearsal on *NewsRadio*, he was relieved of duty in the part later played by Joe Rogan, WNYX's somewhat trusty engineer. "I *knew* I sucked at that," Romano says now. "It's not like I thought I was doing a good job. I knew in my gut and my heart. I was green. I didn't know where to stand on the stage. I didn't know what I was doing. The casting director called my manager and my manager called me at, like, six-thirty in the morning on day three of rehearsal. As soon as I picked it up, I *knew*. He said, 'They're going in another direction'—the standard line they give you—and I said, 'Where are they going? I'll meet them there.'"

After the future collaborators first broke bread, Rosenthal was approached to see how he would build a show around Romano. "They asked, 'Would you have an idea for this guy?' I had what I thought was a stupid, simple answer—I would do a show that *is* this guy rather than make him a gay astronaut from Cleveland. When you're starting with a comedian who's never acted before, it's in your best interest to keep the character close."

Rosenthal knew he wasn't the only one being approached, so he was excited when two months later he was in New York for the holidays and got a call from David Letterman's people asking to meet about Romano's show, which was going to be a Worldwide Pants production. "I meet Robert Morton, Rob Burnett, and they say Dave wants to meet you," he recalls. "They gesture for me to sit behind Dave's desk like it's my office. So the first thing I did was throw them out of my office. That was a twenty-minute meeting. I've never seen David Letterman again. I've talked to him maybe once or twice a year when he calls up and says, 'Hey, you're doing a good job.'"

*Everybody Loves Raymond* started out a long shot—CBS's better slots went to bigger stars—Ted Danson and Mary Steenburgen, Bill

Cosby, Rhea Perlman and Malcolm McDowell. Ray Romano—a gifted working comic but hardly a household name—didn't qualify then. *Raymond* got Fridays at eight-thirty. "CBS hasn't had a hit at that time slot since . . . *Gomer Pyle*," says Rosenthal. "That was the *bad* news. The good news was there were no expectations."

Critics embraced *Raymond* and, more significantly, CBS's president and CEO Les Moonves became a vocal fan of the show. Still, the series was mired in the lowly eighties of the Nielsen rankings until March of its first season. Then Moonves told Rosenthal they were giving *Raymond* a six-episode run on Mondays at eight-thirty. Rosenthal recalls, "Suddenly we were petrified, coming from our protected place— where nobody knows and nobody cares—to Monday." Not to worry— ratings doubled and Monday became the family comedy's new home.

As a first-time showrunner, Rosenthal had one frighteningly golden rule: "Be *nice*. Everybody be nice, because I've worked on shows where it wasn't so nice. Let's start from there because we have to live together. I think it shows in the work. No star trips and if there are it's bang, back in your place. Don't pull that shit here."

Rosenthal credits his leading man with helping him create the right atmosphere in which to create. "Ray's a sweetheart," he says. "When we met, I just talked to him about his family. I found out his parents did live nearby and he had twin boys and a little girl. His brother was a police office who was divorced and living with his parents. I got to know his parents later. After getting to know those details, I then filled in *my* family. Some of the things are a combination of his family, my family, and what the actors bring to it. It's a very happy soup."

Romano confirms that the family that ended up on air was a cross-cultural combination of his and his showrunner's own tribes. "I think the father character is closest to mine in real life," he says. "My father is exactly like Peter Boyle is, yeah. The mother is without a doubt strongly influenced by Phil's mother, her mannerisms, the things she does, her tone of voice. My mother's the same type, but she's very low-key. So it's a combination of the Jewish-Italian family. What was weird was the first time Phil asked if I would wear a Hofstra T-shirt to bed, because he graduated from there. I made sure the next three times I was wearing a Queens College T-shirt."

According to Romano, it took a little time for him to be totally happy with his own level of involvement in the creative process. "There weren't any sparks, but I don't know if he was aware of how creatively involved I wanted to be," he recalls. "To be fair to Phil, he'd only worked with actors before. The show was going to be based on my persona as shown in my standup—what I created—and I wanted to be strongly involved. If it wasn't in my voice, I didn't think I could pull it off." Over the first five or six weeks, it became obvious that Romano had to be more of a fixture in the writers' room.

If Rosenthal sometimes sounds like a bit of a Boy Scout—one whose handbook comes in Yiddish—consider his other guiding principle of showrunning: "Be prepared. Utilize the preproduction time. We have every story broken for the season in July, except for maybe one or two. We were ahead last year, and so we had ten drafts when we started preproduction this year."

This kind of unusual advance work helps the *Raymond* staff keep a sane schedule during the season. "In order to write about life, you have to *have* one," Rosenthal offers. Certainly *Raymond*'s nonsaccharine family comedy has a lived-in quality. Rosenthal learned a valuable lesson reading about how Carl Reiner ran *The Dick Van Dyke* show by having everyone go around the room and say what happened at his or her house the previous weekend. "You talk and all of a sudden there's an episode," Rosenthal explains. "We laugh now because we can't believe we get to put our wives' horrible habits on television."

With all this nice talk and everybody loving *Raymond*, the unpure mind wonders if there is any dark side around here. "I get angry like anyone else," Rosenthal says. "I get insulted if the studio treats us badly." And when was the last time that happened? "This year—I don't know if I should say what happened—I *will* say I resented being put in the middle of a war between the studio and the network over who's going to pay for what," he says. "I felt it wasn't my place to be put in such a position and I was. And I got *very* angry."

Rosenthal now has an overall deal with Disney, one said to earn him $16 million over the next four years—more than enough to

*DAVID WILD*

cover quite a few excellent meals for Rosenthal; his actress wife, Monica Horan; their four-year-old son; Ben, and their one-year-old daughter, Lily.

*Everybody* loves $16 million.

Rosenthal has been meeting other talent with his eye toward creating a new series but Disney has let him stay on with *Raymond*, then develop something for next year. "I'll *always* be connected to *Raymond* and Ray's involvement also grows," he says. "Really, I'd be happy if this was the only show I ever did. How many things do I have to be remembered by?"

*Everybody Loves Raymond* may be remembered for, among other things, prevailing in the court of popular opinion over the more high-profile *Ally McBeal* and *Monday Night Football* so far this season. "Yeah, I thought we'd get *killed*," Rosenthal admits of the *Ally* challenge. "It's the most hyped show ever on television. Now we beat it—this to me is *unbelievable*. This to me is like . . . there's a God." Had things not started so well, might he have put the cast in miniskirts? "Sure, and I thought everyone should go on a diet to the point of anorexia," he says with a laugh. "Actually, no, because the food must be fantastic."

A few days later, Rosenthal enters the *Raymond* stage on the other end of the Warners lot for show day on an episode called "The Article" and heads straight to John Lee's catering table of plenty positioned just across the stage floor from the Barone parents' kitchen. He samples an olive and cream dish. Then he crosses over to a small crowd of colleagues gathered around Brad Garrett, who plays Ray's brother Robert on the show. Garrett is telling tales of his two big recent events, the birth of a baby boy and a small part in an upcoming Woody Allen movie. *Raymond* is very nicely shooting a day later than normal this week to accommodate Garrett.

When rehearsal gets under way, the former character-actor-turned-showrunner repeatedly jumps in and gives his own line readings to show the cast precisely what he's looking for from them. Truth be told, Rosenthal is quite good—though coming out of his mouth, the bantering of TV's most beloved Italian clan sounds slightly more kosher.

During a break before the studio audience enters, Romano sits back in his TV living room for a Turner Broadcasting interview to promote his new book, *Everything and a Kite*. He's asked about any rivalry between *Raymond* and *Ally McBeal*.

"Somebody said my legs were nicer," Romano deadpans. *"That's where it started."*

Around seven P.M.—midway through the filming—John Lee slips out to the entrance to meet a Little Caesar's man delivering well over $500 of pizza, though Caesar renders unto *Raymond* a volume discount and charges only $499. Yes, they feed their studio audience here too.

"It's *nice*," says Lee, suddenly sounding like Rosenthal. "I mean, they have to watch us eat, *right?"*

One more reason—this one cheesy—for everybody to love *Raymond*.

On October 8, the one hundredth episode of *Friends*—the one with the birth—airs, and it turns out to be a blessed event for NBC that helps the network win its first week of the young but already troubled season. A win is desperately needed, as rumors are flying that there may soon be big changes at the top of the network. In such a tense climate, "The One Hundredth" proves a big old-fashioned must-see hit, and within industry circles there's speculation that NBC may have miscalculated by anointing *Frasier* and not *Friends* in the sanctified nine o'clock *Seinfeld* spot, since America's funniest shrink is currently suffering from ratings shrinkage of his own.

During the episode, Phoebe Buffay can be heard saying "vagina"— rather than "dick ditch"—loud and clear on prime-time network TV. There is little public protest, and according to the trades, the Earth continues to spin in the same basic pattern.

There's far more protest on the other end of the Nielsen rainbow, where UPN's *The Secret Diary of Desmond Pfeiffer* resides, however briefly. The show is charged with being racially insensitive and horrifically unfunny. In an unusual move Los Angeles City Councilman Mark Ridley-Thomas calls for the series to be investigated by L.A.'s Human Relations Commission. The network eventually pulls the planned pilot, and instead broadcasts an episode called "On-line Abe," in which President Lincoln gets involved in the Civil War–era equivalent of cybersex.

On Monday, October 5—*Desmond*'s big premiere day, its date with dismal destiny—Jesse Jackson joins a picket line in front of Paramount Studios protesting the show, with chants of "Just take it off the air. Just stop it. Just say no." Remarkably, far worse things are said about the show—on this same day when the House Judiciary Committee votes for an impeachment inquiry on Lincoln's successor Bill Clinton, *Desmond* gets utterly assassinated by America's TV critics.

Freedom fighters everywhere find themselves in the awkward position of standing up for a lousy show to defend to the death *Desmond*'s constitutionally protected right to suck. That said, there's no shortage of excellent reasons to attack and mock *Pfeiffer*—the primary one being that while the "P" in *Pfeiffer* isn't silent, the laughs sure are.

On the far eastern edge of the Paramount lot—surrounded by Joint Operations maps of the Vietnam conflict—the writing staff of *Seven Days* is waging limited warfare on a few scripts.

Tonight UPN's pulpy new time-travel drama premieres with a special two-hour episode. The pressure is on, not simply for *Seven Days*—said to be the most expensive network pilot ever produced, at $10 million—but also for UPN as a network.

Some of the show's largely positive reviews hang proudly on the bulletin board, including this morning's near rave from *Los Angeles Times* TV critic Howard Rosenberg, but there is surprisingly little talk around the office about tonight's big launch. Unlike the rest of the world, they have already seen the pilot. Rather than worrying about the present, or seven days into the past—the amount of time the show's hero Frank Parker can "backtrack" in time to save the world on a weekly basis—everyone here is focusing three days into the future, when the show's eighth episode, "Shadow Play," must start filming.

"You enjoy a good pilot in solitude and then by the time it airs and you could be celebratory, you're in the mire, the Vietnam of doing a series," says Christopher Crowe, executive producer and cocreator of *Seven Days*.

This afternoon the mire finds Crowe meeting first with supervising producer Tom Ropelewski and consulting producer Michael Cassutt, who are helping him run this show, then separately with the other writers. *Seven Days* shoots a freeway drive away near Magic Mountain in a vaguely ominous space that formerly housed research and development for Lockheed. The writers were originally set to toil there too, until it became clear that their windowless facilities would make them even crazier than the job required.

For years now, Crowe has traveled fairly freely between the worlds of feature films and TV—"crop rotations," he calls it. The Wisconsin-born native and former auto racing reporter has written or cowritten numerous movies, including *The Last of the Mohicans* and *The Mean Season,* and directed films like *Whispers in the Dark* and *Off Limits*. He was executive producer for a number of series, including UPN's *The Watcher* and *The Untouchables*, which was syndicated—a show sold directly to stations in each market rather than to a network. Now Crowe has created *Seven Days* with his nineteen-year-old son, Zachary, quite possibly the only cocreator/production assistant combination in television history.

Whatever Christopher Crowe's age—he politely declines to share it—he looks more like a Midwestern Keith Richards than your typical TV geek. Recently Crowe even released his first CD—a wild, poetic, bluesy affair suggesting both Tom Waits and Leonard Cohen. Clearly he's a music lover—the other night Eric Burdon, onetime lead singer of the Animals, sang at his birthday party, which he celebrated with fiancée Julie Park, a former member of Femme II Femme, a group positioned as a sort of bisexual Spice Girls.

*DAVID WILD*

*Seven Days* emerged during a 1997 lunch with Crowe, NBC's Warren Littlefield, and Kerry McCluggage, who runs Paramount TV. As Crowe recalls, "Kerry had a notion—just spitballing, bullshitting like a bunch of asshole kids. He said, 'What if we could get a device to go back in time seven days?'" Right away Crowe saw the possibilities. "Always time shows have dealt with the business of trans-era travel," he explains. "This really was a genre that was not yet explored. You can only go back in your own era and rectify something—it's a natural human fantasy." In creating TV shows, showrunners are often called on to reinvent the wheel, and this wheel just happen to go backward in time.

Next, *Seven Days* was developed as a pilot for NBC—Crowe recalls "great excitement in the trenches about it, then it didn't go." That might have been the end of it, but Dean Valentine—then at Disney, but before long president and CEO of UPN—read the script and was intrigued. Soon *Seven Days* was a go at UPN, a network whose own days were thought by some naysayers to be numbered. UPN was the same network that canceled *The Watcher*, Crowe's twisted Vegas-set series starring rapper Sir Mix-a-lot, which debuted during the network's 1995 launch year. That was around a dark time in Crowe's life, during which he cops to being too intimately involved with some rock-and-roll-ish substances. Nonetheless Crowe remains angry that former UPN president and CEO Lucille Salhany killed *The Watcher* after less than half a season.

It was fun while it lasted. "We got by with fucking murder," Crowe recalls. "We went *nuts*. That show was UPN's highest-rated hour ever other than their space shows and dumb Lucie canceled it."

This time around at UPN Crowe is encouraged to have a Wednesday night time slot, since *Seven Days*—the lead-in to *Star Trek: Voyager*—is a heavily male-skewing show going up against the more female-friendly *Beverly Hills 90210* and *Dawson's Creek*. Still, Crowe has his work cut out for him. "How we do depends on UPN to some degree," he says. "They have to dig out a ditch. Lucie *created* a ditch."

A board in the *Seven Days* writers' room marked "DO NOT ERASE" reads "All Changes Back in Time Are Caused by Parker. Heavies Always Go to a 'B' Plan (the 'Oh, Fuck' Factor)." On another wall there is a diagram breaking down the show into four acts with assorted guiding principles. To hear Crowe tell it, the laws of *Seven Days* were hard-earned. "This is a unique show because you have that backstep and it was giving us fits," he explains. "By its nature this is an odd construction. You don't have the normal rising action and the climatic event. You almost have a climatic event at the beginning. We needed a basic cookie cutter because you need some kind of formula at least to violate."

The board represents that elusive dramatic cookie cutter—a functional architectural plan for building this time-traveling yarn in which the show's hero (played by Jonathan LaPaglia) turns back the hands of time for an elite, covert military intelligence unit that just happens to include an Iron Curtain cutie.

For Crowe, having the formula down allows writers to get to the meat of the thing. "It's always opera, opera, opera," Crowe says. "It's *never* mechanics. You have to be ever vigilant that the opera is right. We're getting it down to where we can dispense with that shit. If you don't have this, you tend to handmake the show—things work but you don't know how. A lot of movies are like that where you have endless time to finger-fuck around. We *don't* have that time."

Crowe, Ropelewski, and Cassutt briefly assess the progress on another recent episode, "Vows," about which Crowe had been concerned.

"It won't be the Emmy submission but it's no reason to jump off the Bludhorn Building," Cassutt tells Crowe, referring to a structure on the Paramount lot. They discuss budget matters, including cutting mounting costs on the episode called "Shadow Play" by moving a scene from night to day. With his tongue at least partly in cheek, Crowe refers less than fondly to the forces of fiscal accountability as "the Doberman cocksuckers." Still, these dogs of finance must be fed. "People have inflated our budget," Crowe says. "The budget now has become legendary, but other people have spent what we spent per minute this season. There were other people with $5 million hours and we had a $10 million two-hour. I think the whole thing worked out pretty well."

*DAVID WILD*

Crowe gives the pair a list of changes large and small he'd like to see made to "Shadow Play," communicating to these showrunning sergeants in shorthand—"clean that," "fix that," "dial that up."

None of this remotely fazes the veteran writers, both in their forties. Cassutt was most recently at *Beverly Hills 90210* but has also written for shows including *Max Headroom* and *Eerie, Indiana*. Tom Ropelewski, who was on UPN's short-lived *Three*, was a network executive back in the early eighties and has gone on to direct feature films like *Look Who's Talking Now* and *Madhouse*.

"The difficult we do immediately," Cassutt explains. "The impossible takes until two A.M." Thankfully, today's changes for "Shadow Play" are merely difficult.

No man is a showrunner to Crowe, who freely admits he's not a micromanager. "I'm not Moses coming down with the fucking Word," he says, confessing he's already stayed away from the set for more than a month at a time. Despite the room's war map decorations, Crowe takes pride in keeping his writing staff "a very unmilitary un–pecking order. Everyone runs the show with me. I look at dailies but if things are going well, they'll never hear from me other than to say, 'Good job.' A lot of guys who do this are fucked up that way—I'm still just a kid with crayons in the basement. I'm supposed to be the Mad Hatter because I say 'Fuck you, make a decision. You *know* what your mission is.' I'm not Bob McNamara in the White House, which a lot of guys who run shows are. I leave it to the boys in the field."

Tomorrow morning, Crowe will get the overnight ratings for *Seven Days*, a first indication of things to come—or possibly not to come. Crowe is not sweating these early numbers. "It doesn't test us, it tests their promotion," he says calmly. "Our show tested great—it's UPN bringing people into the tent. Ratings certainly can have an effect on the atmosphere but I can't worry about that shit."

Next, Crowe meets with the show's other writers for a story-breaking meeting in which various scripts in the works are discussed and potential new ones are "gangbanged" or hashed out by the group around the conference table. Crowe runs this meeting like some Deadhead Poets' Society seminar. He draws on his years of experience in a manner that is stream-of-consciousness and still focused. There is a little Socratic dialogue, a little bullshitting, a little inspirational speaking, lots of swearing—basically the creative process in all its ragged glory.

At one point, Crowe refers back to rules he learned working on *Baretta.* "Baretta was the messiah," he explains. "The bad guy was devil and there's *always* some assholes in the middle."

For *Seven Days*, Crowe's assembled a writing staff that's a mix of "older writers who have industrial wisdom" and "younger writers who think in that fuckin' free-associative kinetic fuckin' uncontainable way." There are six writers in the room today—five men and one woman.

Another element in the mix is not visible today—the show's resident spook. "We have some real fuckin' paranoid government–ex-government types, *professional* paranoids," Crowe says with pride. "The main one is in army intelligence and has lots of access to a lot of shit flying around the Intel business." Harry Cason—a staff writer who nearly went to *Walker, Texas Ranger* before coming to *Seven Days*—explains that "the spook works at home. He was a CIA operative in East Germany. He did a lot of strange stuff."

Crowe calls this meeting to order. "Just to keep everyone up to speed, Harry and I are working on a story wherein the President's illegitimate progeny is kidnapped," Crowe tells the room. Understandably, talk dissolves into a discussion of President Clinton's recent activities, a situation that hardly shocks the been-there-done-that Crowe.

"One of the great truths I've learned over the years is that people *fuck*," Crowe explains deadpan to a room soon full of appreciative laughter. All agree it might be wise to switch the character from a president to a governor.

Moving on to more pressing matters, Crowe works his way around the room, dealing out quick fixes ("Dial up the A story, dial down the B"), mild criticism, savvy advice, subtle admonishments and outright praise to writers in need, all the while chain-smoking his beloved American Spirits.

Crowe reminds his team that TV can't compete with action films,

that it must be character-driven, emotional, primal—"opera." This is
how to make the viewer connect, care—"and *that's* our big fuckin'
mission," he explains. "We are creatures of simple emotion." Crowe
then offers suggested viewing and reading to help solve their problems—to a writer who's struggling with an episode involving mutiny
and rock-and-roll, he recommends not only Shakespeare, but *The
Caine Mutiny* and *Crimson Tide* as well.

"It's earn while you learn around here," Harry Cason whispers
with a grin.

Highbrow and lowbrow commingle in curious ways in the *Seven
Days* writers' room—two of the most common words out of Crowe's
mouth today are "verisimilitude" and "buttfuckery."

A bit of a History Channel junkie, Crowe is not one to dismiss the
power of the medium. "Church and synagogue are not attended the
way they once were," he says, "so it kind of becomes our job to pass
along the moral jungle drums. We are priestly and rabbinical in a way."

When Crowe's sermon at the Paramount lot is over, he asks, "Is
everyone engaged now?" The troops responding affirmatively, Crowe
sends them back to their trenches—oops, offices. "No one's sitting
dead in the water, *right?*"

One more mission accomplished, Crowe golf-carts across the lot to
the *Seven Days* editing rooms—just across the hall from where *Desmond
Pfeiffer* supposedly comes together. Crowe watches a future "backstep," then tries to smooth over a small skirmish that has erupted
between various editors, the sort of turf war any showrunner must
settle. To lighten the mood, Crowe tells a joke about two brain sur-
geons that ends with one telling the other, "Don't worry, it's not
episodic TV."

Crowe goes over to the next room to check out a trailer for the
"Come Again" episode. The trailer is amusing, but aware of his audience's tastes, he requests more action be thrown into the mix. Harry
Cason pops in, and asks his most fearless leader if he has any notion
of how much is at stake for him financially when *Seven Days* airs in a
few hours.

"No, I'm in massive debt because that's my life and I don't even ask about it," Crowe explains with clear disinterest in the topic.

"He could make, like, $25 million if this goes five years, and he doesn't even want to *know* about it," Cason says of his boss.

The next morning, the *Seven Days* overnight ratings come in and unlike *Desmond Pfeiffer,* it doesn't look dead in the water. Indeed, the show appears to be a relative shining light for the sixth network. The lingering question is, How long will there *be* a UPN on which to shine?

A call is placed to Paul Simms to check if there has been any progress whatsoever on the *OverSeas* pilot, once meant to be filming this month.

No return call is forthcoming.

From the start, the 1998–1999 fall lineup looks so weak it seems likely the networks will go to their bullpens early to keep up any appearance of staying in what's looking increasingly like a losing game. For all that TV *tsuris,* here is Ted Harbert—former chairman and president of ABC Entertainment—kicking back on a cloudy afternoon having a leisurely lunch at La Loggia, a tasty Italian spot just across from CBS Radford Studios in Studio City, with a big grin on his preppily handsome face.

Why is this man smiling?

Consider that word "former" in front of "chairman." From January 1993 to early 1997, Harbert was responsible for all prime-time and late night entertainment programming for ABC, but that's not his headache now. Harbert has crossed the great network suit/creative type divide. He's traded places from being the network to feeding the network, arguably a better spot in the food chain during a time of widespread layoffs and withering ratings. In leaving ABC, he negotiated himself a dignified exit and signed an exclusive two-and-a-half-year deal with DreamWorks to develop and produce new television shows. This is not uncommon—a production deal having become the standard valuable parting gift given to parachuting TV hotshots.

First, Harbert became executive producer of a sinking ship of an Arsenio Hall sitcom known, however briefly, as *Arsenio*, but now for the 1998–1999 season, he's helping steer a seemingly sturdier craft—a new sitcom for ABC with the unlikely title *It's like, you know . . . .*

Harbert's smile might also be explained by the funny man sitting beside him, Peter Mehlman, the creator and fellow executive producer of *It's like, you know . . .* , as well as the longtime *Seinfeld* writer whose contributions to popular comic culture include "yada yada," "spongeworthy," and "shrinkage," that delicate male condition with which the greatly missed George Costanza once famously grappled.

Both Harbert and Mehlman are casually dressed this afternoon for lunch, though it's two distinct levels of casual. Harbert—in a polo shirt and jeans—looks like a young CEO on vacation, which in a sense he is. Mehlman, on the other hand, wears khaki shorts and a sweater and looks like a wonderfully mad English professor on safari. On *Seinfeld*, characters were often identified by their noteworthy, eccentric behavior—"close talkers," "low talkers," etc. Were Mehlman to have popped up as one of Elaine Benes's love interests on the show, the gang might have tagged him a "shorts wearer"—a cool, casual dude, Mehlman even wore shorts to the big pitch meeting at ABC to sell them on *It's like, you know . . .*

"I just feel like I have more energy in shorts," explains Mehlman.

"It's not the first time—*all* the best writers wear shorts to pitch meetings," ABC's Jamie Tarses confirms later. "Writers are not known for their inclination to dress formally when they come to the network.

*Any* kind of dress is commonplace." Indeed, another gifted former *Seinfeld* scribe, Larry Charles, is said to be partial to wearing pajamas to work.

For his part, Harbert has worn shorts to work a couple of times. "I honestly felt like I was this . . . rebel, this *revolutionary*," he says. "The fact that I get to wear jeans to work is unbelievable."

Spoken like a recovering suit.

"Ted's in a great place," says Mehlman with a grin. "He's gone from the Joint Chief of Staff into the antiwar movement and *everybody* knows where there's more fun and more sex."

This somewhat odd couple first met in the summer of 1996 on a golf course in Malibu, an entirely fitting beginning for a show that would take as its topic the life of L.A.'s peculiar moneyed class. Later DreamWorks suggested they get together off the links. "There was a little bit of an arranged marriage, with DreamWorks just saying, 'Gee, why don't you guys go sit in a room and see if you don't kill each other,'" Harbert recalls. "We didn't."

*It's like, you know* . . . concerns a cynical New York journalist played by Chris Eigeman who comes to town to write a book about disliking Los Angeles and then finds himself becoming caught up in the strange world of his old college roommate Robbie (Steven Eckholdt), who now lives in the guest house of the wealthy Shrug (Evan Handler). Their Hollywood Hills neighbor is none other than onetime *Dirty Dancing* diva Jennifer Grey, who plays . . . Jennifer Grey, complete with nose job jokes and stalled career references. Then, since this is a show about Los Angeles, there's the adorable A. J. Langer—a veteran of *My So-Called Life*—as the adorable masseuse/process server/auxiliary babe.

Insomuch as such a thing is possible, Mehlman fell into becoming a showrunner. After graduating from the University of Maryland, Mehlman wrote for the *Washington Post*, then wrote and produced for Howard Cosell on a show called *Sports Beat*, before becoming a freelance magazine journalist. Looking for a change, he moved to Los Angeles, where he met up with Larry David—a fellow University of Maryland alum who was starting a little sitcom starring a standup comedian named Jerry Seinfeld. Instead of submitting a sample script, Mehlman offered an article he'd written in the *New York Times Magazine*. That was promising enough to land Mehlman a freelance gig and before long a staff job on what would eventually become one of the greatest sitcoms of all time.

"I consider myself to have absolutely *no* network TV experience," Mehlman says matter-of-factly. "I've just been on *Seinfeld*. This is *not* something aspiring writers in this town are very happy to hear."

*Seinfeld* would eventually make Mehlman rich beyond his ex-journalist imagination—as happened to others who played a role in *the* comedy of the nineties, offers arrived from those anxious to contractually acquire some *Seinfeld* magic. In Mehlman's case, he signed a deal with DreamWorks in 1997. He cashed in, but hardly jumped the first time he got the chance. "Why would I want to go anywhere else?" he asks. "I didn't care that much about money. I was a freelance magazine writer—that's *not* a field you go into if you're really interested in money. I was already making in my third episode at *Seinfeld* I think $15,000 an episode. Two episodes in I was making more than I would in a year as a freelancer. So what did I care? It was *all* gravy."

Still, even Mehlman could find room for a little more gravy. "It's basically *all* a pact with the devil," Mehlman explains, grinning. "They throw this money in your face and the next thing you know you are taking notes from a network and nodding your head."

Mehlman now takes considerable pride in not being desperate in a system that breeds paranoia and pandering. "To tell the truth, I'm probably a network's worst fucking nightmare because I think I have *plenty* of money," he says. "I don't really care about syndication. All I care about is putting on the show I want and if it goes, it goes. With that being my attitude, it's nice to have Ted there who *does* care about those things."

A waiter comes by the table to take the pair's lunch order and announce today's specials. "It's like Jerry said, 'If they're so special, why aren't they on the menu?'" Mehlman adds after ordering. Talk turns to a high-speed freeway chase occurring on nearby streets during this lunch hour. Mehlman points out that *It's like, you know . . .* already has an episode in the can called "The Getaway," about a freeway chase.

Ted Harbert insists he's thrilled to have made his own clean get-away from being directly in the line of network fire, even if the choice wasn't exactly optional. He gives every appearance of being in the happiest of exiles. Harbert also says he's happy now that *It's like, you know . . .* is sitting out the bloodbath of fall premieres.

"You bet, bub," says Harbert. "It gets increasingly ugly. So ugly now that nobody cares. We in this community try to make it such a big deal—the fall season is here! Viewers come during premiere week and they check out a few shows, but there's certainly no sense of excite-ment, except maybe for *Felicity*. A lot of shows fall off the second week. You already see people saying, 'Okay, I looked at it, I don't have to watch that anymore, thanks.' There's just not a marketing system available that can let the viewer get excited about thirty-six new shows coming on. It's a stupid system and we keep on doing it."

Harbert pauses to correct himself. "*They* keep on doing it," he says.

The aforementioned stupidity would seem to make starting mid-season the far wiser move, but it's still generally not the first choice of most showrunners. "Everyone gets in there and pounds away for that fall spot because there's still that thing about being on the start-ing lineup. A lot of it is male ego, guys who grew up in Little League and still want to be on the starting team. It's silly. It makes *no* sense."

"Since we're so much smarter . . ." says Mehlman.

"And more advanced . . ." adds Harbert.

"We're *not* doing that," Mehlman says.

Not that Harbert and Mehlman particularly had a choice—ABC didn't choose to put the poorly testing *It's like, you know . . .* on the fall schedule.

To Harbert, what's happening to the networks is what happened to radio networks in the sixties when all the targeted, formatted sta-tions came out and conquered by dividing, the same as happened to general-interest magazines like the *Saturday Evening Post, Look,* and *Life* with the arrival of target-specific magazines. "Hopefully there's enough of an appetite on the part of the viewers to watch well-done drama and comedy that they'll keep at least a few networks alive," Harbert says. "I don't know that they're going to keep *six* networks alive. I think that's rather improbable."

Another problem is the deathly impact of massive, around-the-clock overkill—for too long too many have been exposed to too much of a mediocre thing. As Harbert puts it, "Everyone in the eighteen to forty-nine bracket has been watching TV for so long, they've seen one of everything. They've seen *fifty* of everything."

*It's like, you know . . .* dissects El Lay peccadilloes in a manner not worlds away from how *Seinfeld* brilliantly sliced the Big Apple. While it's no doubt still finding its voice in Episode Six—a process that took even *Seinfeld* some time—the show aims to take a long quirky look at superficiality and wealth, at people who order Evian with Perrier ice cubes. Like *Seinfeld*, it's not stooping to conquer, making research-unfriendly references to John Updike and John Irving and "safety schools" in a single episode.

The first time he met officially with Harbert, Mehlman explained he wanted to do a show about wealth—after all, writers are told to write what they know. Sadly, outside the Hollywood Hills extreme wealth may not be perceived as the most readily relatable experience—though it never hurt *Dynasty* or those *Beverly Hillbillies*. Such issues will likely be researched by ABC, though Mehlman's not interested: "Every time they say, 'Yeah, but are people in Ohio going to understand this?' I just go 'Yeah.'"

*Seinfeld* proved there is a large discerning audience out there somewhere in America, but Mehlman believes that the show barely changed the fundamentally bland quality of network broadcasting.

"Do you know what the impact of *Seinfeld* is on the networks?" Mehlman asks. "*Zero*. The characters *still* have to be likable. We thought we had disabused people of that. You can go very, very far on pure funny, you know. The one thing I notice is they seemed to like the music of *Seinfeld*, but other than that not one iota of impact. I think actually there's a certain resentment toward *Seinfeld*. You had two guys who never did a sitcom in their lives and turned the whole thing on its ear. Establishments don't like that."

A longtime part of the establishment, Harbert sees things a little differently. "I *still* think the network has value," he says. "They are the distributors, they're paying most of the bills, and throughout entertainment, those who pay the bills get a vote." Still, in his days as a suit, Harbert witnessed up close that a good showrunner is generally not a passive one. As he puts it, "The guys that are regarded as the biggest pains in the ass, you'd probably have to put at the top of the list."

Mehlman doesn't come across as a pain in the ass, but he does appear to know what he wants. Asked about the casting process, he reports, "I'd say you could sum it up in the word—*hell*. Actually the female roles went relatively easily." Getting Eigeman as his male lead was more of a fight. "The network didn't really like him very much—they thought he was cold and distant." Mehlman says the actor, most familiar from Whit Stillman's preppy art house films *Metropolitan, Barcelona,* and *Last Days of Disco*, had impressive credits but hardly the stuff of which dreamy mall tests are made. "I kind of had to make this passionate speech in Chris's defense," Mehlman says. "They went along with it and now they love him."

One might imagine Harbert has the network rigged with his old ABC ties, but he admits there've been advantages and disadvantages to being reunited with the company he ran: "Yeah, I know how the whole place works and I know everybody," he says, "but I also think early on it was a little awkward for many of them to deal with a guy who used to be their boss. Now *they're* in an authoritative position."

Mehlman—no company man—is quick to point out some other potential awkwardness and political conflict. "You have what Ted was saying, then you have the dicey relationship between Jeffrey Katzenberg and Michael Eisner, then you have Jamie and Dan," he explains. Katzenberg—one of three principals of DreamWorks SKG, along with Steven Spielberg and David Geffen—had a famous falling out with his onetime mentor Eisner, who runs Disney and thus oversees ABC. Additionally, the head of DreamWorks Television is Dan

McDermott, who happens to be the former husband of ABC president Jamie Tarses, who replaced . . . you guessed it, Ted Harbert. "I mean, Jamie and Dan, *that* I can live with," Mehlman says with a chuckle. "That was a nice clean *divorce*."

For now Harbert believes the advantages outweigh the disadvantages. The first couple of times Harbert returned to ABC—which has a half ownership stake in the show—he sensed his presence there was strange for others, but soon it became a kick for him. "It was really good to be able to go into that building and not have to worry about all the things being in that building entailed. That building represents just years and years of neck-hurting tension and more problems than I could deal with. . . . I am certainly glad that I don't have to be responsible for the set of problems that ABC and every network has. It's very hard to find a network president who says, 'God, I *love* my job. I can't *wait* to get to work in the morning.'"

Lunch over, it's time for Harbert and Mehlman to head back to work. *It's like, you know . . .* is operating out of the same offices across the street where *Seinfeld* was once created, which Mehlman says "feels kind of right," though the former *Seinfeld* stage is now occupied by *Working*.

Mehlman recalls that the first table read for *It's like, you know . . .* took place the morning after he attended the last *Seinfeld* taping. "About one in the morning I finally went up to Jerry—he was sitting in the apartment set between takes—and I said, 'Man, I've *got* to go.' Jerry said, 'Here's the baton, run with it.'"

"*Wow*, I didn't know that," says Harbert.

Also resolutely unknown is when their show will get its day in the prime-time sun. "The good news for us is that ABC has three time periods we'd be good for," Harbert offers. "After *Spin City*, after *Dharma & Greg*, after *Drew Carey*. Who knows which show they'll pull off at some point to put us on?"

The *It's like, you know . . .* offices are but a few minutes away by foot, but Harbert hands the restaurant's valet parking attendant a ticket. "Because we're in Los Angeles," Mehlman explains with a sheepish grin. "We *drove*."

Ohmigod! They killed Warren Littlefield!

Okay, all they did was relieve NBC's entertainment president of his must-see duties. Not for the first time, the rumors were true. Apparently, the seminar that famed New Age lecturer and author Deepak Chopra (*Seven Spiritual Laws of Success*) led for the network's programming executives earlier this month about how to live up to their potential was too little too late.

Still, Littlefield's run was nothing to sneer at. In the October 27 calendar section of the *Los Angeles Times*, Brian Lowry points out that Littlefield had occupied his position long enough to see eleven counterparts fill the same seats at ABC, CBS, and Fox during his tenure at NBC. An even more remarkable statement appears in the same paper's business section, where Sallie Hofmeister reports: "The cost of *ER* and other hit shows, coupled with an erosion of the network audience caused by cable and Internet, is threatening NBC's status as the only television network to make a profit."

Scott Sassa, thirty-nine, is named NBC's new Entertainment president. Furthermore, the stage is now set for Sassa to take over for West Coast president Don Ohlmeyer by the turn of the century. Sassa—a well-regarded former rising star at Turner Broadcasting—joined NBC only a year earlier as the president of its owned and operated stations, and now he is the man anointed to bring NBC into the new century. Not bad for a former cable guy.

NBC's changes come during a particularly disastrous week of ratings when the network fell to fourth in the eighteen to forty-nine demographic. *Wind on the Water*—the network's *Dynasty* meets Hawaiian surf-and-turf drama, with Bo Derek as the family matriarch—proved another ratings wipe-out and gets shut down for good after only two airings. Meanwhile, all the other new NBC series are floundering except the protected *Jesse* and the surprise hit *Will & Grace*, with even the much anticipated *Encore! Encore!* getting pulled for the November sweeps.

TV advertisers are guaranteed certain minimal ratings, and when those numbers are missed they must be offered "make goods," free ads to compensate for the shortfall of eyeballs. More and more with only six of thirty-six new fall comedies or dramas living up to advertiser expectations, 1998–1999 was looking like the year of the make good. Four nights after the debut of the last new fall show to premiere—Fox's *Brimstone*—UPN fills the *Desmond Pfeiffer* hole with the first midseason replacement, only to have *Reunited* with Julie Hagerty record what are reportedly the worst prime-time ratings in network history.

Try making *that* good.

# First Sweeps and the Occasional Well-Timed Death

**Beatniks are out to make it rich**
**Oh-no, must be the season of the witch**

**"Season of the Witch" by Donovan Leitch, 1967**

**M**ax and I just had dinner with Warren on Friday."

Inside Stage 18 on Mary Tyler Moore Avenue near Newhart Street at the CBS Studios, *Will & Grace*'s David Kohan stands on the floor during show night. Between takes of Scene K of "The Big Vent"—the twelfth episode of the show's season—Kohan takes a moment to speak warmly of Warren Littlefield, the duo's longtime booster and recently deposed network president. "He's doing well," reports Kohan, who's wearing a suit but no tie today. "Why *shouldn't* he be doing well? Twenty years of GE stock options, a little production deal, and he's out of a job where you have *no* life."

Kohan—who's just broken from one of the evening's many midshoot huddles with his partner Max Mutchnick—is learning firsthand about that "no life" part himself. "Writer/producers have *no* lives," he says with a sly, exhausted expression. "I have no life, and what life I *do* have, I'm making a mess of."

Were they running most other new NBC series, Kohan and Mutchnick might be well on their way to plenty of personal time. *Will & Grace,* however, has been looking like a shining point of light for the Peacock. Indeed, *Will & Grace* could very well go down in the books as Littlefield's last hit while running NBC, though after a strong start the well-received show's ratings have become increasingly wobbly during sweeps as NBC's Monday evening of programming has increasingly faltered and CBS has surged with the help of *Everybody Loves Raymond* and the effective launch of Ted Danson's *Becker.*

"Monday nights are *murder,*" Kohan says as he runs off to confer with Mutchnick and fine-tune the next scene. These have been exciting but trying times at *Will & Grace*—the table read for "The Big Vent" went poorly last week, with the network offering prodigious notes. Even as the episode is being shot tonight, the writers furiously rework lines between takes, with impressive results. Repeatedly, with a studio audience looking down at them, Kohan and Mutchnick inform the gathered writers, "We need a line here," instantly daring them to beat whatever is on the page in the last draft of script. More often than not, somebody delivers.

Tomorrow the whole process begins again with yet another table read for an episode entitled "My Fair Maid-y," set to feature a guest turn by Cyndi Lauper as Will and Grace's cleaning lady.

Back in their bungalow office a week and one episode later—with their two desks pushed up against each other like dueling pianos— the now casually dressed pair remain hard at work during what's officially the tail end of a brief show hiatus.

Mutchnick finishes up a phone conversation, during which he gets what sounds like inside information on *Will & Grace*'s upcoming People's Choice Award nomination for Best New Comedy Series, while Kohan is just back from the writers' room, which is still working this morning.

"There is no such thing as hiatus," Kohan explains. "Hiatus means we only work from ten to eight."

For all that, Mutchnick adds that the pair are getting a bit calmer about the job. Kohan concurs: "That trough of despair that you fall into before a major rewrite," he says, "it's beginning to get shallower." And as everybody knows, in television shallower can often mean better.

Only a few months into the season, Kohan and Mutchnick look less like novice showrunners and more like grown-up players. They've already come a long way from the humbling days on *Boston Common*, which failed despite exposure on NBC's Thursday night schedule.

"There's a big difference between getting a show and creating a show that's a hit or is *perceived* as being a hit," says Mutchnick. "They are *totally* different monsters."

Kohan stresses that in TV success is largely a matter of perception and that *Boston Common* was in the top ten for six weeks, while *Will & Grace* has so far cracked the top twenty-five once—though it has cracked the top ten for the key demo one week.

"That doesn't really mean anything in terms of how a network perceives you," Mutchnick adds.

Of course, one man who perceived *Will & Grace* as a hit is now out of his job. The pair got news of Littlefield's departure reading the trades here in the office, and Mutchnick felt a sense of loss. It was Littlefield who suggested that *Will & Grace*'s lead characters—pitched as supporting characters in a larger ensemble piece—should be the center of the show. It was Littlefield, Mutchnick reports, who brought the pilot script to James Burrows when Don Ohlmeyer balked slightly at the project, a move that led them to a powerful friend and collaborator and did wonders to earn them a pilot order.

Despite the change in administration, the pair aren't worried that the new NBC team will want to disassociate themselves from their predecessor's darling.

"It's not the Republicans vs. the Democrats—they're *not* going to dismantle something just because the other regime originated it," says Kohan. "It's much more realpolitik."

Truth to be told, there were also rough patches with the old regime. For Mutchnick, one of the season's lowest points came when the two were called into Littlefield's office during the show's first hiatus break, after successfully completing the initial five episodes.

"They were worried that we were working too hard and we were going to burn out," Mutchnick recalls, looking agitated by the memory. "It was one of those classic situations where things were going so well they'd better *find* a problem, *create* a problem. It was a *horseshit* meeting. I found that to be *totally* insulting. Instead of being calm and nurturing, they thought, 'Oh my god, we have a hit, we better start to *schvitz* about it.'"

Much like an unwarranted dressing-down in the principal's office, the experience had shaken Mutchnick. "We were on *such* a high and we got called in and it has put a permanent mistrust in all of it," says Mutchnick. "Because of that, I've never been able to quite relax and I think it's unfortunate they're in the business of doing that."

Kohan remembers Littlefield explaining that this was big business and that they would have to be naive to think the network wasn't going to check in. "On one hand we're going to tell you you're doing a good job," he remembers Littlefield saying. "On the other we have to take a micro-look at this show."

The pair didn't storm out of Littlefield's office.

"Unlike some showrunners, we don't do the whole 'fuck you' thing," says Mutchnick.

"We have *mothers* to please," Kohan explains.

"They rarely waste time with the bad cop thing," Eric McCormack—who plays Will Truman—confirms later. "Which is great because it's really not conducive to comedy. Max definitely has the higher passion in terms of being impatient, excited, and angry. He gets very defensive of the show—not toward us, but maybe toward the network. He'll be the mama bear very often."

"They're lucky we're like that and we have careers because of it," Mutchnick says. "We play ball. As businessmen, you have to. It's not 'Fuck you, I'm doing my art.' Well, no, you're *not*, you're selling toilet paper. You have to pay attention to that stuff. It's all about choosing battles."

Both Kohan and Mutchnick say that working with Burrows on

*Will & Grace* has been a big advantage—he's a draw to actors and the dean of TV direction—but even that creative union is not without its tense moments.

"Usually it seems to me the role of the director is to take what's written and make it work to the best of his ability," Kohan says. Burrows is more assertive than that, he explains: "Jimmy will say, 'I think I can direct it better if it goes like *this*.' But ultimately the director is at the mercy of the writing and the cast."

"Jim also did *Union Square*," Mutchnick points out with a naughty chuckle.

Burrows, they say, often pushes them to pick up the comedic pace, more in the *Cheers* tradition. For Kohan, any resulting tension "has made us more effective, but on the other hand there are scenes where Max and I don't necessarily mind if something meanders if it tells a funnier story or a funnier side of character."

The new NBC boss has given no indication of getting heavy-handed. As Mutchnick says, "To his credit the first thing Scott Sassa said to me on the phone when he called was, 'I really like your show; hopefully we won't talk to you too much and fuck it up for you.' He came to meet us and he was very nice."

Nice goes a long way, but Mutchnick wants something else—a new time slot: "I just said it to David Nevins at NBC this morning—someone has *got* to explain to us why we're on Monday night, why they're burning off their best product on Monday night. I'm thinking why don't you take the losses you will incur because of a contractual obligation to another show in another time slot and *fuck* it because you want to nurture your hits. The stuff that isn't working, move it."

Translation: Mutchnick wants Thursday. *Bad.*

NBC's Monday night is collapsing and he wants off, and soon. "The night's a *disaster* for NBC," he says.

Later tonight in Manhattan, Nathan Lane—star of NBC's once hyped and now failing *Encore! Encore!*—will break up the crowd at a Creative Coalition Spotlight Awards dinner by declaring that the best way to get rid of Saddam Hussein is to "put him on the NBC fall schedule."

DAVID WILD

Kohan reports that Burrows thinks *Will & Grace* is right where they want it to be—where expectations are so low they can't lose—but Kohan's more in the mood to let it roll. "My attitude is let's come out swinging," he says. "I *believe* in this show. They're like, 'Subject matter, content, blah, blah, blah.' Nobody gives a shit—people just want to laugh and be entertained, enjoy the characters and maybe identify with something."

Until the right slot comes along, there's still work to do. The "My Fair Maid-y" episode they just finished has proved another difficult one, and the pair found themselves in the awkward position of letting go of Cyndi Lauper, who was already an MTV icon when they were still in school.

"It didn't work out," Kohan explains. "We brought it to the table and we'd written something we thought was very much in her voice. Then she sort of somnambulated through it at the table. Maybe that was partially our fault because we didn't get the script to her early enough. Then, because of story problems, we had to do a *major* rewrite that evening—I mean a page one rewrite—and that part had been cut down."

Mutchnick was hoping to see some of the spark he'd seen from Lauper on a *Mad About You* appearance (for which she won an Emmy), but found himself less than mad about her in this role. The role was recast and given to veteran character actress Wendy Jo Sperber. Mutchnick doesn't seem particularly pained by this tough call. "It's *never* scary letting an actor go," he offers. "Fuck 'em, they're *silly* people. It's scary letting writers go—*that's* what's scary."

If that infamous NBC meeting was the most trying day of the season for Mutchnick, his most uncomfortable was when he and Kohan let go a few of their staff writers. "You let a high-level writer go on a show that's considered a hit," he explains, "you're putting out a big message to the community—you did *not* work out here." When it happens in the middle of the year and not the appropriate dip—*that's* scary."

It is another cost of being the boss—the polar opposite of the pride they take in paying lots of people good money for creatively satisfying work. "I feel like I got the shit beat out of me on a lot of shows," Mutchnick says. "I feel thankful we're in a position we can make people feel good about what they're doing for us."

So far this season, there have been a few blowouts between the two partners, though any fights tend to be sporadic and short-lived. Kohan quickly shoulders most of the blame.

"This has been a *hard* year for me," Kohan says quietly. He explains he's just split up with his wife and is trying to balance his showrunning with even more pressing personal matters. "My time in my life is split between work and fatherhood and that's *it*," he says. "I see my daughter Olivia every morning and then I come to work. Then on weekends I see Olivia. *That's* been my life. I'm in retreat mode and sometimes it gets in the way of my effectiveness at work on the floor or even in the writers' room."

"I've certainly fucked up relationships this year," Mutchnick continues. "I would need to come home to some pretty high confidence or someone who's going to acknowledge you're doing a *shitload* at the office and you're exhausted when you come home and that's just the truth. I've run into that situation when someone says, 'Just let it go. Just let it go.' *No*, not when I have to wake up and pray for a twenty share. You *don't* just let it go."

"I found it was easier to let it go when I was married," Kohan explains. "Now I pick Olivia up every Friday night and go to *shabbat* dinner, and once I'm with her it's gone. When I'm alone it's harder to shed the stuff of the day. It was easier when I had somebody else. I just happened to have gotten myself into a marriage that was *not* a good one. With the right person, it could *absolutely* work."

So not every painful thing in life can be blamed on the rigors of showrunning?

"No," Kohan answers with a half-smile. "My marriage really disintegrated when I was in development."

Norm Macdonald is in a Hollywood sound studio working on recording a comedy album. He's joined today by his former *Saturday Night Live* colleague Will Ferrell to perform a sketch Macdonald originally envisioned doing with his late friend Chris Farley. In the sketch, two heterosexual, middle-aged married fellows—after watching a football game together—spontaneously decide to try a little sodomy. The sketch ends with Ferrell's character screaming out in agony, "Oh, God, mother of all things holy, please let this nightmare stop."

Somehow, it's pretty funny stuff and classic uncensored comedy à la Norm—Beckett meets buggery with a little absurdist heteroanxiety thrown into the edgy, potentially offensive mix.

It's also the sort of material one is highly unlikely to find on any network sitcom—even post–*South Park*.

Asked how his sitcom is going—after all, the pilot was originally supposed to have been filmed by now—Macdonald becomes uncharacteristically quiet, almost tactful. "Yeah, I want to work on it," he says, without much apparent conviction or interest. "I don't want to rush it."

On Sony Studio's Dubbing Stage 11 in Culver City, "Pickup Shticks" is being played.

"Pickup Shticks" is one of the three episodes of *Cupid* that will air during November sweeps—on the remaining week ABC will offer Arnold Schwarzenegger experiencing the joys of motherhood in *Junior* to no appreciable ratings bump. Before "Pickup Shticks" can air two nights from now it must pass through this final stage of postproduction, during which *Cupid*'s crack mixing team gets Winant to sign off on its wrap-up work. After this, copies will be struck and sent off to the network for general public consumption.

The room looks a bit like mission control, and indeed it is here that showrunners get to exercise one last bit of control before parting with the products of all their TV labor. Everywhere around this building, sitcoms and dramas are being touched up and reworked, fixed and sometimes salvaged before heading off to their final Nielsen destinies.

Happily, *Cupid*'s shtick has just received a major pickup of its own—ABC has surprised some naysayers in the media by ordering more episodes of the show despite shaky ratings. Instead, it is the future of *Cupid*'s time slot neighbor *Fantasy Island*—mixed just down the hall—that is currently in question.

Scott Winant is due here any minute, but no one is surprised when a call comes saying that he's running twenty minutes late—or "Scott time"—which leaves a few moments for a game of pool on the table that rests in front of the multiplex-sized screen. Winant's been run especially ragged lately, since at the same time he's trying to make sure that *Cupid*'s aim stays true, he's also executive producing *Anna Says*, an ambitious half-hour pilot starring Tracy Pollan, the actress married to *Spin City*'s Michael J. Fox. Pollan—who among other roles played one of Fox's girlfriends on *Family Ties*—is planning on making her return to TV in a half-hour show that will mix a traditional four-camera shoot and a live audience with the sort of single-camera style usually seen in a drama. Between this show and other projects, Winant has been so busy lately that the other night he couldn't even find time to return phone calls from the network and instead heard from one of his producers the good news that *Cupid* was definitely going to be able to make more episodes.

This *Cupid* mixing team also works on *Martial Law*—a very different show, especially considering that the latter show's sizable martial arts star is only now fully grappling with the English language. The dialogue-heavy *Cupid* is a much easier show for Robert Edmondson, who does sound effects—not many sound effects with Trevor and Claire—but far more challenging for Sherry Klein, who must try to keep all the talk—and in the *thirtysomething* tradition, there's a *lot* of talk on *Cupid*—crystal clear. That can be especially challenging with exterior scenes shot in Chicago—apparently because Chicago turns out to be a *windy* city. Still, this team knows all the digital tricks of the

*DAVID WILD*

trade that expedite the process, and as a rule, the team knows what Winant wants. Klein goes back to the *thirtysomething* days with him, and in these circumstances, a shorthand develops. With a laugh, Klein points to a board that offers helpful interpretations of some typical showrunner responses. "I see," for instance, translates as "Blow me."

Technically, Winant doesn't have to attend this session—he has associate producer Tony Palermo to oversee things on his behalf. "I'm the orderly for this asylum," Palermo explains. Still, despite everything else going on, Winant wants to make the trip over here. He's always been known for his attention to detail, and at least in the nuance-heavy shows he's chosen to make, details actually *do* matter.

Winant arrives and greets his mix-masters with a tired smile. "This is where the executive walks in and they give me the impression that I actually *have* influence," he explains dryly. "They nod, I leave, and then they make their own decisions." Still, he's happy to be here where problems seem more approachable. "I'm lucky I work with very talented people who make me look good," he adds, "plus I use this as an excuse to get out of the office."

Everyone grabs a notepad and soon the pre-tweaked "Pickup Shticks" is played back not on the giant screen at the front of the room but on a more standard-sized TV set closer to the room's controls. The episode that unfolds is gripping, easily the best since the strong pilot, and one that intriguingly explores some of the darker sides of the show's potentially too-sweet premise. Our fallen Cupid, Trevor, finds himself confronted by some earthly temptation in the shapely form of former *Twin Peaks* star Sherilyn Fenn—he wants her badly, but if he bites this forbidden piece of tasty human fruit, he'll lose his immortality. To make matters worse, the previously icy Claire is now defrosting with another man. The episode also concerns Sure Score, a sort of creepy paramilitary organization dedicated to teaching men how to make sexual conquests by subliminal mental suggestion.

Both Jeremy Piven and Paula Marshall dig deeper than they have in previous episodes, with Piven exploring the torment or madness implicit in his character—depending on whether he's in fact a god or just another nut. The net result is a standout episode that is unusually smart, hot, and artistically searching—an altogether sexy and serious piece of work—one that has risen far above the show's potentially goofy concept.

The network's not happy with it, however, especially the dramatic darkness of Piven's performance, which in the episode's final moments is many miles from warm and fuzzy.

"They want the happier *Cupid*," says Winant with a pained look as he sneaks a quick bathroom trip and a smoke on the balcony. Here Winant begs to differ with ABC. "This one I *really* like because I feel like we're owning our ten o'clock time slot. I don't like assuming the audience is not sophisticated enough. I hate this notion that in order to play the middle we tend to talk down. I think this episode was not written down to the audience at all and we dealt with a lot of things that are all out there but are taboo on television, and we touch on those things without getting exploitative."

Some showrunners might just be satisfied with mere survival—an elusive enough grail—but Winant claims that's never his primary focus. "I work really hard and take pride in my work and the things I can't control I don't worry about," says Winant. "I kinda learned it on *My So-Called Life*. I did nineteen episodes, I'm *very* proud of those nineteen episodes, and then it didn't get picked up and then it had this second life on MTV. Ironically, it's almost like getting canceled gave it this mystique that paid off. So I don't invest in the pickup, I invest in the work."

That may explain how Winant seems able to filter out the mixed reviews and the less-than-stellar ratings. Most Sundays when Saturday's overnights get faxed to his house, Winant doesn't even bother looking at them, waiting until the workweek to assess the *Cupid* report card.

Winant is learning that Saturday night is the loneliest night for TV and is ready to take his Olympic arrow to audiences in a different time slot. He would love Tuesday or Wednesday at ten, but understands that it's not going to happen. "I know that after *Monday Night Football* ends, that there's a spot that opens up," he says. "Although that's not ideal, it's better than where we are. I'll take that."

**D A V I D   W I L D**

Amid its veritable assortment pack of bad news, the 1998–1999 season is, thus far, underscoring the painful erosion of adult viewers on Friday and Saturday nights—particularly for anything more challenging than the ultraviolence and simplistic moralizing of a *Walker, Texas Ranger*. Already *ER*'s John Wells and NBC have endured a painful attempt to launch *Trinity* on Fridays, a night under the spell of ABC's preteen block built around *Sabrina, the Teenage Witch*.

Despite *Cupid*'s struggles and a commitment to what he proudly calls aberrant programs, Winant has recently signed a profitable new two-year overall deal with 20th Century Fox Television to develop new series. "I think I've *always* been doing this," Winant says, "but I may be more in fashion now."

With that, Winant makes his fashionable way back into the dubbing stage to give his relatively minor notes to the mixers.

After viewing the final scene one last time, Winant announces, "I've got to be going to the next crisis," and makes his way out to the studio parking lot. He's already due at a casting session for the Tracy Pollan pilot.

A week ago, Winant was in New York shooting some scenes with Pollan; next week he will be shooting more here in Los Angeles. All this from a guy who is running a show in Chicago. He's asked if that distance is becoming less of a problem. "It's just hard," Winant says, "and the cast feels abandoned."

Like a lot of other busy father figures, Scott Winant understands that even in showrunning, quality time just doesn't cut it.

Always, but never more so than during sweeps periods, TV shows—and by extension the hearts, souls, and pocketbooks of showrunners—become well-paid pawns in a larger network chess game, though in reality most shows are fundamentally rooks.

With sweeps month drawing to a close—and not even halfway

into a season that is long and looking longer every day—more than a dozen shows have been canceled or are on hiatus—that is, residing in TV limbo.

A fine line seems to exist between the living and the dying. For example, after reportedly verbally committing to making five more episodes of *The Secret Lives of Men*, ABC changes its corporate mind and ultimately does not order from Witt-Thomas-Harris more of the show that has been losing 35 percent of its substantial *Drew Carey* lead-in. The show's well-known creator Susan Harris (*Soap, The Golden Girls*) announces in *USA Today*, "If ABC cancels the show, I'll retire." This threat is not enough to stop the show from going the way of *Costello, The Brian Benben Show, Desmond Pfeiffer, Living in Captivity*, and *Getting Personal*. That's the same direction in which *Conrad Bloom, Encore! Encore!, Holding the Baby, To Have and to Hold, Vengeance Unlimited*, and *Trinity* currently appear headed.

Though no one likes to say so, most hiatuses—or should that be hiati?—never end. Here's the ugly truth, kids: Hiatus is usually a slow death sentence.

During sweeps months, the high-profile demises of Jimmy Smits's beloved character Bobby Simone on *NYPD Blue* and Jack Kevorkian's ailing patient Thomas Youk on *60 Minutes* aren't the only examples of death on TV—they're just the best-timed and highest-rated.

As Thanksgiving beckons, *Seven Days* finally receives its official back nine pickup from UPN—a welcome promise of more days to come. This is no huge surprise, really, since *Seven Days* has begun to establish itself as the struggling network's highest-rated new series.

At nine-thirty A.M. on November 24, *Seven Days'* Christopher Crowe sits in his blue bathrobe at the computer in his cluttered home office in the hills outside Pasadena, reworking a script titled "Last Card Up," which starts filming tomorrow morning. His home looks like a rock star's lovely, lived-in country estate, with its pleasing catch-as-catch-can decorations, portraits of the Rolling Stones and other pop culture greats, and a recording studio off the kitchen where the *Seven Days* music gets recorded. The extensive grounds here include an elegant pool, a fountain, and an impressive rose garden. Crowe's script-strewn writing space includes a sizable library of books, a guitar and plugged-in amplifier, old auto racing memorabilia, a TV, a VCR, videotapes, and a bowl of what a visitor can only pray is last night's chili. "It's postdivorce decor," Crowe explains before excusing himself to get dressed. "You know, whatever someone else didn't want."

Today promises to be one of reckoning between Crowe and those Doberman penny pinchers at Paramount. It's been dubbed Sphere Day at *Seven Days,* and that means he's needed on the set to oversee the partial dismantling of his televised dream.

On the forty-five-minute drive to the set this morning, Crowe explains that *Seven Days* continues to go considerably over budget—"I used to have three children before *Seven Days,* and now I only have two," one Paramount executive jokes. It's been determined that one show expense that ought to be scaled back is the Sphere, the impressive futuristic structure that allows time travel on the show. A giant sphere—more than thirty feet high—occupies Stage One, and while it doesn't actually go back in time, it nonetheless manages to eat plenty of Paramount money. "For financial reasons we may contract the scope of our major sphere set, which is real expensive to light and do with black lights—it's like a rock-and-roll show," Crowe explains. As a showrunner, Crowe hates to see the Sphere diminished, but even his own sphere of influence is limited.

Still *Seven Days* lives—though Crowe says he never lost any sleep over whether the show would get picked up for the rest of the season: "I figured that if there is a network there will be a *Seven Days.*" Crowe believes UPN's dire ratings can't be blamed on the current administration. "They're doing their best to turn it around," he offers. "But it's a *momentous* task—networks are like great big ocean liners, you *don't* turn them on a dime. People's viewing habits are such that when you turn on the TV you go to a home base network. Then you'll dip out if it's boring you. You turn to Fox or whatever, then it's the hub of the wheel for you—and UPN is *not* many people's hub.

"What is a network really?" Crowe asks with a rhetorical flourish as he looks out at the freeway. "A network is a circus tent. It's like there are four circus tents in town. Well, if you put a fuckin' great act inside a tent, *eventually* it will work, but it's slow. There's no magic to it. Word leaks out, 'Hey, there's a pretty good fuckin' act in Tent A!' 'Never been there,'" Crowe says in another voice. "'Yeah, they've got naked girls and midgets!'"

Despite ratings that sometimes suggest otherwise, UPN is still not a cable network and can't go headfirst into the naked-girls-and-midgets direction yet. Instead, the struggling network has just announced it will focus first and foremost on serving the programming needs of young men—the exact audience tuning into *Seven Days* and *Star Trek: Voyager* on Wednesday nights.

Crowe is for the most part proud of *Seven Days*, and pleased with the consistent ratings—"the viewers have given us a few," he says ruefully—but he confesses a few lesser recent episodes that were standard action fare pain him. "Some troops *are* expendable," he says as he looks out at the road. "You do see those episodes coming. Oh, fuck, *do* you see them coming."

Crowe says getting *Seven Days* this far is important for more than cash-flow reasons. "You want to succeed because it's your life's work— if you're an earnest man you want to do a good job and it's *terribly* disappointing if you disappoint people," he says. "Are you going to be crushed if it doesn't work? No, but it keeps you at that damn typewriter." For Crowe, failure is a blow and success a pleasant distraction. "I've been hot and cold so many times, so all I know is I drift to the typewriter and try to do something that excites me and hopefully others," he says as the car pulls up to the stage with the Sphere. "Along the way there's *massive* compromise."

In the face of such obstacles, what makes the showrunner run?

"The lucky thing is every once in a while doing a show you get to dig in, make a little stand. Within this greater context—which is entertainment and craft and not a hell of a lot more—there are moments along the way when you can honestly have an artful moment. Those fuckers, those *fuckin'* moments, are the ones that propel you through it, I swear to Christ. Those are the same epiphanous moments that you have playing in a rock club, painting a painting, any artistic enterprise—those little moments in this circus that are as true as true can be."

Crowe enters the mammoth futuristic space to see approximately fifty crew members and a bunch of extras in various stages of hurrying up and waiting. It turns out that there's just been a temporary reprieve for the Sphere. Apparently it has been discovered that a signed lease makes it impossible to give up this space anytime soon—meaning today may not be the Sphere's last big trip. Crowe confers with director/producer John McPherson and producer Chip Scott Laughlin about what Sphere exteriors can be shot today and spread out over a bunch of future episodes.

"There's no bulletproof plan at this point," Crowe says, looking simultaneously relieved and frustrated. "None of it makes sense. What we were going to do was lose this facility and move this to a smaller situation. Then we learn today we can't lose this set so now we're figuring out what to do. Our plan is not as good as it was yesterday and now we're . . . vamping."

Vamping can take a lot of time between those epiphanies.

The time-traveling *Seven Days* is not to be confused with *7th Heaven*—the WB's wholesome hit about a minister, his wife, and their sizable congregation of offspring that only *seems* as though it comes directly from another era. That quality may have helped *7th Heaven* become one of the blessed exceptions to the general downward slope of the 1998–1999 TV season, with its ratings up nearly a third.

*7th Heaven*—the single biggest hit on the WB—comes from Aaron Spelling and offers family-sized portions of *Waltons*-style moral grounding in the midst of the Bill and Monica daze. The show represents a tubular throwback with enough postmodern wisecracking and issue-oriented topicality to makes things sweet but not sickeningly so. Think *Father Knows Better* with more generous servings of multigenerational sex appeal. A TV dinner for the whole family, *7th Heaven* is served up to a growing number of consumers, some of then twice weekly. In an unheard-of move, the network broadcasts new episodes on Mondays and reruns called *7th Heaven Beginnings* on Sunday nights. The Camden clan delivers the prime-time equivalent of comfort food, but it can be surprisingly tasty stuff. A show in which good prevails and kids occasionally honor their parents, *7th Heaven* represents a sort of the anti–*Melrose Place*—another Spelling show it has now overtaken in the battle for our Nielsen souls.

*7th Heaven* also turns out to be one of still relatively few series for which the creator turns out to be a she. "She" in this case is Brenda Hampton, who's sitting today in her office just a few floors below Spelling. Though she's much younger than her better-known recent mentor and collaborator, the fortysomething Hampton is quick to explain that she too grew up with the TV industry.

"My father is a TV repairman," Hampton explains with a smile. "So I have family in the business." She grew up in the Atlanta area and remembers that "we would either have ten TVs in the house that he was fixing or we'd have none." Surprisingly, even with that sort of early access to the TV trade, Hampton took her sweet time getting into the biz herself.

"I got into TV late because I worked as a technical writer for a top secret testing project," she explains. After graduating from the University of Georgia, Hampton answered an ad and found herself writing training manuals for the United States and British navies.

While hardly a direct path to showrunning, the job had its own rewards. "Well, there were five hundred men on the island and five women, so it was definitely *fun*." After a year in this job—she'd tell you where but then she'd have to kill you—Hampton came back to Atlanta and substitute-taught for a year in a tough school. Then she went back to writing manuals—this time on the only slightly less top-secret matter of burger preparation for the Crystal Hamburger Company. Then it was on to Chattanooga, where Hampton ran an award-winning magazine for the Tennessee Valley Authority power plants.

Thus empowered, Hampton set her sights on either Manhattan or Boston. On a trip to New York, she was sitting on the steps of the Metropolitan Museum when a man came over and introduced himself. He was a standup comedian. A year later they got married, and shortly after that she found out he was gay and had AIDS. "We stayed married for ten years," she says quietly. "Then I left and the next year he died."

During that marriage, Hampton got to know standup herself, and even wrote some comedy for, among others, Roseanne. Her more steady gig, however, was writing speeches for executives, and in the mid- to late eighties she ended up working in corporate communications for NBC, even writing speeches for its chief executive, Bob Wright.

Hampton's move West was precipitated by a book contract; she cowrote a book about cancer. In Los Angeles she hooked up with a scriptwriting partner, Bill Kenney, who had won an NBC writing contest she'd earlier helped organize.

"We wrote a spec script, got an agent, and a job in thirty days," she remembers. The pair got on the staff at *Sister Kate*, a short-lived 1989–1990 sitcom about a nun starring Stephanie Beacham, formerly of *The Colbys*, and featuring a pre–*Beverly Hills 90210* Jason Priestley, run by the team who did *Mister Belvedere*. "It was only on for like a season, but it was *fabulous*," Hampton says of the gig. "Jeff Stein, Frank Duncan, and Tony Shehan were the executive producers, and they only hired us. So we'd see a run-through, sit in their office, laugh a little, and go home." It was a lovely introduction to TV writing—and a welcome counterbalance to writing a book about cancer.

From *Sister Kate*, she and Kenney were off to 1990's misguided *Bagdad Cafe,* which failed despite the talents of Whoopi Goldberg and Jean Stapleton and whatever advantage comes from being based on a German art house hit. On her own, Hampton went on to *Lenny* and then *Blossom.* "Don Reo, a great showrunner, ran both shows and the staff did both shows as well," Hampton says. From Reo,

Hampton learned two guiding principles—to stay organized and not take things too seriously.

After she'd worked on *Blossom* for a few years, Paul Witt and Tony Thomas asked Hampton and writer David Landsberg to create a show at CBS for Dudley Moore, who'd just failed for the network in the imaginatively titled sitcom *Dudley*. The result was *Daddy's Girls*, notable for featuring future *Felicity* star Keri Russell and Harvey Fierstein in the same cast, though only the former played one of the title characters.

*Daddy's Girls* lasted on CBS for a few weeks in the fall of 1994, but with an order for thirteen episodes the staff kept right on working. "I think we *still* get a residual from some foreign market," Hampton says with a laugh. "It was a very funny show, and we had so much fun because we would still get all these notes. We'd say, 'It's not *on,* guys,'" says Hampton, laughing at the memory.

As for the show's title star, Hampton says, "Dudley was the greatest." She still remembers when she called him to discuss his character. Hampton delivers Moore's ultimately farsighted response in pure *Arthur*-ese: "*Whatever* for?"

With *Daddy's Girls* flung into the trash heap of sitcom history, Hampton found herself doing nothing for first time she could remember. "I had saved some money," she recalls. "So it was delightful."

Soon she had more than enough to do when opportunity knocked in the form of a staff job at *Mad About You*—then entering season four. The work was tougher than anything she'd done. "You work until four-thirty in the morning, then come back in at ten or eleven the next day. The hours are *excruciating.*" Hampton was trying to adopt a child and didn't think she could keep those kinds of hours. She was looking for a different situation when her agent at Creative Artists Agency called her and asked if she'd like to go over and pitch a show to Aaron Spelling. She was excited because "I'd never met him and he's a legend." She'd also never written a drama. "I'd never done hour, so I put together seven characters rather than try to do story," she says. "I came over, pitched *7th Heaven,* and Aaron's enthusiasm made me give the greatest pitch I ever gave."

*DAVID WILD*

It must have been a great pitch for a drama king like Spelling to be swayed by a writer whose experience was entirely in sitcoms. "She was so exciting," Spelling recalls later. "We didn't want it to be all about issues, but also comedy with the kids. And to be honest with you, I didn't think there was much chance to sell a family show to WB at the time."

Now that Hampton and Spelling have a hit on their hands, he remains her nonsecret admirer. "She's *marvelous*," he says, "and not only is she executive producer, and the head of the staff, but there's only like two other people on the writing staff. Most shows have a staff of between six and eight. She must write like eight to ten scripts a year. Don't ask me where she gets the time. She's delightful and very strong. She doesn't take a lot of trash from anyone."

In creating the show, Hampton was influenced by some of "those funny little morality plays" she enjoyed growing up, like *The Andy Griffith Show* and *Father Knows Best*.

Doing the show means collaborating closely with Spelling. "He is hands-on," reports Hampton. "I go up and I try to pitch six episodes at a time and for us that's thirty stories—about five an episode. It's *very* casual. I go straight through the six episodes and then he might say, 'You know that little B story you had in Episode Two would work better for Four, wouldn't it?' He is the only person I have ever heard in my ten years of listening to notes who benefits the show. He's working for a reason. He's *good*. He's smart on every aspect of show business—he's the king of casting, business-wise he's a genius, creatively he's brilliant. There's *nothing* missing."

Hampton and Spelling rarely argue. Just yesterday they screened an upcoming episode together and Spelling told her he didn't like the last shot of the show. Hampton disagreed, as did the episode's writer. Still, they cut it Spelling's way. When they saw it the next morning, "We looked at it and said, he's right again," she says, shaking her head. "I've learned not to argue the point immediately because he can see things I can't because I'm *nowhere* near as experienced."

Perhaps that's why Hampton lets Spelling, his partner E. Duke Vincent, and their production team do what they do best while she spends most of her time right here focused on the writing of the show. It works out nicely for everyone, including Hampton. "I go home at six-thirty to seven at night," she reports. "I come into the office at ten or ten-thirty and I don't work weekends and I don't work holidays. I have a very nice life and I make a *lot* of money."

Hampton very rarely goes to the set despite its being only a twenty-minute drive away. Most recently she made the trip because former Monkee Peter Tork was making a guest appearance and Hampton wanted to get an autograph for her niece. "When I go, I'm the *pope*," she says with a laugh. "They clear a path, they have a chair for me. I have no need to be there. I love to go out there, but when I get there it's just to say, 'Thank you.' It's not to yell at anyone, or fix anything."

Though Hampton's not separated from her show by half a continent like *Cupid*'s Scott Winant, she too runs her show long-distance. "I watch the dailies; if I don't see something that I had on the page, I pick up the phone. It's worked out beautifully—they just do a great job for me and they love the scripts and they want to see them shot just like I envision them. They have never said no; they have never said we can't afford that. They *always* make it work. I'm still very involved with the actors—and if there's anything on the technical side, I'd get involved but that so rarely happens."

Hampton says being a woman has been largely a non-issue in her career. "This is the first business where I have been treated according to what I am contributing. I've *never* been treated differently in the ten years that I've been doing this." As a boss, she says, "I'm really nice as long as people are doing their job, but TV is an art of time and the second someone's not doing their job I come down on them. I don't have the time." As for her writing staff, she let a few people go the first season, a few the second, and none so far this season. "I have a very small staff," Hampton says. "We don't table; there are not ten people. I have a few people who all go off and write."

However they're doing it, it's working. Hampton keeps her show's popularity in perspective. "Yes, we're number one on the WB but we're still battling it out at eighty-sixth place," she says. She takes pride in her moral Nielsen victory for a show that debuted with less

*DAVID WILD*

than great expectations. "We got very low publicity, and the show has steadily grown since Episode One," says Hampton. "When it's implied that a network stayed with us because of the quality of the show, I can't imagine a network canceling its fastest-growing show—although we did start very low. Our story is that we have steadily grown—which is *not* the spin on it from the network."

With *7th Heaven* on her track record, Hampton's much in demand to spread the Nielsen-friendly love to other shows. She's already endured a less than idyllic journey on *Love Boat: The Next Wave* for UPN. "Last Christmas Aaron asked me to get involved," she recalls as a look of horror crosses her face. "It was probably the worst experience I ever had. Catherine LePard from this show and I created a very good show for that network and they had absolutely *no* respect for either of us. I couldn't *wait* to get out. The WB is *very* respectful—I haven't had a note on a story since year one. Listen, I'm happy to take notes because I'm not paying for the show. We worked very hard at giving them what they wanted, but there was *no* giving them what they wanted. We had a clear vision and they changed theirs every day."

Eventually she asked Spelling to hire her old *Daddy's Girls* partner David Landsberg to steer *The Love Boat*. "I thought he could deal better with *that* network than I did," she says. She says "*that* network" not unlike the way President Clinton said "*that* woman."

Hampton doesn't plan on creating any new shows for UPN soon but she is planning to spend part of her Christmas holiday developing a new show for WB, one that could potentially follow *7th Heaven* next fall. She's reluctant to give any details that will likely change. "I'll tell you this—they called me last summer and they wanted *Moonlighting*," she says. "So I wrote it for them, and it sat there for three weeks. Then they said, 'We don't want *Moonlighting*, we want *My Three Sons*.' I said, 'All right, pay me for the *Moonlighting*, I'll give you *My Three Sons*.'" In fact, Hampton says she's now giving the WB *four* sons.

In the meantime, Hampton has another family to think about—her own. She has a daughter with whom she is looking forward to spending her holidays. Zoe will be twelve in January, and she's been in the States for over a year. "It took almost three years to get her out of Vietnam," Hampton says, still sounding amazed at the process. "You would think someone like me who protested the war in Vietnam would know something about it, but I didn't realize the big difference between the North and the South. I got involved with a corrupt agency and orphanage, but I felt this child was shown a picture and told I was coming to get her, so I went and got her, but it was *not* an easy process."

At a crucial point, Hampton got some help from the cousin of her *7th Heaven* leading man Stephen Collins, who happens to be a congressman from North Carolina, in expediting matters. By Christmas, Hampton will marry the man who is Zoe's tutor and start what she calls "a wonderful funky family."

So it is today that Zoe—who just happens to be a big fan of mom's show—sits across from her mother in an elegant office, learning all about her strange new land of plenty in a neighborhood called the Miracle Mile.

Rob Thomas—the young creator of *Cupid*—takes a meeting with David E. Kelley, the far more famous creator of *Ally McBeal, The Practice,* and *Chicago Hope.* Kelley wants to discuss the possibility of Thomas's running a new series that he is currently creating for ABC. Thomas feels honored by this interest from the likes of Kelley, but at the same time, he finds the talk of a new job premature. Thomas reminds Kelley that he still has his own show, *Cupid,* on the air. If for some reason *Cupid* ends, he might well be interested in working on Kelley's new project.

Later, Thomas will wonder if Kelley already knew something that he didn't.

# Comfort, Joy, and Cancellation

> The trumpet of a prophecy! O Wind,
> If winter comes, can spring be far behind?

**Percy Bysshe Shelley**

**D**uring the early days of the Yuletide month a most remarkable bicoastal rumor takes hold among the naughty and nice in gossip-friendly Los Angeles. *South Park*'s Trey Parker and Matt Stone are said to have applied for and won the job of being copresidents of Comedy Central, offering their services as replacements for the now Fox-bound Doug Herzog.

### "Park" Pals Ponder Prez

Under that headline, a front-page story in the December 3 *Daily Variety* spreads the word that Parker and Stone covet the job and have even flown to New York to meet with the man who will make the final call, Tom Freston, chairman of MTV Networks, Comedy Central's corporate parent.

This makes for a rudely touching seasonal success story: two unrepentant network-bashing ruffians, only a few years ago scrambling around Hollywood for their next nonfigurative meals, quickly go from low-budget video Christmas cards to running a network of their own. The lunatics are programming the asylum.

"I heard it's already a done deal," one top Hollywood agent confides over lunch later the day that the story runs. In reality it is nothing of the sort. Only days later, the rumor du jour is that former NBC's chief Warren Littlefield is one name in consideration for this same giggle-rich gig. Once again the TV fates have conspired to demonstrate how the walls that formerly separated the networks and cable are coming tumbling down.

As the final results of November sweeps sink in it is becoming clear that among the networks there is no real winner other than the WB, which has felicitously moved up nearly 13 percent in households and 19 percent in the eighteen to forty-nine demographic. That's true growth—although it doesn't stop WB president Garth Ancier from leaving the network to pursue other opportunities, namely taking Warren Littlefield's old job at NBC. To varying degrees, all the other network victories can be filed under "P" for Pyrrhic. CBS just beats out NBC in terms of total households, while NBC squeaks past Fox in the all-important eighteen to forty-nine demographic race. Worryingly, virtually everyone is down in household numbers—CBS and NBC by 8 percent, Fox and ABC by 5 percent. UPN, meanwhile, has watched in horror as its total viewership has dropped a nose-bleeding 41 percent.

Does this mean there's a significant ratings meltdown? Is cable now battling network TV *mano a mano*, much as Santa Claus and Jesus did in Parker and Stone's *Spirit of Christmas* video? That—as a certain chief executive might say—would depend on what your definition of "is" is.

"Nothing could be as unstable as the network business," a speaker declares at the California Cable Television Association's Western Cable Show in Anaheim. That speaker is not some lone cable rabble-rouser but Robert Wright—chief executive of NBC Inc., which also happens to own CNBC as well as stakes in MSNBC, A&E, Bravo, and AMC, among other cable outlets.

Still, on soundstages and in the corridors of power around town, the cycle of network life continues, even at UPN, where the ratings free fall appears to have bottomed out after those early weeks of September when the network discovered how low it is that low can go. In fact, UPN is already starting to aggressively promote one of its upcoming midseason shows, on which much is riding, an animated version of the popular comic strip *Dilbert*, itself a crowd-pleasing send-up of contemporary corporate absurdity. Perhaps *Dilbert* can turn the battered UPN into the comeback kid?

Hope springs eternal—at least until spring.

Larry Charles, forty-two, isn't wearing his pajamas to work today— not that there's anything sartorially wrong with that.

"Yeah, I don't want to be a walking cliché," explains the former *Seinfeld* writer, the man who can claim credit for making "not that there's anything wrong with that" into a nineties mantra of comic political correctness. Charles explains that he mostly wore his pj's when he was at *Mad About You*. "I was working eighteen hours a day, seven days a week," he recalls. "I'm looking for simplicity, and it's so much easier just to put on a pair of pajamas than to decide what I'm going to wear with what."

Sitting today in his already cluttered new *Dilbert* office in Culver City, with a homemade shrine to his family across the room and the latest issue of *Tricycle: The Buddhist Review* on a coffee table, the casually dressed Charles looks like a lanky, friendly mix of Kramer and Rasputin. Charles went on from the first four seasons at *Seinfeld* to serve as a showrunner for *Mad About You* and is now in the process of creating *Dilbert*, an animated series based on Scott Adams's comic strip set to debut in January on UPN. America's favorite line-drawn bureaucrat has his work cut out for him in his new network workplace.

Charles was born in the same neighborhood in Brooklyn that produced Mel Brooks, Woody Allen, and *Seinfeld* cocreator Larry David. An exceptionally well-read fellow with a philosophical bent—

*D A V I D   W I L D*

the bookshelf behind him includes works of Kierkegaard and Nietz-sche, not to mention R. Crumb—Charles ended his formal educa-tion after a single year at Rutgers.

"I had a teacher there named Mark Crawford who is this big angry black man, and he wore a black cape and a black beret and chain-smoked Kools," Charles recalls fondly. Crawford became a mentor to him, and at the end of the semester Charles remembers Crawford telling him that if he was serious about being an author, he should quit school, just go out and live, travel, and write. "He said, 'Look at me, I can have tenure next year, but I'm going to quit and go finish my novel." So it was that Charles quit school, traveled around the country. A year or so later, Charles was predictably down-and-out in New York City when he spotted his former teacher on the street. "I see him, and I go 'Mark, Mark, I quit school. I'm like living. I'm living life. How are you doing?' He said, 'Well, I got tenure.'"

After working at a variety of odd jobs back East, Charles made his way to Los Angeles in 1976, not knowing anyone. Wanting to break into comedy, he would write jokes and stand in front of the Comedy Store club on Sunset. "I didn't know how to get into show business, and I stood in front like a drug dealer with jokes," he remembers.

As Charles tells it, comedians would try out his comedic wares and come out and buy them afterward for ten bucks or so a joke if they liked how something played with the Comedy Store crowd. He believes he sold his first joke to Jay Leno—then the king of the Com-edy Store along with another standup guy named David Letterman. "They both worked for Jimmy Walker at the time," Charles recalls.

Meanwhile, Charles had yet another connection to the stars. "My mother lived in Florida, and Phil Foster from *Laverne and Shirley* had come on to her once in a restaurant," he says. "She told him, 'Look, I'm not going out with you but my son is in Los Angeles, why don't you sit down with him?'" Remarkably, Foster did just that and invited young Charles over to Paramount, where he started hanging out with the *Laverne and Shirley* crew. He was nineteen and felt he was being groomed to be a writer on the show. More a seeker than a careerist by nature, Charles couldn't wait for that break. Instead he had what he terms "a self-destructive episode" and left town to follow an old girlfriend.

When he came back to L.A. as the seventies ended, Charles called an old associate who was working at *Oui* magazine about writing some pieces for that porno mag, only to discover that her husband had signed on with a new sketch show called *Fridays* that was looking for young writers. Charles hitchhiked to his interview and made quite an impression. In fact, he believes, the show's producers fired writers they had just hired so they could hire him instead.

Though *Fridays*—which debuted in April 1980—was written off by many as a lame ABC clone of NBC's *Saturday Night Live*, the late night series, in retrospect, has turned out to be an important breeding ground for future *Seinfeld* players. There Charles met Larry David and Michael Richards, the Man Who Would Be Kramer. "Larry was immediately a mentor to me," Charles recalls.

The *Fridays* job was intense and paid a hell of a lot better than his last job—as a bellhop in the Catskills. "It was a *gigantic* culture shock," Charles recalls. "In the course of a week, I went from making $150 a week to $1,500 a week. It was a time of great drug abuse in the industry. Everything was like a rock-and-roll dream come true. Creatively it was great too because anything you could think of content and structure-wise, you could do. You could be Edward Albee or Harold Pinter."

Like most good things—particularly good things fueled by illegal substances—*Fridays* had to end. "*Fridays* crashed partially because of drugs," says Charles, who today compares the trajectory of the show to a drug experience. "We had a couple of tremendous peaks, then the thing started to collapse and finally fell apart," Charles recalls. "It became a bad trip. Everybody was just burned out. It's really a job for young people, which fortunately I was at the time."

After the death of *Fridays*—it was canceled in the fall of 1982 to make way for an extra night of *Nightline*—Charles imagined he would become "some kind of Charles Bukowski character in a rooming house somewhere, writing little stories and working in a factory, which I had done."

*DAVID WILD*

First, Charles took the time out to plunge into a depression; then from 1982 to 1985 he figured he'd take the time to learn how to really write "without the deadlines and the drugs," while his long-time girlfriend, whom he married in 1985, brought home the proverbial bacon. After that, he hooked up with comedian Richard Belzer, doing a program for Showtime called *The Richard Belzer Show* about the life of a comedian, as well as collaborating on a book entitled *How to Be a Stand-Up Comic*.

Charles's TV writing career had stalled in part because of a succession of agents who came and went: one from AIDS, one from drugs, one he says simply "disappeared from the face of the earth," perhaps joining a federal agent relocation program. Finally, Charles says he hooked up with the right, nondisappearing agent and things started to come together for him.

In 1989 things came together for him on *The Arsenio Hall Show*.

"I needed a job," explains Charles, who dreamed of penning mind-blowing nightly monologues of the Richard Pryor variety for Hall to deliver. "Arsenio seemed into it, then he chickened out a little bit," Charles says. "It was too hard for a lot of reasons, not necessarily his fault. I got fired by Arsenio, but it was kind of a mutual thing. I fired him also."

Getting sacked by Arsenio turned out to be a professional and personal blessing. Around this same time, Larry David told him about a sitcom that he and Jerry Seinfeld were putting together. The idea sounded promising, even though David, like Charles, had no sitcom experience (and Seinfeld himself had been let go after a brief run as Frankie, the governor's joke writer, on *Benson*). Still, he was thrilled when Larry David called offering a job on what would become *Seinfeld*.

Charles could hardly be prouder of the *Seinfeld* experience. "Both publicly and privately, *Seinfeld* broke so many rules," he says. "The reason it all happened was that Larry was *always* true to himself. We both felt, and Jerry did too, we'll do thirteen episodes the way we want to do them, then we'll go back to our lives. If you go into this business thinking of job security, it's an absurdity."

Despite his love for the show, Charles would leave *Seinfeld* relatively early, after four seasons, and start what would become a tradition among the show's writers by signing an overall deal with NBC's production unit—not that there's anything wrong with that either. "I think I had like one of the first deals that was made at that time," says Charles, who'd become supervising producer at the show. "Now it's de rigueur that people get these big deals. I did eighty episodes. I really poured my heart into it, but I hit the glass ceiling. It was made clear to me that I was never going to run the show."

Though he hardly looks the part of the ambitious company man, Charles was tiring of being perceived as the junior partner at *Seinfeld*. Here as elsewhere in life, Charles chose to follow his instincts— "I'm always willing to throw the dice," he explains—because he felt it was time leave the nest. It didn't hurt any that the overall deal with NBC was going to pay him three times the money he was making to create shows of his own.

What Charles created was *Middle Man*, a sitcom of sorts for NBC starring Wayne Knight, *Seinfeld*'s own Newman, which Charles fondly describes as "this bleak, Beckett-like pilot about a middle manager at a strange multinational corporation in a California desert." For Charles, "The creative process of *Middle Man* was amazing, I *loved* it, and of course it was a complete and utter failure." Coming off the high of *Seinfeld*, the fact that *Middle Man* didn't get picked up by the network—even with Jerry Seinfeld personally warming up the audience for the pilot—was a blow. "It was like, *wow*, failure," he remembers. "The fact that I felt so positive and it was received so poorly threw me for a loop."

After that, Charles tried a few more projects for NBC, but then in 1995 the network came to him with another proposal. He was told that one of the network's big shows was in trouble—*Mad About You* starring Paul Reiser and Helen Hunt. "It was very valuable property to both NBC and Columbia TriStar that had not yet reached syndication," Charles recalls. "It was stumbling for a variety of reasons." Two new showrunners had come in and quickly quit before the first episode. "It was a rudderless ship, a runaway train," he says. The show's cocreator Danny Jacobson had moved on, had come back, and was holding down the fort until someone new arrived to run things.

Charles considered the offer and concluded that "the difference between *Mad About You* and *Seinfeld* was I would be able to explore more emotional issues, more complex relationships, which is something I was going through since I was married." In that way, the job could mean more to him than simply keeping a runaway train on the TV tracks.

Finally, *Seinfeld*'s other Larry was running a show—if not *the* show of shows.

"Here I am in pajamas going into these big meetings with the heads of the corporation," Charles recalls. "It was a multimillion-dollar responsibility, particularly at that time when they were trying to get it into syndication. There was a *lot* of pressure at the time because they were close to saying, 'It's not going to work out, we're going to cancel it.'"

Charles came into *Mad About You* with, he says, "a tremendous amount of vitality and sort of reinvented the show with the cooperation and enthusiasm of Paul and Helen." At the time Charles would tell his assistant that he was going to write a book called *Zen & the Art of Showrunning*.

"You're not so Zen," he was told.

He learned that, paradoxically, the job requires detachment and involvement at the same time. He also learned that the reality of running a show is "you're totally isolated—it is all on your shoulders. The first thing that struck me was, 'Wow, I can't go home until the job is done and the job is *never* done.' So for two years, I did not go home essentially." The system Charles inherited on *Mad About You* was "relatively dysfunctional," he says. "It really did require eighteen-hour days, often seven days a week for weeks on end. Coming home I would be just a silhouette climbing into bed as my wife and kids were getting up. We really did not see each other for two years, which was damaging, no doubt about it."

After two fulfilling if exhausting seasons at *Mad About You*, Charles was ready to move on. "I felt like I did with *Seinfeld*, that I had said everything I had to say," he says. His two seasons saw the show hit a new high with the surprisingly unflinching look—for a sitcom, anyway—at a temporary breakdown of Paul and Jamie's marriage and the couple's subsequent march toward parenthood. "There was nothing more for me to do," he says. "As far as I was concerned the show ended the day they had a baby." (*Mad About You*'s dwindling ratings this season suggest Charles was not far off.)

In working out Helen Hunt's schedule for the film *As Good As It Gets*, Charles came to know the film's director, James L. Brooks, a TV legend in his own right with credits like *The Mary Tyler Moore Show* and *Taxi*. When Columbia TriStar offered Charles a deal, part of what spurred him on to take it was the chance to work with Brooks developing a show. As Charles sits here in the *Dilbert* office— he also has space in Brooks's nearby office—their series still has plenty of developing to do. "It's a TV show, but we haven't decided what it's going to be," Charles explains with a fittingly vague smile. "The great thing is I have another mentor like Larry David, I get to sit with Jim Brooks every week, sort of like a guru. I sit at his feet and we talk about ideas."

A man who wears pajamas to work may seem an interesting choice to turn *Dilbert*—Scott Adams's wildly popular celebration of the surreality of the modern workplace—into a weekly TV series, but Charles was an aspiring cartoonist growing up and even corresponded with Al Capp of *Li'l Abner* fame. When he finally read one of the *Dilbert* books he "saw something. It's really this epic vision, philosophy of life. It's very heavy and very complex, very multifaceted and anthropological. I got very excited about this as a TV show. This office is a microcosm for the universe. *Dilbert* is a big Kafkaesque story of a little logical man in a big illogical world."

With talk like that, it's little surprise that when he went to meet with Scott Adams, Charles "wove a spell" and got the job. A spell might have needed to be woven, since there had already been a failed live-action *Dilbert* pilot for Fox. Still there was interest, since *Dilbert* has become the most popular comic strip of the nineties, appearing in nearly two thousand newspapers worldwide and in numerous best-selling books, reaching an estimated 150 million readers daily. Even in broad TV terms, that's a serious presold audience.

Adapting a show from the strip has turned out to be a different sort of challenge for Charles. At *Mad About You*, he was in a sense a custodian—albeit an exceptionally gifted and well-paid one—but here at *Dilbert* he is building a new system from the ground up.

First, he got a personal seminar in animated comedy from his friend George Meyer, co–executive producer on *The Simpsons*. Though the animation process is famously time-consuming—especially for all the animators in Korea—Charles is finding the pace of *Dilbert* far more relaxed than that of *Mad About You*. He says that now, at eight P.M., he finds himself asking, "Isn't there something *else* I can do?"

The first season of *Dilbert*—just now starting to come back from Korea in near final form—concerns the efforts of Dilbert's employer The Company to create and market a new product. Conveniently, that's exactly what Charles, Adams, and UPN are doing. As for the dysfunctional state of *Dilbert*'s network home, Charles admits, "There were moments when we worried about it, but the truth is that as long as I produced the thirteen shows and it came out the way I wanted, I knew it would have a life *somewhere*."

That life features Daniel Stern—previously the retrospective narrator for *The Wonder Years*—who gives voice to the beleaguered title character, while longtime David Letterman associate Chris Elliot is his less than fully supportive canine pal Dogbert, and *Suddenly Susan*'s Kathy Griffin plays Dilbert's overworked colleague Alice. "With no wardrobe, no makeup, it's more fun," Charles explains.

To ensure that the fun never stops, Charles still clings to Larry David's counsel—"If it makes you cringe, don't do it."

"I've tried to follow that," he says. "That's a very simple rule to live by in television."

Simple, but one that could keep a showrunner off most network programming.

"Exactly," he says. "Larry taught me this too—it's liberating to say no. You lose power from yes."

A noncringing Charles explains that *Dilbert* premieres on January 25. Beyond that, he has "no expectations. I know the show is great, but that's *all* I know. Will people watch it? Will people like it? Will UPN succeed? It's all irrelevant to me."

Perhaps Charles is still working on *Zen & the Art of Show Running* after all.

There is a sinking feeling at *OverSeas*.

More specifically, what's sinking is the shoes of a few dozen NBC executives and agents gathered at Renmar Studios in Hollywood for the first table read of Simms's new pilot. The inside of Soundstages 8 and 9—once home to *I Love Lucy*—has been transformed into LaShangria, a tiny fictional Third World nation somewhere in the India/Afghanistan/Pakistan neck of the woods. It is here that the American representatives of the International Foreign Aid Foundation will work on *OverSeas*. Inside the stage, twenty-four tons of dirt have been dumped as part of an effort to create a believable strange land to be trampled upon by a hopefully hilarious crew of American strangers. Close by, there's even a sizable faux lake, part of the massive preparations for this first run-through in the jungle. One imagines that being in this place—walking distance to Melrose Avenue—is just like being in LaShangria, if such a place in fact existed.

Today various executives—including NBC's Don Ohlmeyer, and Bernie Brillstein and Brad Grey of Brillstein-Grey—and assorted agents will not sit in the bleachers, as audiences will do next week on show night and for many happy seasons to come, God and NBC's Scott Sassa willing. Instead, Simms has chosen to make things more atmospheric. For the table read, Simms has set up folding chairs in the dirt of the town center, with the main camp's tents in front of them and a slightly sinking feeling below. Most of the *NewsRadio* writers who've come by to support their boss are wearing sensible shoes and sneakers, but other VIPs are facing a tiny footwear disaster. Still, the mood remains high with anticipation as everyone grabs a script.

There was some early discussion of doing the show not inside a soundstage but outside, perhaps out in a Malibu ranch as *M\*A\*S\*H* was done. Simms, however, yearned for the energy of a live audience. "The idea—and I admit it's ambitious to the point of possible failure—was doing this outdoor show *with* an audience," he explains, surveying the LaShangria landscape with a grin.

When Simms and the cast take their preassigned seats on the dirt and begin reading the script, it becomes clear that this is not the only ambition evident in *OverSeas*. Dressed in a blue sweatshirt and sipping a Big Gulp from 7-Eleven, Simms listens to his words like everyone else. Today is nearly four years to the day that Simms had his first table read for *NewsRadio*, and he seems motivated to do more than simply beat the dreaded sophomore slump.

It has taken too long to get *OverSeas* to this stage. "Originally we were planning on shooting in April, but I felt like we didn't have the cast together," Simms recalls. "Then we thought we were going to be shooting in October, then Phil got murdered by his wife and I realized I was going to have to help out a little bit more on *NewsRadio,* so it's been all stretched out."

Weaning himself from *NewsRadio* in the post-Hartman era became a gradual process for Simms. "The first three episodes were like how we used to do it, then it was just me going to table reads and taking a look at the rewrite but not actually putting it through the computer," Simms says. "The past six episodes, I'd go to the table read and say what I think. Then I'd go down on shoot night. This last shoot night I missed—that's the first *NewsRadio* script I didn't write or even read or even go to shoot night. This will be the first time I get to see a *NewsRadio* episode I don't know *anything* about."

These days a steady stream of *NewsRadio*s are being served up twice daily in L.A. through the modern miracle of syndication. "I'm not getting checks yet," he explains, "but it's been great because now people see it and know it. Like the woman at the newsstand I go to knows what I do."

Simms admits to some odd, slightly mixed feelings about *NewsRadio* going on this season without the benefit of its best-known cast member. "Yeah, it's weird," he says quietly. "You're proud you get over the hump but you still have the feeling it's not the same. I still like it a lot—this is more me on a personal level. Not that it's worse or better, but without Phil, it's not the show we were doing all those years."

Still no ratings-buster for NBC, *NewsRadio* remains on the NBC schedule during a season when the network has enough other worries.

"It's all going down the toilet," Simms says with a fleeting, canary-eating grin. "*Some* surprise." For Simms, audiences are suffering from sitcom-fatigue, which figured into his concept of *OverSeas*. "I just can't see another living room or office, and I don't care about people who live in New York, L.A., or Chicago anymore, he says. "I've seen every story about dating do's and don'ts strip-mined to *death*. Everyone's done their version of that, just like everyone's done their version of who gets the corner office."

Simms has caught a dangerous jungle disease—he yearns to do something different both in style and in content. With *OverSeas*, Simms feels he's found "something personal, it's a ha-ha comedy but it's also about ideas about America and bigger problems. With these people, if the well dries up, they are literally without water as opposed to 'I went out with a girl last week and she dyed her hair and now I'm not sure if I want to go out with her anymore,' you know."

Casting *OverSeas* has also been a long haul. "With *NewsRadio*, I went into it knowing I wanted to use Dave Foley and Phil Hartman and Andy Dick," Simms recalls. "With this I went into it not having anyone in mind."

*OverSeas* features a main cast of nine—only two of whom are played by familiar faces. These were the last two cast: Joe Rogan from *NewsRadio* signed on as Jack, the closest the show has to a male lead, while character actor James Rebhorn (*The Game*) will play Mr. Johnson, a gambling-addicted former high school coach, the leader of the International Foreign Aid Foundation camp.

Simms finds the current culture of casting exceedingly strange. "You have actors who you've never heard of who've done one show and they won't read," he reports. "You can meet with them but they won't read, and I have to hear what people sound like. The biggest name we looked at was Jason Bateman, who I *really* liked, but by Wednesday last week we narrowed it down to three guys."

Simms was ready to offer the role to one of those actors when some of the *OverSeas* team went to dinner. They discussed how the role of Jack was the hardest to cast. "It's not the lead exactly, but you want a cute guy who's funny who seems like he's lived a little," Simms says. "Thinking if I could have anyone on the air, I said I could only think of two people, Matthew Perry from *Friends* or Joe Rogan from our show. Our director Tom Cherones said, 'Why don't we have him read for it?'"

Initially NBC was reluctant about poaching Rogan—"You know what the network people thought of *NewsRadio*," says Simms—but the actor's reading convinced even the faithless. The current plan is to stagger the schedules of *NewsRadio* and *OverSeas* so Rogan can do both for the rest of the season—assuming *OverSeas* doesn't go under. And what if both shows make it to next season? "In the incredibly unlikely chance *NewsRadio* gets picked up for next season," Simms explains, "we'll figure that out."

Also late in getting cast was the part of Mr. Johnson, originally written for a well-known TV character actor Simms had worked with, whose name he will utter only off the record. Then there was a period when Simms was talking to Patrick Warburton, best-known as Elaine's dim-witted, face-painting Puddy on *Seinfeld*, first for the part of Jack. After Warburton did a fine three-episode arc guest spot on *NewsRadio* in the fall, Simms considered rewriting Mr. Johnson as a younger man to fit the actor.

"We were talking to him for a while, a monthlong negotiation, then ultimately last Thursday or Friday, I said all right, enough," Simms recalls. The cost of getting Warburton on board *OverSeas* became prohibitive. Instead, Simms chose to keep Mr. Johnson middle-aged—older if not wiser. "Look, I loved them both, but the part always called for one grown-up," says Simms, "and James is definitely that."

The rest of the ensemble cast looks younger, with arguably more

obvious sex appeal than that of *NewsRadio*—partly a reaction to the
heat Simms took from the network last time around. "There are a
thousand theories from the network on why *NewsRadio* wasn't a
hit—it doesn't have heart, it needs more sex appeal," says Simms.
"The only reason is it didn't get big numbers. I'll *always* think it has
more to do with scheduling."

The table read goes okay—this is no total bungle in the jungle,
though too much time seems dedicated to setting up the situation,
leaving less time for comedy. Afterward Simms admits to feeling "a
huge relief," having made any forward motion. "When I did *News-
Radio.* between the time I pitched the idea and did the table read was
a month and a half and that's the right time. The more time, the
more overthinking goes into it." With *NewsRadio*, there was only
one large rewrite of the pilot script. Today's table read is of the
eighth draft of *OverSeas*.

After the table read, executives huddle in the dirt, while the
agents and *NewsRadio* writers disperse. "The actors are welcome to
leave," a stage manager announces. The message gets delivered with
a warm laugh and a smile, but to any thespian who has gotten this
far with a pilot, this is a real nerve-wracking moment. It is now—
when the network and the studio, both from NBC in this case, give
their laundry lists of desired changes—that things, including actors,
have a funny way of changing. Without any audible protest, the cast
heads across the soundstage to the catering area, where they hash
over how the table reading's gone.

The NBC team—including Ohlmeyer—has its collective insight
delivered to Simms. Ohlmeyer himself has been hands-on with the
show since the departure of Warren Littlefield, a change that Simms
credits with speeding up the process of getting *OverSeas* on the boards.
"The fact that Don and I were meeting and talking about the script
built a fire under some people there," he says.

Ohlmeyer's notes are mostly familiar to Simms. He still wants each
character's point of view made clearer. He also found one of the
female characters too vague—a criticism Simms deems fair.

"Everyone's going to have their favorite parts but if I pick and choose that we'll have a hodgepodge of crap," Simms says. "We need a simple clear story and a taste of each of these people," says Simms. "Their note was make sure it's not a bunch of dumb people in the jungle. The ironic thing—actually it's more *painful* than ironic—is the notes were *so* similar to the *NewsRadio* pilot. They want to know why the characters are there. Look, they're there because they're there—we'll find out later. That's what I always say—twenty-two minutes is what we have. I knew what the notes would be—what they always are. More, more, more—and make us *laugh* but make us *care*."

Simms balks slightly at one note—that the Hindi-English translation got a little tedious. "It's a show about two groups of people, no fake language, no subtitles. They're not going to *happen* to speak English with an accent. The road we're starting to go down is a cliché—back off on the foreigners. Focus on all these white people and use all these mute brown-skinned people as background and set dressing."

Still, things could have gone worse, *much* worse. Simms wasn't ordered to alter the show's basic scenario—which has happened after other pilot table reads—nor was he told to lose any actors. "No, I wasn't worried," Simms says. "But look who I fired off *NewsRadio*—Ray Romano." Simms spotted Romano doing standup on TV and brought him out to be "my special find." Soon that special find was told to get lost. "Ray's even said he felt like he didn't know what he was doing and was pushing too hard," Simms says. "I never talked to him about it and I always felt terrible I couldn't find the nerve to call him—someone else called his manager. But he and I have exchanged notes and I've said how much I like his show."

After receiving NBC's notes today, Simms comes back up to his office and talks things over with some *NewsRadio* staff, then writers Joe Furey and Brian Kelly start reworking the script while Simms takes a nap. At three A.M. Simms heads off to seek sustenance at Taco Bell before getting back to the business of being funny on deadline.

A few days later, the *OverSeas* team is preparing for the big network run-through on Thursday afternoon.

"This is going to be *really* weird because there's going to be a partial audience of real people," Simms warns beforehand. "They're going to get up and wander around with us." According to Simms, a studio run-through yesterday for Brillstein-Grey and NBC Studios was "as they always are—just *death*."

Today's run-through is hardly death but it feels a bit surreal as fifty or so game civilians, numerous NBC executives including Ohlmeyer and Scott Sassa, and other invited guests follow the cast through the action scene by scene, a minor migration occurring with each new location. The script continues to evolve—with the Hindi translation slightly played down. There's some smart, funny stuff here, possibly too smart for its own good, since it's hard to imagine Henry David Thoreau references testing all that well.

Afterward, Simms sits down with the test audience, takes their comments, and answers all their questions. Normally Simms can seem like a wise guy but talking with civilians he seems deferential and less sarcastic than in virtually any other circumstance. After the session is over, Simms refuses to cut off an older man's rush of comments even though Scott Sassa's outside waiting to give Simms his own notes. Finally, Simms runs to Sassa, who's waiting by his car.

Sassa's notes seem clear-cut—he wants Simms to be more upfront about what Jack's motivating problem is by the act break. Simms agrees. Sassa also wants the pilot to be "just funnier." Simms declares himself happy to accommodate. "Funnier," he says with some confidence. "That's easy."

The next week, after still more rehearsal and rewriting, it's finally show time, and this evening the bleachers are completely filled. Right before the scheduled seven P.M. start time, Simms—wearing a sweatshirt that reads PHAT FARM—stands on the set with Joe Rogan, scans the audience, and pulls out a cigarette.

"Is the fire marshal here tonight or can I smoke?" Simms asks his star.

"Risky on the pilot night, man," Rogan warns him.

Rogan—a standup veteran—is asked about what kind of leader Simms makes. "What kind of *leader*?" the actor asks disbelievingly. "He's like a bad frat boy. *Terrible*. He's got no leadership ability *whatsoever*. If he led by example you would be a video game–playing vampire who chain-smokes. That's *really* not the guy to follow—but he is a very great writer and a lot of fun and probably the best executive producer you could ever have."

As for how he feels about being tied to Simms for a potential second show, Rogan says, "I couldn't care less."

Simms warms to this notion more. "He's Tony Roberts to my Woody Allen. No, Clint Howard to my Ron Howard."

"Yeah," adds Rogan. "I look *really* goofy and don't get laid."

Brad Grey checks in with Simms. "This is an ambitious show," he says, looking around the set. "I'm very optimistic about it. The truth is what's great about this, and so energizing about it, if it works—which we're all hoping it will—it could take us to a new place in terms of what prime time is today. Hopefully we'll send a little bit of a message—I hate to even *use* that term—that not every person coming out of school is interested in going to Wall Street or a law firm."

No, the ones who think they're funny want to write sitcoms.

Finally, Rogan goes center stage to introduce the rest of the *Over-Seas* cast to the studio audience and kick off the show. "This is what we think is going to be your solution to your boring sitcoms," he tells them. "A sitcom in the jungle. It's gonna be fun. It's going to be . . . *different*."

The script has changed yet again. One new line Mr. Johnson delivers to Jack seems apropos this evening as words to live by for any showrunner who still gives a damn—"God bless you and your misguided optimism."

Midway through the filming—a process that will last until the wee hours and be followed by an early morning group jam in Simms's music room—Scott Sassa is spotted standing next to Simms by a TV monitor. He is asked what he thinks so far.

Sassa looks over at Simms's sweatshirt and offers only a grin and these words: "He be Phat."

Brad Grey stands a few feet away, no doubt ready to do a little business. Perhaps Sassa would like to skip the normal research and meetings, and commit to a time slot for *OverSeas* right now?

In the way of an answer to this query, Sassa offers a nonreply that must be considered masterful in its Sphinx-like elusiveness, one that suggests the guy's indeed got a bright future ahead of him running a network.

"What's a time slot?" Sassa says with a smile.

Some seasonal questions are perennials: What exactly do you give *Friends* who have everything for the holidays?

Perhaps in another town and another business, a fruitcake might do the job, but not here. Sometime before Christmas, Warner Bros. decides to give each *Friends* cast member $200,000. On December 22, Michael Fleming reports in *Daily Variety*'s "Dish" column that the studio first planned on giving the actors Range Rovers, then decided to go with $100,000, an amount that subsequently gets doubled, in hopes of providing that extra bit of comfort and joy.

The studio has good reason to want the show's magnificent, telegenic six full of goodwill and cheer. Early in 1999, Warner Bros. will be heading back to negotiations with NBC. Many are anxious—possibly even desperate—to add time to the one and a half seasons left on the cast's old deal. Everyone's looking to make a new deal. More than ever *Friends* seems to be in the catbird seat—one of network TV's few sure things, a smash not only on NBC but also in syndication, where the show beat *Seinfeld* this month for the first time.

The cast of *Friends* should be getting the sort of gift that keeps on giving.

Like death, the television industry occasionally takes a holiday.

Most showrunners grab at least some semblance of a break—

though in December the more substantial summer hiatus—the Big One—still remains months and a TV eternity away.

*Cupid*'s Scott Winant—who has been pulling double duty working on the Tracy Pollan pilot *Anna Says*—is leaving the day after Christmas for a very intensive family ski trip in Mammoth.

Shortly before the holidays, Winant received a gift from ABC. What he found wrapped up under the programming tree wasn't quite what he wished for. Yes, he got a brand-new, shiny time slot, but not the Monday night at ten P.M. slot he spoke of in November—instead, he got Thursday nights at nine P.M. This finally puts *Cupid* on a night when adults are watching TV—the problem is, many of those adults are otherwise engaged watching *Frasier* and *Veronica's Closet*, part of NBC's diminished but still dauntingly popular lineup.

Winant and *Cupid*'s creator Rob Thomas are trying to be optimistic about this Thursday go-round, set to start in the new year. "I think *Frasier* is an excellent show but if someone presents a viable alternative, there will be some people who will check us out," Winant says. Now he hopes ABC will let people know that an alternative exits.

Underneath his calm demeanor, it seems obvious Winant is growing weary of the rather low profile of *Cupid*. "I've never had a show that seems so . . . *invisible*," he says. "I run across people all the time who don't even know that *Cupid* is on the air. This is the hard part for me because we work *very* hard, and we've done a number of episodes we feel *very* proud of, yet it's almost as if they've evaporated and we have to start all over again."

Creatively, Winant is quite satisfied with the first two *Cupids* that will be run on Thursday nights in January, particularly the second one, set to air on the fourteenth, which he calls "our *homage* to Cervantes's *Don Quixote*."

Winant takes a beat.

"Yeah, you *know* how the audience is *dying* for that," Winant says with a laugh. Still, he's trying to stay positive and remains thankful that ABC hasn't shut down the show as it recently did with *Fantasy Island*, *Cupid*'s former lead-in. "It's just *anti-network* to renew a show with a seven share," Winant says, referring to his *Cupid*'s poor Nielsens. "They believe in this show and the work we're doing. I know that the support is there. I also know the support won't *always* be there."

The move to Thursday takes place as Winant has been going bicoastal to finish up the *Anna Says* pilot for Tracy Pollan, who is coincidentally much in the news due to Michael J. Fox's going public about his battle with Parkinson's disease. Right after New Year's, Winant is to oversee final postproduction on the show, but already he appears pleased with the result. "What I am happiest about is that we sold it as a somewhat hybrid show—having more film elements than a sitcom," he says. "Even as I was selling it, I didn't believe we'd *really* accomplish that because the network tends to be nervous about that sort of thing. Ultimately we did do that."

Winant says he has no clue what ABC will do to replace *Cupid* in that Saturday night slot.

"I don't know," Winant says. "Maybe just dead air."

Perhaps dead air could score an eight share.

"It *would* be peaceful," says Winant.

Wherever it resides, *Cupid* is still alive, which is more than can be said for many other members of the network's freshman prime-time class of the 1998–1999 season. With few exceptions like *Friends*, *Everybody Loves Raymond*, *JAG*, *The Practice*, and *7th Heaven*, even returning shows are struggling to keep the ratings up. As for the new shows, back in a far more innocent time—September—a TV executive predicted that by the end of the year thirty of the new shows would already be dead or dying. He wasn't too far off. Here's one medical diagnosis of how things stand at year's end.

Stillborn: *Hollyweird*.

Dead If Not Buried: *The Secret Diary of Desmond Pfeiffer*, *The Brian Benben Show*, *Costello*, *Buddy Faro*, *Encore! Encore!*, *Conrad Bloom*, *Mercy Point*, *Secret Lives of Men*, *Guys Like Us*, *To Have and to Hold*, *Living in Captivity*, *Fantasy Island*, *Wind on the Water*, *The Army Show*, *Trinity*, *Holding the Baby*.

Dying or Seriously Ailing: *Vengeance Unlimited*, *Hyperion Bay*, *DiResta*, *Legacy*, *Brimstone*.

*D A V I D   W I L D*

Under the Weather: *Cupid*, *Maggie Winters*.

Healthy If Not Hits: *Jesse*, *Martial Law*, *The Hughleys*, *Will & Grace*,
*Seven Days*, *Sports Night*, *Charmed*, *Felicity*, *The King of Queens*,
*Two of a Kind*, *That '70s Show*, *L.A. Doctors*.

Remember, though, it's always wise to get a second opinion.
Some healthy patients die; some supposed goners survive to a ripe
old age. To wit: Back at the dawn of the 1990s, there was a little sitcom on NBC roundly judged to be in critical condition, as well as far
too smart, too New York, and too damn unsexy to survive.

You might have heard of it—it was called *Seinfeld*.

Over the holidays one year ago, *South Park*'s Trey Parker and Matt
Stone went together to China, taking time near the Great Wall to
digest their great good luck in the wake of their first brush with
fame and fortune. Sensibly, the pair decide to go their own ways this
year. Stone heads off with his girlfriend to Australia, where, he discovers *South Park* is even bigger than at home. Parker, meanwhile,
takes his parents and sister to England. He too finds *South Park*
everywhere he goes. "We actually had separate vacations," Stone
reports when he gets home. "That was strange. We went through
withdrawals, but I have a picture of Trey in my wallet and Trey has a
picture of me."

Can that *possibly* be true?

"No," he confesses, though one still wonders.

'Twas the night before Christmas Eve and all through the Warner Bros. lot, not a prospective ABC midseason pilot is stirring, except for *The Norm Show*.

In recent months, what buzz there has been on the new sitcom Bruce Helford and Norm Macdonald have been creating together has not been particularly good. "I hear Norm wants out," one industry insider tells me. "The network doesn't like it." Macdonald himself has come off noncommittal about the show's progress. "It's coming along, I guess," is about all he reports. The fact that the schedule keeps getting pushed back, including a last-minute one-night delay of the pilot filming, cannot be encouraging.

On the other hand, delays are to be expected—it's hardly unheard-of for writing to bog down or for actors to be hired and dismissed. Both happened here. Then only a week or so ago the news came that triple Emmy-winner Laurie Metcalf—Norm's dream costar from the start—was joining the cast of what's now being called, with modified minimalism, *The Norm Show*. True minimalism would have been *Norm*—like *Roseanne*, where then neophyte sitcom writer Macdonald first met actress Metcalf.

Now on this freezing—for Burbank—eve of Christmas Eve, a packed studio audience gathers in the bleachers of Stage 12 to be duly entertained. Bruce Helford stands in the center of the floor, nervously talking over some last-minute details with director Andy Cadiff.

Once the show is under way, it's clear that bad buzz or not, *The Norm Show*—or at least the pilot meant to launch it—is significantly better than the norm. The sitcom's somewhat reluctant leading man appears surprisingly ready for prime time. Wisely, Helford has opted to let Macdonald be Macdonald. As was the original concept, Norm plays a social worker, but it turns out he's working in the field first and foremost to avoid doing far harder time in prison. On the show, he's Norm Henderson, a former professional hockey player sentenced to five years of public service for gambling and tax embezzlement. There are lines in the pilot script that *scream* Norm—"You're a huge whore" in particular, though off-screen Macdonald might prefer his beloved phrase "crack whore." There's another moving moment when Norm

*D A V I D   W I L D*

tells a prostitute client, "Okay, fine, I'll go to jail, young lady, but you're going to have to give me a few pointers on how to please a man."

Macdonald blows only a few lines tonight, such as when he calls the hooker—played by guest star Nikki Cox from *Unhappily Ever After*—"Trailer" instead of "Taylor," arguably not a bad rewrite. He appears to be on his best behavior—muttering "Fuck" under his breath only a few times tonight. More importantly, he displays real chemistry with Metcalf, who plays his more caring colleague. Metcalf, a Steppenwolf Theater Company veteran, is the sort of unfailing actor's actor whose very presence raises the overall level of the play.

Throughout tonight's taping, it feels cold inside the stage, and some of the VIPs on the floor—including ABC's Jamie Tarses and Tony Jonas of Warner Bros.—can be seen wearing L.A. winter gear as Helford paces intently, making last-minute fixes and conferring with Macdonald. Right before the second pass at the episode's last scene, Tarses and Helford hug in celebration, and possibly for a little extra heat.

Things wrap up at 10:15. Apart from one large Japanese tour group with a bus to make, the studio audience sticks around and appears charmed by the show.

"Watch for Norm on ABC," the crowd is told as they leave. Of course exactly when, where, and if the masses will be able to see these social workers remains an entirely open case.

Afterward, as frigid executives scurry out and head off to their assorted holiday plans, Norm Macdonald and Laurie Metcalf sit backstage outside the trailers that are serving as dressing rooms tonight, grabbing a brief moment or two of post-pilot peace on earth. All over the frigid village of Hollywood—as the industry prepares to sing "Auld Lang Syne" to the 1998 part of the 1998–1999 television season—viewers face the upcoming moment of TV truth, whether to watch Dick Clark's *New Year's Rockin' Eve* or a special double shot of *South Park*. Before that, though, in this chilly place where network TV dreams and nightmares both come true, old acquaintances Macdonald and Metcalf simply sit and receive stray compliments for work well done—not a bad way to end the year in a business where old acquaintances generally *should* be forgot.

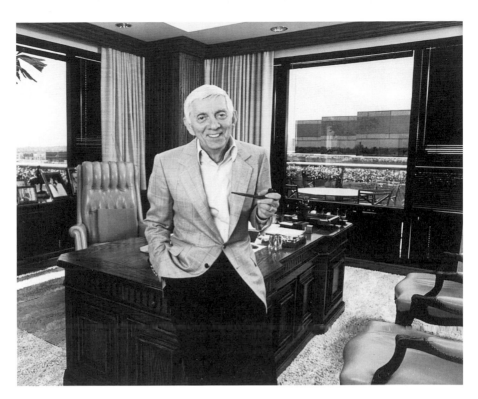

**Your Showrunner of Showrunners** Aaron Spelling—who was writing TV when most of today's showrunners were only glimmers in their agents' eyes. Spelling is in his office the personalized pinball machine is to his right, the gargantuan mansion to his left.

**Ohmigod, They Made a Killing!** Adorable cable terrorists Trey Parker (right) and Matt Stone, the wiseass (and now multimillionaire) founders of *South Park*.

**Power Trio** Kevin Bright (standing), Marta Kauffman,
and David Crane in a rare quiet moment together,
on the set of their smash sitcom *Friends*.

**A Perfectly Matched Pair** Ray Romano (right) and creator Phil Rosenthal of *Everybody Loves Raymond* reflect on a pressing eyewear decision.

***Cupid*, before the Slings and Arrows** (from left) Scott Winant and Rob Thomas during the making of the *Cupid* pilot with guest star George Newbern and the show's leads, Paula Marshall and Jeremy Piven.

**Amazing *Will & Grace*** Partners Max Mutchnick and David Kohan with the cast of their breakout sitcom *Will & Grace,* one of the few new hits of the 1998–1999 season: (clockwise from top left) Megan Mullally, Sean Hayes, Debra Messing, Eric McCormack, Kohan, and Mutchnick.

**Heavenly Mother** *7th Heaven* creator Brenda Hampton, who left a career in sitcoms behind to bring the family drama to life again.

>>>

**Like Minds** The cast of *It's like, you know . . .* with former *Seinfeld* writer Peter Mehlman and recovering network boss Ted Harbert, well before their show's midseason launch. Harbert (kneeling), Mehlman (standing) and the cast: (from left) Steven Eckholdt, Chris Eigeman, A. J. Langer, Jennifer Grey, and Evan Handler.

**All You Need Is Love** Amy Lippman and Christopher Keyser—the creative team behind *Party of Five* and its new spin-off, *Time of Your Life,* starring Jennifer Love Hewitt.

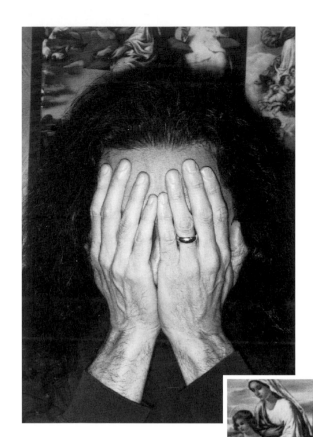

**Hello, Larry** *Dilbert* showrunner Larry Charles faces life after *Seinfeld*.

**The *Norm* Conquest**  Bruce Helford (left) and his sardonic partner-in-crime Norm Macdonald of *The Norm Show* (now simply *Norm*) at rest in their natural habitat—the writers' room.

**As the Crowe Flies**  Showrunner Christopher Crowe celebrates the end of an extended (and often trying) first season during the wrap party for *Seven Days*.

**Mustn't-See TV** The *NewsRadio* team gathers moments after shooting what would be the show's final episode. Series creator Paul Simms is seated at center with a showrunner's best friend—a dog, not a network.

*JANUARY*

# Cupid Goes to Hades

**Slump? I ain't in no slump. I just ain't hitting.**

**Yogi Berra**

*L*ike other flighty life-forms, TV critics migrate on a seasonal basis, and January finds much of the nation's opinionated flock heading West. They seek the relative warmth, comfort, sustenance, and easy column inches at the Ritz-Carlton Huntington Hotel, in Pasadena, California, for two weeks the great winter home of the Television Critics Association.

Executives must take time to face the press, answer for past mistakes, hype the future, and generally feed the hungry television publicity machine. Nowhere is there a keener need for a more diverting dog-and-pony show than at UPN's day of the Winter Press Tour. Ever since the network hyped its fall season back at the June Press Tour, it has wound up with more dogs than ponies. Network presentations are all about spin, but it's hard to spin a 40 percent decline in viewership. Apart from the relatively encouraging launch of Christopher Crowe's *Seven Days*, there's little to crow about. There is the further horror of having to justify such a performance in light of a season when UPN's upstart rival the WB is flourishing. In other words, UPN's press tour looks to be a moment of media reckoning.

The morning's schedule begins with a light breakfast in the Salon Foyer—perhaps UPN might have sprung for a full breakfast if only the reviews of *The Secret Diary of Desmond Pfeiffer* had been slightly kinder. The media here today, however, seem in a mood to bite the hand that feeds.

The moment of truth comes shortly before noon, when it's time for the Q&A session with UPN's top two executives, Dean Valentine, president and CEO; and Tom Nunan, president, Entertainment.

Valentine gamely takes the Salon stage, dons a huge Lincoln-esque black top hat, and begins to address the expectant crowd.

"Fourscore and fifteen days ago, UPN brought forth upon this nation a new sitcom, conceived in silliness and dedicated to the proposition that a television show about the Lincoln White House was created funny," he proclaims. "We were wrong. And you guys were right. I'd be lying if I said I wasn't disappointed in our fall performance."

Valentine's strategy seems clear—he will metaphorically eat his Abraham Lincoln hat, show the assembled press predators his executive neck, and pray for the best. There is mild laughter from the reporters, who then get back to sharpening their teeth on UPN-provided breakfast pastries.

Valentine casually tosses in a little bit of good news—or in this case, some less bad news. About *Seven Days*, he says, "There is reason for us to be pleased," but then adds the glaringly self-evident truth that generally "we have to try harder to be better." That said, he turns the conversation over to Tom Nunan, a former executive at NBC and Fox, to talk about some of UPN's future plans. These include a new show from *Fall Guy* actress-turned-producer Heather Thomas, through Meg Ryan's production company, which Nunan describes as "an animated comedy that Meg may or may not lend her voice to called *Quints,* which some people have described as sort of an irreverent female version of *South Park.*"

The importance of *Dilbert* to UPN, symbolically and otherwise, becomes vividly clear later when at sundown it comes time for the *Dilbert* Q&A session, to be followed immediately by the gala event for the evening, the Dilbert Zone—which the UPN schedule describes as "a spectator event not to be missed!"

The *Dilbert* press conference draws an overflow, standing-room-only crowd of TV critics with its panel featuring Larry Charles, *Dilbert* creator and series co–executive producer Scott Adams, as well as Chris Elliot, Kathy Griffin, Larry Miller, and Gordon Hunt from the show's voice cast. The questions this evening mainly go to Adams, who is asked for his most *Dilbert*-like experiences in bringing *Dilbert* to TV.

"I was very disappointed that it was not worse," Adams says. "I was kind of expecting that I would be feeding the comic strip for months just based on going to the meetings in Hollywood. But I managed to stay fairly insulated and I get to do a lot of work from home, so a lot of silliness, Larry protects me from."

It takes another reporter's question to remind Adams of the earlier, failed attempt to make a live-action *Dilbert*. Adams admits "smarting" from that experience and points out he is much more involved this time. Later he will add that last time the show's talking canine character Dogbert was done as an animatronic being "which I think they spent upwards of twenty-five dollars on. It looked *every* bit of it."

Adams cuts a pleasant, preppy figure—he looks less like *Dilbert* than the emancipated ex-PacBell corporate refugee that he is. Charles, meanwhile, isn't wearing shorts today either, but is typically casual-cool, in sweatpants and a tattered T-shirt. Suffice to say, the *Dilbert* partners don't look like two guys who would have been best buddies back in high school.

Surprisingly, there are no questions for Charles this evening about his illustrious sitcom past with *Seinfeld* and *Mad About You*. He is asked about the process of animation, and speaks of the advantages, of how all the various stages allow for honing, for getting closer to the creative goal.

One reporter presses strongly on why *Dilbert* has been so long in the making.

"Hey, Bitchy McGee! Take it *down* a couple notches," Kathy Griffin says, jumping in with mock annoyance.

"Kathy, I can fight my own battles," Charles offers with a grin.

DAVID WILD

"Well, apparently he thinks this is the *Love Boat* panel," Griffin says. "We don't take that *shit* here at *Dilbert*."

Charles is asked about the sudden proliferation of prime-time animation and if all the cartoony midseason competition—including upcoming shows such as *Family Guy* and *Futurama*—worries him.

"Well, there's going to be a natural attrition rate, it seems to me," Charles answers reasonably. "Certain shows will succeed and fail based on their own merits. . . . I think people are looking for something else, some other form to get excited about in television."

Too sly to engage in straight-ahead hype, Charles offers his own twisted version of a hard sell. "*Bugs Bunny* or *Popeye* or *The Simpsons* or any great cartoon you can point to—they work on *many* different levels. . . . I think we tried to sort of fashion *Dilbert* the same way, so that a child can enjoy it on a certain level and a teenager who's stoned in his dorm room can enjoy it, and adults can enjoy it, and elderly people and dead people, *whoever*."

Dead people—now there's a woefully untapped demographic group.

Asked about the perceived burden on *Dilbert* to salvage UPN's season, Charles says, "They don't return my calls. The only pressure we get is to produce a great show and we believe everything else will fall into place. I mean as far as how *they* feel about it, that's something you'd have to ask them, I think. In my opinion. Scott?"

"So Dean hasn't been sending you his bills and showing you his mortgage?" Adams adds with a smile.

Dean Valentine—bravely sitting in the heart of enemy press territory—laughs heartily and smiles his most genuine smile of this tough day.

From there the crowd is directed into the Dilbert Zone, where cast member Larry Miller—a veteran standup comic—is pressed into duty to serve as master of ceremonies. The slightly forced highjinks include adult games such as Dunk the Boss special, Find Alice's Résumé, and a Time Clock Shredder. The participants compete for a prize that's seeming less and less useful with every passing season—a new thirty-two-inch TV. Later Larry Charles—already frustrated that the voice cast weren't asked more questions—calls his time in the Dilbert Zone "maybe the nadir of my professional career."

As the festivities proceed for what feels like *Dilbert*'s L.A. media bar mitzvah, Dean Valentine can be spotted, deep in thought, chilling by a *Dilbert* ice sculpture. Charles objects to the bar mitzvah comparison. "I have a twelve-year-old daughter and she's going through the bat mitzvah route this year," he explains. "As vulgar and ostentatious as some of these bar mitzvahs are, they're *entertaining* on some level."

In only a few hours, *Cupid* will move from its old Saturday time slot from hell into a brand-new Thursday time slot of death—and they call this programming progress.

On the bulletin board in his office at *Cupid*'s Santa Monica office, the show's creator, Rob Thomas—recently promoted to executive producer along with Scott Winant—has a faux *Variety* headline:

### Alphabet Ankles *Cupid* as Sac Lamb Against Peacock

This fake trade story was written as Thomas's initial, gallows-humor reaction to sensing that his beloved creation was about to be thrown to the ratings wolves. "We were all *so* praying for Monday at ten and then we find out Thursdays at nine—that headline reflects my mood there without any spin," says Thomas, who's wearing jeans and a very Chandler Bing shirt this afternoon.

After Thomas found out *Cupid* was being counterprogrammed against must-see TV, he endured his bleakest period with the show. First there was the announcement of the move to an unprotected slot with the wildly inappropriate *Vengeance Unlimited* lead-in. Then ABC expressed doubts about an episode turned in—the *Don Quixote*–influenced *Cupid*. ABC felt that this show wasn't as accessible as the one running tonight. Thomas was beginning to feel *Cupid* slipping away from him.

*DAVID WILD*

The mood rebounded slightly this week when a big vote of confidence arrived in the form of a sizable promotional campaign on behalf of *Cupid* on Thursdays. "That makes me think ABC is serious about trying to make a dent because if they were abandoning us they wouldn't have all this," Thomas says, sounding almost hopeful. "I swear I watched ABC constantly this week—not necessarily because I am interested in the shows but because I cannot *believe* how much promotion there is. One of my goals for today was to call Jamie and Stu at the network and say thank you."

Of course, as a rule, networks don't look for thanks so much as for ratings.

"Essentially they want us to get a three in the key demos, which is not that high," Thomas says. "We were getting a 2.2, 2.4 on Saturday night. They want a number—they don't want a miracle."

Of course, a miracle may be needed for *Cupid* to build on a show as dissimilar—not to mention poorly rated—as *Vengeance Unlimited*. Still, in some ways Thomas would rather have this unlikely lead-in than continue to be linked with *Fantasy Island*.

"As someone in television, there's part of you that roots for those sorts of things to fail," Thomas confesses. "I would hate to think that whatever I'm working on creating is competing with the revival of *Petticoat Junction*.

"The great thing is that at least now we're on a night when our target audience is in the house—they may be watching NBC, but they're *there*," Thomas says. "Maybe they'll flip over. Maybe we can plan so our best jokes are during their commercials. Our running joke here is that we want to run from eight-thirty to nine and nine-thirty to ten." Such an unprecedented stop-and-start slot would allow *Cupid* to face off against the more vulnerable *Jesse* and *Veronica's Closet*.

There's some solace in that *Cupid* is living to shoot another day, though Thomas admits even the show's December pickup wasn't a total party. He says that before ordering more episodes of the show, ABC let it be known this renewal was contingent on Thomas stepping up as executive producer, replacing Ron Osborn and Jeff Reno, the more seasoned hands who had originally been brought in to help run things at the show because of Thomas's relative inexperience.

"The pickup was a celebration for some people, but that's when Ron and Jeff were let go and so it wasn't like *I* could celebrate," he recalls. "It was *extremely* awkward and they're very bitter and somehow in their minds I've been blamed for this. It's created a lot of animosity."

Despite only one year of prior series TV experience writing at *Dawson's Creek*, Thomas is now sharing responsibilities more equally with Winant.

Thomas quickly acknowledges that he is far better equipped to run things today than he would have been back at the beginning of *Cupid's* season.

"The learning curve is unbelievable," he confesses. "The way I write the scripts is so different. Before I really wrote and Scott knew how to do everything. Now I'm thinking production all the time. I know what we can do and what we can't do."

Exactly how much Thomas has learned becomes evident when he conference calls to Chicago this afternoon for a "tone meeting" with the Windy City team that today includes Winant and James Whitmore, who is directing the upcoming episode entitled "Botched Makeover," which includes some au courant swing dancing and a cop show within the show called *Sunset & Vaughan*. Earlier in the season, Thomas for the most part sat back until Winant asked him about some script issue. Today he seems confident, often driving the conversation, even from halfway across the country.

Winant remains the calming voice of experience at *Cupid*, but he seems to be allowing Thomas a lot of leeway, as if helping the talented younger writer to gain his showrunning legs.

"We're going to have a financial problem on this show and I'm anticipating the usual howling from the studio," producer Howard Grigsby informs Thomas.

The episode is "cast-heavy," and Thomas runs through script changes he could make to address such bottom-line concerns. Though it takes more than a half-hour to do so, everyone on the line tentatively agrees on a few small characters Thomas will write out to cut the "Botched Makeover" budget. The "Flower Delivery Guy" and "Receptionist" may lose their small speaking parts. A "Nurse" could disappear entirely.

There are also other pressing matters that need to be attended to immediately, such as casting the key part of Kristy—a frumpy, dowdy, orthopedic shoe–wearing writers' assistant at *Sunset & Vaughan* who blossoms during the course of the episode's hour. Negotiations are under way to get *Saturday Night Live*'s Molly Shannon to take the part. The network is said to be offering Shannon "25,"—presumably $25,000—for the guest spot, though Thomas discovers there are a few scheduling problems still to be resolved. (Apparently more than a few—the part eventually goes to former *Melrose Place* player Laura Leighton.)

Whitmore poses questions to Thomas about other characters in the episodes, some of whom will be cast in Chicago to save travel expenses. The director wants to make sure he knows exactly what the creator is looking for, so that he can find it for him. "Who's the old man?" Whitmore asks Thomas.

"He's Dennis Hopper if Dennis Hopper would do one day on *Cupid*," Thomas explains, playing the name game that often serves as instant casting shorthand.

Finally, Whitmore asks the big question the show has gone out of its way not to answer—whether Trevor really is Cupid.

"We're playing either-or, you know, *Miracle on 34th Street*," Thomas explains.

"So who *is* Trevor?" Whitmore asks, pressing a little further.

"I couldn't answer that question, and I *created* the guy," Thomas answers, laughing.

If Thomas doesn't want to give away too much about his title character, he speaks more directly of the actor who's made him flesh and blood. "Jeremy will fuckin' *nail* this, I guarantee you that," he says of Piven.

Finally after one hour and fourteen minutes of teleconferencing, Thomas hangs up with the Chicago contingent. In all the commotion of the meeting, no one has mentioned tonight's big Thursday night debut. No one wishes anyone else good ratings luck—something they're all going to need.

So does Thomas expect to be here a year from now, calling the shots during a second season of *Cupid*?

"I think I'll have a better idea tomorrow morning," he answers before getting back to "Botched Makeover" script changes. "Then I can make a much more educated guess."

Until the overnight ratings come in the morning, *Cupid* is looking very much either-or.

*The Sopranos* debuts early in the month and is immediately embraced as the most impressive new drama of the 1998–1999 season—proof that series TV can work. Unfortunately for the networks, this proof happens on HBO.

The show—about the tortured mid-life crisis of a New Jersey mobster—was created by the Garden State–born David Chase, who previously worked on *Northern Exposure* and created *I'll Fly Away*, the acclaimed but low-rated 1991–1993 NBC series about the dawn of civil rights. When it came time for Chase to develop a TV series, Brillstein-Grey suggested he try a sort of *The Godfather: The Series*.

"I had *no* interest in that," he says. "*The Godfather*'s been done. I'd seen the spoofs, I've seen its pale imitations." Then Chase remembered an old movie idea he couldn't sell years before about a mobster and his mother, and realized it could work as a TV show—"In my first crude thinking, *Eight Is Enough* meets the Mob," he says.

The pilot was originally created for Fox. "All the people I dealt with, the younger vice presidents, liked it, but above that it got massacred," Chase recalls. "Then I think we sent it to every other network. They all professed admiration for the writing, but they said things like, 'We just can't find a place for it on our schedule,' 'Doesn't fit into our long-term planning,' 'We really tried hard to make it work over here,' whatever that could *possibly* mean."

Even in the throes of rave reviews, strong ratings, and a near instant order for a second season for *Sopranos*, Chase is wise enough to understand full well what all those network excuses ultimately meant—thirty-one flavors of no.

Q: What's the difference between the Mob and the television business?

A: The Mob has a clear-cut code of conduct.

There's nothing quite like being surrounded by *Friends*.

Everywhere one looks around the office walls of Bright Kauffman Crane, there is another magazine cover of the assembled *Friends* or a solitary *Friend*. Every once in a while there is also an image of Kirstie Alley from *Veronica's Closet* as well as the occasional shot of Christina Applegate from *Jesse*.

"I'm in *Veronica's* land," Kevin Bright announces as he makes his way past the reception desk toward one of the editing rooms.

Bright, in jeans, a gray T-shirt, and sneakers, is taking one last pass at the episode of *Veronica's Closet* before it off-lines tonight—then it will be locked and ready to air next week. He has just come from a *Friends* table read this morning of "The One Where Chandler Proposes"—with Marta Kauffman reading for Lisa Kudrow, who is in Manhattan collecting a New York Film Critics award for her work in *The Opposite of Sex*. In the next few hours he must oversee final editing of the *Veronica's Closet* episode, as well as the same night's *Friends*. His schedule seems exhausting but Bright still looks relaxed, having gotten some recent R&R during a trip to Oahu over the holidays.

In the hall, Bright passes a framed check in the amount of $5.02 written to the "Cast of *Friends*," a wacky wise-guy offer of false support from Albany, New York, radio morning men who were apparently inspired in this generosity by a past cast renegotiation. The check remains uncashed.

In the hall outside the editing room, Bright takes a phone call from Matthew Perry, who wants to recommend a woman singer for consideration on a *Friends 2* soundtrack album that is in the works. "Tell me one thing first, are you dating her?" Bright asks slyly. "Because that *will* impact how I say no."

Ducking into the room, editor Jay Sherberth comments to Bright on *Jesse*'s win at last night's People's Choice Awards—tying with *Will & Grace* for Best New Comedy Series.

"Congratulations, by the way," he tells the boss. "I saw you on TV."

"I wasn't there," Bright answers quietly.

"I swear to God," the editor says.

"It wasn't me—you're the second person to say that," Bright says. "Last night my son had his final performance in *Grease*, my nine-year-old son, so what was the choice? The People's Choice Awards— the suspense about who's going to win doesn't drive you there."

Bright takes a quick look at the written notes from Marta Kauffman and David Crane before doing the first pass with just the editor and himself. "Then it goes out to Marta, David, and the network and the studio," Bright explains as he puts his feet up on the board.

Each of the Bright Kauffman Crane sitcoms has its own distinct editing style. "*Friends* is the fastest-paced; *Veronica's* close but not exactly the same," he says. "The scenes tend to be a little longer. You generally have an A and B story, and you don't have that third storyline, which is what makes *Friends* go so fast. *Jesse* is very slow compared with the other two." Bright is less involved with the postproduction on *Jesse*. "You can only be in two places at once," he points out.

This episode of *Veronica's Closet* is presently two seconds over-time—no big deal but Kauffman also has two pages of notes to be addressed, while Crane has only one.

Many of the notes are about whether the selected take is as good as it gets. Kauffman, for example, wants to know if there is a better version of Ron Silver's reading of the line, "When I say this conversation's over, it's over." Bright finds one and the fix is in within a matter of minutes. TV editing today is a relatively quick digital process—more takes are called up and viewed on demand. Other notes are tougher fixes—of one relatively slow scene, Crane wonders, "There aren't any more jokes in this scene, are there?" Apparently there are not. Eight frames are cut here, a few others are added there—small change when it takes thirty frames to add up to a second on screen.

A big word in the editing room is "help." Actors and actresses get "help" by taking out anything unflattering. Bright takes pains to make sure his *Veronica's Closet* leading lady is as well served as possible by the camera angle. There is also help from a state-of-the-art laugh machine. Today Bright finds one spot where the machine has gone too far. "We were probably trying to help a laugh along that was small and made it bigger and now it gets in the way," he says. Each TV show has its own library of laughs because the audience sounds different on each stage. "We'll take a real laugh from the audience from the show and put a little machine on top of it just to make it blend," Bright admits. Eventually, all the assorted giggles and guffaws get blended to nearly organic perfection.

Some of the choices make impact in subtle, possibly subliminal ways that only a director like Bright would notice—at one point he asks for a longer shot. "It feels like if you cut close it puts too much pressure on the joke," he explains. Some jokes can't handle any extra pressure.

After taking a quick call from Kauffman, Bright closes the closet on *Veronica* and ambles next door to where editor Stephen Prime is already at work on "The One with Chandler's Work Laugh." This editing room is filled with Grateful Dead and Beatles memorabilia, and Bright walks in ready to rock.

"Let's just start from the top and see what we can cut," Bright says.

In this strong episode, Rachel finally discovers Monica and Chandler's long-hidden love connection, Ross hooks up with Chandler's famously annoying ex-girlfriend Janice, while Monica finds herself put off by Chandler's toadying to his boss. The notes are light, a single page each from Kauffman and Crane. Kauffman suggests a few trims.

Crane begins with the preface—"Overall this is a great fuckin' show"—then lists some changes, including possibly cutting a Clinton joke and restoring some moments from an early edit that he misses.

"The One with Chandler's Work Laugh" is running over by eight seconds—unless the lame Clinton joke made by Chandler's boss goes, a change Bright wants to avoid making.

Stray moments of no apparent consequence disappear. Bright and Prime cut a useless shot of Monica getting her muffin at Central Perk, making the entire scene that follows feel measurably more perky.

Bright requests that some jazzy music be added to the scene at Chandler's work party where we hear Bing's fake laugh for the first time.

"Put in something David Sanborn-ish," Bright says.

"Sanborn or a knockoff?" Prime asks, since in TV the price difference between buying the rights to a recording by a name artist and a reasonable substitute can be significant.

"Knockoff," Bright tells him.

As he watches the show unfold, Bright notes standout cast contributions—notably an inspired moment when Lisa Kudrow does inspired improvisation with a duck. "She *saved* this take," he says admiringly. "And she's genuinely afraid of the duck—she *hates* the flapping."

Moments later Bright tells Prime, "I think you need a little bit more of Rachel's tail"—not an ungentlemanly aside, but an entirely professional request that he add another beat at the end of a joke from Aniston. Sitcom showrunners spend a lot of their time in search of the perfect beat.

In the end, Bright accommodates virtually all of his partners' requests, though he leaves out a couple of moments Crane "kinda misses" and leaves in the intentionally lame Clinton joke he's convinced works.

Normally after today's *Jesse* run-through, Bright would go back for one last look at the edits, but this evening he's got to do some assistant coaching of his son's basketball game. "You'll peck at that,"

Bright tells Prime, as his assistant delivers his keys for the short ride over to the Warners lot.

On his way downstairs, Bright assesses the 1998–1999 season so far. It's been an imperfect but mostly impressive one. All three shows are still on, fixtures of NBC's fallen but still dominant Thursday night. The creative and ratings strength of *Friends* is clear. Bright feels that with the reinvigorating influence of the Monica-Chandler relationship, the show is having "the best season since the first." The show, he says, has surpassed his goals.

Bright sees *Veronica's Closet* as improving, despite continuing to get very mixed reviews and only okay ratings considering its heavenly slot. He attributes some of the progress to the addition of Ron Silver to the cast. "I think what was lacking in the show was a nemesis, someone for Veronica to spar with," Bright says. "Everyone was working for her before so it was much harder to create that dynamic. That's made the show stronger."

As for *Jesse*, Bright says, "I think *Jesse* is doing well, but I don't think we've really found the compelling heart of the show yet. Audiences like Christina very much and they like her in this relationship with Bruno Campos. I think the rest of the show has been a little less clear."

For Bright, things have been slightly problematic as *Jesse* creator Ira Ungerleider and the staff try to integrate a family show with a romantic comedy. "It's sort of hard to involve your brother and your dad in your relationship," he says. "They can get in the way, but doing that week to week is just a tough thing. It's been trickier than we thought." This helps explain the recent announcement that veteran character actor George Dzunda—who plays Jesse's dad—will be taking a less regular role in the show. "So far things are pretty good," Bright adds, "but that one has some evolution left."

Before he goes, Bright is asked if he's happy in retrospect that Bright Kauffman Crane's most evolved sitcom *Friends* didn't land the *Seinfeld* slot.

"Nooo," he says instantly. "Let me put it this way, I'm not unhappy where we are. I always felt *Friends* would be a stronger show than *Frasier* at nine. It has nothing to do with *Friends* being a better show than *Frasier*, just that in this particular time slot, I thought we'd earned it. I said to NBC, 'Don't you just want to try us out there *once* and see what would happen?' Part of it, selfishly, is that somehow this time slot gets more attention. Starting out at eight, somehow we get taken for granted, don't get the focus that we should, but critically this show has gotten such a great response this season. *Obviously* we're getting looked at."

It is also obvious that *Friends* is about to go into a new period of negotiations, with NBC trying to make enough peace with its tense partners at Warner Bros. to keep the *Friends* gravy train on track longer.

"You know what, we know we're coming back next year so right now that's not a big deal," Bright says, getting up to head across the street to *Jesse*.

In truth, the future of *Friends* is a very big deal—one that could impact the economies of television and possibly that friendly little village called America.

On January 20, Patricia Heaton—who plays Ray's wife, Debra, on *Everybody Love Raymond*—gives birth to her fourth son, Daniel Patrick.

No one besides immediate family could be happier than *Raymond*'s showrunner Phil Rosenthal, who has had an increasingly hard time hiding Heaton's pregnancy under the harsh light of prime time, as her normally petite five-foot two-inch frame went from her usual 105 to 162 pounds.

"It was difficult," says Phil Rosenthal. "I love Patty, I love her family, I love all of her kids—all four of them. They're adorable and everything, but it really does put a straightjacket on the show. I think she's done. I *hope* she's done. I got a special letter from the Pope, who said, 'I like the Debra episodes so knock it off.'"

*DAVID WILD*

The situation kept getting more difficult to work around. "Those last couple shows right before—she was nine months pregnant on the show and we were trying to hide it," says Rosenthal. "We didn't do a very good job. Anybody paying attention could see that she was pregnant." Rosenthal didn't want to add another kid on the show, so he chose not to write in the pregnancy.

By the end, Rosenthal explains with a laugh, he and the rest of the *Raymond* team were getting desperate. As he tells it, "You had to hide her behind the laundry baskets, behind tables, then I brought a steamship onstage."

Paul Simms may be wearing a T-shirt that says NIRVANA, but a glum, fatalistic mood has fallen upon the *NewsRadio/OverSeas* office on this grungy, rainy afternoon. All the hard work and great expectations evident here a few weeks ago are now fading into something more like frustration. Simms, longtime colleague Joe Furey, Brillstein-Grey executive Michael Rosenfeld, and *NewsRadio* cast member Maura Tierney pop into the music room for a brief jam session, but it apparently fails to lift anyone's spirits.

Right after the New Year, Simms oversaw the editing of the *Over-Seas* pilot, which was then sent off to NBC. Since then he has been hanging out waiting for a network order—the showrunner's equivalent of waiting by the phone for that all-important second date.

"I talked to one network person right when the taping was over," Simms remembers. "I said, 'Test this *immediately* so we can start making it.' They said, 'We don't want to test things anymore—we think we should make our *own* decisions.' Now we're waiting on testing results, and it's been eerily quiet."

NBC is testing the show both by putting it out on cable to sample audiences and by showing it to focus groups. Simms is clearly not encouraged. "I don't know who's going to make the decision and I think that's sort of the problem now," he says. "They've had it for like two weeks, and it's sort of like, 'Well, we're going to see about the testing.'" Right after the taping, Simms still felt *OverSeas* had good momentum going. He recalls Sassa telling him, "Yeah, I liked it, it looked different, I have a few thoughts about this and that but I don't want to go into specifics."

Simms, Furey, and others did attend a story idea meeting last week at NBC. "The assumption was they wanted us to start writing so that we could be ready to go in February and shoot it," says Simms. "They really liked the stories, but since then it's been . . . nothing but silence."

To break the silence on this slightly gloomy day, a tape of the *OverSeas* pilot plays in Simms's office, although no one here seems driven to watch the episode yet again. "That's okay," Furey explains, "I've seen it 28,000 times."

*OverSeas* comes off even more ambitious today than on show night, in part because director Tom Cherones has shot the sitcom with Steadicam flourishes that highlight the show's unique set fully. The humor mixes high-, middle-, and lowbrow—with references to both Henry David Thoreau and the horror flick *One Bad Monkey*—but it's all delivered in a less Pavlovian manner than on the conventional sitcom. The *OverSeas* pilot isn't perfect by any means, but it's demonstrably different in a medium that could sure use some fresh jungle air.

At NBC's press tour presentation, Scott Sassa stressed that he wanted shows with more diversity in setting and cast, as well as— here's what got the headlines—less sex. During the same event, his only reference to the *OverSeas* pilot—with an exotic locale and a nookie-free pilot—came off noncommittal in a forum where enthusiasm is typically boundless.

Part of the frustration evident on Simms's face today—and there's no shortage of it—could be because he's gone slightly against his own strong-willed, slightly eccentric personality. He's played his share of network ball, and he still feels he's losing this game. He's made his corporate bed, but right now he doesn't feel too cozy lying in it.

"It is disappointing now because we did *so* many drafts and I really feel like we worked with Ohlmeyer and all the people there in a way they were happy with," he says, looking down. "Part of the problem is if Scott picks this up, this will be the first show he's green-lighting. I wouldn't feel this bad if we spent three months on this, a reasonable amount of time. But because of a lot of other factors—Phil and *NewsRadio* and that stuff—it stretched out to nine months, and I think that could have affected the network perception."

Simms feels that if NBC wants different, he's got the different market covered. "A show like this—even if critics *hated* it, they'd have to say at least NBC is trying something different," he says. "It's up and down every day but at this point I don't think it's going on NBC. What do *you* think?"

Michael Rosenfeld from Brillstein-Grey, to whom he's addressed this last big question, pauses before confirming Simms's increasingly dark suspicions. "I would agree," Rosenfeld says quietly.

"Then it's a battle to see if they'll give it back to me so I can put it on another network," Simms says, playing out ugly scenarios he still hopes to avoid. "But they own such a big piece of it, I don't know."

Simms hasn't been invited to the focus group tests to gauge audience response.

"They don't invite me to much," Simms says, looking down. "I don't know—I think they're disappointed."

Asked if he's disappointed himself with *OverSeas*, Simms says, "No, I think it could be better, even some of the way it looks, but it's a pilot—it's 'Here's the idea.' It's not perfect but we're proud of it."

Sitting on Simms's couch, Furey offers his support for the show. "You look at the pilot of almost any famous TV show and they're *never* 100 percent there in terms of what it's going to be."

"As a prototype to say, 'Here's what it's going to look like, here's who the people are, now let's make six of them,' in that sense it's good," Simms says. "But on the other hand we've spent *nine* months working on twenty-two minutes of television, which is ridiculous."

Here's the problem with pilots—how can a prototype be judged if no more of the product is manufactured?

For Simms the left-field success of NBC's *Providence*—a midseason entry about a pretty doctor who proves you *can* go home again and get ratings doing so—may be working against *OverSeas* right now. The former drama's surprising good fortune has reduced the need for NBC to rush more midseason shows into production. Ironically, early on the female doctor character in *OverSeas* was a plastic surgeon looking for a more meaningful life, much like the lead character in *Providence*.

One might think that if a midseason launch doesn't work out, NBC could wait and find a spot for *OverSeas* on its fall schedule.

One would be wrong.

"To do that they'd have to pay a lot of holding fees to keep the actors—a *big* chunk of money," Simms explains. "If they were willing to pay that huge chunk of money, that would mean they were excited. If they were excited, they would put it on for midseason."

Inside the bad news–friendly TV community, *OverSeas* has gotten a reputation as a pricey pilot.

"It's a little more expensive than most sitcoms," Simms says. "Some agent was telling me it's got a reputation as *ridiculously* expensive. It's not like we're paying any huge stars. It's not like *Apocalypse Now*, although that's the way the process of making it has felt."

"The goal really ultimately is to get Marlon Brando at the end," Furey adds dryly. "*Then* the network will like it."

Simms looks at the phone. It does not ring.

A promising if imperfect show about public service and the curious impact of American culture, *OverSeas* appears to be going down a road in the Hollywood jungle that's been paved with good intentions.

*The Norm Show* is now open for funny business just down the hall from the Olsen twins on the second floor of the same generic office building on the Warner Bros. lot that houses Bruce Helford's other creation, *The Drew Carey Show*. Starting in March, *Norm* will follow *Drew Carey* on ABC Wednesday nights. This supposedly "troubled"

pilot now has an order from the network for nine more episodes, and the buzz is of the good variety.

Helford is busy downstairs at the moment, and the mood in *The Norm Show*'s clean, well-lit writers' room appears casual, what with all the Koosh paddles and Nerf objects, here presumably to encourage a sense of play. The closest thing to a drug is a pack of lemon Zinc lozenges. A tired-looking Macdonald stands in the room's doorway, listening to the writers with a hard-to-read, there-and-yet-not-quite-there look on his unshaven face. Macdonald's wearing two hats these days at *The Norm Show*—as a writer and as the title star. To hear Macdonald tell it, he finds that only the first hat fits comfortably.

Acting he finds less thrilling, though Macdonald has a different name for the art of the thespian. *"Memorizing,"* he calls it with a suggestion of contempt. "I don't presume to call it *acting*," Macdonald explains. "But the *memorizing* is tremendously difficult. Any side issues like publicity, taking pictures, and so forth are just unbearable."

This afternoon, with the second episode of *The Norm Show* about to go into production, the pressure is on to finish up the first couple scripts and "break" some stories for the episodes to follow. "If we don't have two scripts by tomorrow, we're *so* fucked," executive producer Bruce Rasmussen tells Macdonald, who flashes a brief, devilish smile.

On a board toward the back of the room there's a list of "Ideas We Like," with the following possible *Norm Show* storylines written underneath

> *The funeral idea*
> *N and L accidentally date*
> *New guy comes in*
> *L wants female friend*
> *N is going bald*
> *N gambling arc*

"N" is Norm, "L" is Laurie Metcalf. The job of the assembled writers in this room is to take those sort of bare-bones "Ideas We

Like" and make them work, at least on paper. Everyone in the room spends a few minutes brainstorming other story ideas. One storyline is quickly shot down when someone points out it's dangerously close to something already on *Two Guys, a Girl and a Pizza Place*. A safe-sex idea is put forth, though Macdonald seems ambivalent. "Safe sex?" a cringing Norm says to nobody in particular. "My least favorite sort of sex."

At 11:45 A.M., Helford—in crisp blue jeans and an Oxford shirt—arrives in the room, and the atmosphere turns slightly more businesslike, if still far from stuffy.

Helford pulls out a copy of Cheryl Holliday's script for what will likely become the third *Norm* episode, titled "My Name Is Norm," in which Norm is wrongly placed in rehab. There are notes sprawled all over the cover.

"Good episode," Helford tells Holliday, the only woman at the table right now. "Should we talk jokes or just structure?" he asks. It is decided to focus on structure. Helford goes to the board, erases some old notes, then proceeds to diagram a reworked structure for the episode's first act. Short of stature, Helford doesn't comfortably reach the top of the board.

Lanky as he is laconic, Macdonald grins at this sight. "Do you write up or down?" Macdonald asks Helford.

"I write down," says Helford.

"Because if you write up you're an optimist," Macdonald says. "If you write down you're a homo."

Helford accepts Norm's dopey joke and gets back to work.

"My pitch is *this*," he tells the room, pointing to his schematic, which reads:

> *L can't reach kid*
> ———————————
> *Kid worships N*
> *N is able to connect w/kid*
> *N proves kid likes him + not L*
> ———————————
> *Kid begins screwing up life as he emulates N*
> *N has burden of being role model*

*DAVID WILD*

Not a real knee-slapper, perhaps, in its current form, but chances are it will be when the humor finds a home in the architecture of the story.

The room at *The Norm Show* already feels pretty settled. Normally Helford and Macdonald would've waited for an order from ABC, then rushed at the last minute to staff up. Exercising considerable confidence, Helford insisted on doing their scribe shopping early for *The Norm Show*. "That's why most midseasons are terrible," Helford explains. "They usually have a really good pilot and the rest of it is shit because they couldn't get a good staff together."

There are five writers around the room today. For the pilot Macdonald brought some protection in the form of Frank Sebastiano, a *SNL* veteran who cowrote his film *Dirty Work*. Helford didn't want him in the beginning, but now calls Sebastiano "fantastic." Executive producers Bruce Rasmussen and Ron Ulin are *Roseanne* vets, with Rasmussen having been raided by Helford from *Drew Carey*. Rasmussen and Helford were both hired before the pilot was shot. "I said to Warner Bros., 'We've got thirteen ordered, I want to act like it's a series,'" Helford remembers. "They kept saying, 'What if it all blows up?' I said, 'Then you're going to get stung for some money because if we don't hire now we're going to be scrambling."

Talk turns to another pressing *Norm* matter—the addition of a currently unnamed and unformed younger female character suggested by ABC. Everyone in the room has taken to referring to this mystery woman as Trixie La Boom Boom.

Is breathing life into Trixie something the writers *want* to do or something they *have* to do?

"We have to," says Macdonald.

"We *want* to have to," adds the more tactful Helford.

Macdonald whispers to Helford across the table regarding the status of another *Norm* concern. In a future episode, viewers will meet the father of Norm's coworker Danny, an older gentleman who takes quite a liking to Norm. In the end, the character turns out to be gay. Macdonald's convinced the only man for the part is Jack Warden, the great, vaguely macho veteran character actor who played Macdonald's father in *Dirty Work*.

Helford places a calls and gets a final answer from the show's liaison at ABC. "On the Jack Warden issue, did we propose our proposal to ABC?" Helford listens and shakes his head no. The network loves the idea of Warden as a guest star but not the $50,000 fee Warden's said to have requested. Their limit, it's said, is $25,000.

Macdonald explains he is willing to pay the difference personally, with some additional help from Helford. Macdonald refuses to try to nickel-and-dime the actor down—though it may cost him some of his own nickels and dimes.

"They apologize profusely," Helford explains. "They feel bad because they know how badly you want it. They can't justify the money. So the question is, how much do you want him?"

"It's going to be decided by the outcome of the Super Bowl," Sebastiano adds, referring to Macdonald's penchant for the occasional wager.

Helford reasonably suggests that perhaps this discussion about Warden should be off the record.

"I don't know," Macdonald says after only a moment's thought. "It makes me pretty heroic, doesn't it?"

On the way to lunch in the ritzy Warner Bros. Executive Commissary, Helford and Macdonald consider how *The Norm Show* got such early bad buzz.

"We went through a *lot*," Helford confesses. "This *wasn't* easy. There were a lot of story things we wanted to fix, and casting was a nightmare. It was not trouble—really just the birthing pains of getting a show in pilot form."

Early on *The Norm Show* nearly faced a huge problem—namely, no Norm. For a time, Macdonald balked when he feared he might be creatively castrated by this sitcom experience.

"We had a little bit of a thing about my character because I didn't want to be *too* good." Macdonald admits. "But then we ironed that out."

Helford initially made the character of Norm too tame for the real Norm. "I think I made the character too much of a do-gooder," he admits. "It was more apparent to Norm at first."

*DAVID WILD*

"I got freaked out," Macdonald admits. "Bruce said he didn't want me doing something I hated for seven years." The pair briefly considered slowing down the process and waiting so *Norm* would become a fall show for the 1999–2000 season, but they opted for a major rewrite of the script and for keeping the show on its midseason fast track.

*The Norm Show* had to figure out who the hell Norm was. If Macdonald's more at peace with his character, he's less thrilled with the title, which came about when Helford noticed that people kept asking him, "So, you working on the Norm show?"

"It wasn't my idea," says Macdonald. What might he have preferred? "Virtually any other title because if it's a *huge* failure, I don't want my name on it."

Helford's happy with the show's name, like *The Drew Carey Show*, because "there are so many generic names for shows, like *Almost Perfect*, *Everything's Relative*, and all that stuff. I don't know what they mean."

"I like when they do a person's name and make a play on words, like *Grace Under Fire*," Macdonald adds with tongue firmly in cheek. "They *named* the character Grace. I mean they could have named the character Nothing and called the show *Nothing but Fun*."

If the road to *The Norm Show* was riddled with delays, the pilot brought good tidings too. Helford came away more impressed than ever with his reluctant star. In rehearsal, Macdonald's performance was loose, arguably too loose. Yet on show night, Helford recalls, "He took nothing jokes and *ran* with them. Norm's writing has gotten better and better. Having Norm in the room was *huge*." Macdonald has an oddball way of keeping whatever he touches within spitting distance of the edge.

Now Helford—a loud drum-beater for his own shows—is doing what he can to ensure that *Norm* gets the best possible shot. "They are going to promote us during the Oscars on ABC," he reports. "Then we are right behind *Drew* so I have a little bit of control—I want to make sure that the first three episodes of *Norm* get the lead-in of original *Drew Carey* episodes." By the fourth episode, Helford hopes audiences will be hooked.

For Helford, launching *Norm* is a way to pay off on the Warner Bros. gamble on his talent, a big-stakes wager. He admits to feeling "this huge guilt" to make good on the studio's fiscal-backed vote of confidence.

This guilt impresses Macdonald. "Most people don't, which is why *you* make it," Norm tells his partner. "Most are lazy, they have development deals, sitting in offices *not* working on a show in an abandoned office with a secretary."

Brooke Shields walks by on her way to lunch.

"Look at the celebrities," Macdonald says, scanning the star-studded power lunch room.

On the way back to the writers' room from the Executive Commissary, Macdonald and Helford run straight into the cast of *Friends*—minus Courteney Cox and plus actor Michael Rappaport—who are sitting at an outside table having lunch.

"You guys *really* are friends," Macdonald proclaims with audible amusement. "Good to see you."

"I didn't recognize you," Jennifer Aniston tells Helford, with whom she has worked before.

It is explained that Macdonald's doing his own sitcom.

"Oh, how great," Aniston offers sweetly.

Of course, *The Norm Show* will be on a competing network.

"That's all right," Kudrow says comfortingly.

"Are you still on *Saturday Night Live?*" Aniston asks.

"No," Macdonald responds.

"I thought you still were," she explains apologetically.

"It's been like three or four years," Macdonald says before correcting himself. "No, it's been like eight months."

The *Friends* folks are misinformed that *The Norm Show* is about Norm and five pals who all hang out at a coffee shop.

"Hey, I'm worried here," says Schwimmer.

As Helford explains the actual setup of *The Norm Show* to Schwimmer, Norm mentions he recently caught Kudrow on a talk show and passes along a favorite memory from his old Letterman appearance while at *SNL*. "When I went out and shook his hand he whispered in my ear, 'My show is *shit*'—all angry."

"You won some award, right?" Macdonald asks Kudrow. "You got the Golden Globes?"

"No, no," she says, and tells him about the New York Film Critics Prize.

"What about the Golden Globes?" Macdonald insists.

"No, nothing," Kudrow admits.

"Well, the New York Film Critics are more prestigious," Macdonald says comfortingly.

"Also, they don't expect you to throw them a big party brunch," Schwimmer chimes in.

Everyone commiserates about Golden Globe politics.

"They nominated that dude from *Dharma & Greg*—you know, *Greg*—that's *crazy*," Macdonald exclaims in outrage. "Isn't that *crazy?*"

On Thursday, January 28, the *Los Angeles Times* reports that "production shut down this week on ABC's first-year Jeremy Piven drama, *Cupid*, which has failed to catch on in the ratings." The same morning, on page one of the business section, there is a significantly larger story under the headline "Disney's Profit Declines 18% in 1st Quarter." According to the subhead, "Weak TV Ratings, Costs Cited."

Sadly, the actual headline in *Variety* is not worlds away from the fake one that Rob Thomas dreamed up weeks earlier:

### Alphabet Loses Heart
### In 'Cupid,' Ends Prod'n

The programming gods giveth, and the programming gods taketh away.

"*Cupid* has been a labor of love for everyone at ABC from the very start," reads the network statement. "The writing was phenomenal, the production was first-rate, and the tremendous talent of its stars, Jeremy Piven and Paula Marshall, really gave the show life.

Unfortunately, despite everyone's efforts, the audience just didn't respond."

In the show, *Cupid*—whose title character may or may not be the genuine god of love—is banished from returning to the comfort of Mount Olympus until he brings a hundred couples together. As heartbreaking as it is to say, it's looking like the guy's not gonna last one hundred episodes. *Cupid*, alas, won't even survive until Valentine's Day.

The powers-that-be at ABC believed in *Cupid*, which is to say they believed in *Cupid* until paying for such belief became too expensive a proposition to justify. This is how it works. This—in the end—is how we know that TV isn't a religion, just big business with a twist of art added for taste.

# Love, Sweeps, and Maggots

There's no business like show business.

Irving Berlin, 1928

I t was Love at first sight, although truth be told, the Love part worried him.

February is another sweeps month, but it is also a time when many showrunners—and showrunning wanna-bes—are focusing on the future in the form of new pilots. Christopher Keyser—who along with longtime writing partner Amy Lippman created Fox's *Party of Five*—stands by the camera on Stage 20 on the Sony lot during day two of filming the pilot for a spin-off series for the 1999–2000 season, to star Jennifer Love Hewitt, tentatively titled *Time of Your Life*. Love—as Hewitt is called by those who know and, yes, love her—can be seen a dozen yards away in the fake New York City apartment building that is to become her new TV home when her character Sarah leaves behind *Party of Five*. A few hundred yards behind Hewitt is the midsection of the airplane that will whisk Sarah across the country from the Bay Area *Party*—it is coincidentally the same nonfunctional vehicle that her character flew in during *I Still Know What You Did Last Summer*.

As a snow machine starts up, Love—a teen superstar of the big and small screen who's now only a few days from her actual twentieth birthday—takes her place in the open window. Sarah is trying to get the attention of someone who—this being acting—isn't actually there. Apparently this will be one of the final shots in the pilot episode of what everyone here is hoping will be many more good *Times* to come.

"Start to see him," the director instructs the actress.

Seconds later, Love attempts in her patently adorable way to get the attention of the currently nonexistent man by yelling "Hi, hello, yoo-hoo, hello" out to the building's courtyard.

"Cut, *good*," the director announces.

"Was that a great performance or *what?*" Hewitt says self-mockingly to Keyser afterward. "I've been working on that."

Between takes, as the issue of proper snow buildup on Sarah's windowsill is debated and resolved, Chris Keyser recalls the first time he ever encountered Love: "We were told that Jennifer Hewitt was coming in for a meeting. Then she was introduced as Love—like this was some hippie name which we didn't understand. But the first time we saw Love, it was just instantaneous. You think, 'Wow, this person is incredible and you *have* to have them.'" Hewitt wasn't much like the Sarah that Keyser and Lippman had imagined her to be. That Sarah was sort of a tomboyish girl who was in love with Bailey, someone who he would never really see as any kind of serious love interest. "Obviously Love is none of those things," Keyser says. "We completely changed the character to fit with who she was when she came in," Lippman confirms later.

At the audition Love stood in the hallway with seven or so other girls who were wearing lots of makeup and sexy clothes. "I just remember thinking, 'Okay, I am the *biggest* dork on the planet right now,'" Hewitt says. Still, like the trouper she's universally thought to be, she gave it her best shot. As she was walking out, the casting director came up to her and asked what she was doing the next day. Even when they offered her the part, young Hewitt felt she had to confess to Keyser and Lippman about her already checkered past on forgotten series like *Byrds of Paradise, MacKenna,* and the fittingly titled *Shakey Ground.* "I warned them I could possibly be a curse on the show," she explains. Duly advised, they proceeded anyway with the Love-ing of Sarah. Originally envisioned to be on for nine episodes, Sarah struck a chord. "Ever since then," Hewitt says, "it's just been sort of like a pleasant surprise."

Anybody addicted to *Party of Five* knows that the lives of the Salinger orphans and their inevitably attractive fellow travelers have been full of assorted unpleasant surprises and sundry Job-like torment. Offscreen, things have been somewhat less painful—after struggling through a rough first season in the ratings, the show became a slow-burning success, an exquisite downer of a youth drama. Not bad for the first series created by Keyser and Lippman, who met back at Harvard, where he was a law student and she was an undergraduate.

Lippman grew up in Los Angeles, as well as San Francisco, loving show business from a short distance. She remembers begging her mother to slow down on a corner of the Fox lot where one could see the old *Hello, Dolly!* set through a crack in the fence. Keyser grew up on Long Island, in Merrick. The pair met at a playwriting class, one that also included Conan O'Brien and future *King of the Hill* cocreator Greg Daniels. Lippman was impressed by an apocalyptic one-act play Keyser wrote. "It was a little Thornton Wilder and really very good," she recalls. She thinks she and Keyser became friends because he was intrigued that she was going to go to New York to become a writer. Keyser was in his last year at law school, and Lippman feels he was beginning to consider making the same move himself. So it was Lippman who blew her future partner's shot at the Supreme Court?

"He was *never* going to be a lawyer, it's too dry for him. He just went to law school so he could play for three more years in Cambridge."

Lippman didn't write for the *Harvard Lampoon*, but proudly identifies herself as a *"Lampoon* wife." Her husband, Rodman Flender—now a film director *(Idle Hands)*—worked at the *Lampoon* along with O'Brien, Daniels, and Paul Simms. She quickly cops to the existence of what she terms "a significant Harvard Mafia" in the TV business, though personally when she left Cambridge she was more interested in writing plays. "That's what I was thinking when I moved to New York—and then you have to make a living," she says.

Her friends were going off and writing for *Saturday Night Live* and *Letterman*. Comedy was not her interest, and she found there was precious little work for an aspiring drama writer in New York. "So I spent two years in soaps before I escaped with my life," Lippman remembers. "In fact, I just got like a thirty-dollar residual check this morning from one of them." Lippman wrote for a "terrible" soap called *Loving* and then briefly in Los Angeles for *Santa Barbara*, which she insists was "actually a really funny, well-written soap." Still, soap writing was a bitch. "It goes against all your instincts because stories *never* end," says Lippman.

Early on Keyser and Lippman dreamed of being taken under the wing of one of the established showrunners, but that wasn't to be their route. David E. Kelley did give them their first assignment for *L.A. Law* but Lippman recalls Kelley telling them afterward, "I'm going to give you another script but I'm not going to put you on staff because I will rewrite you from top to bottom and you should have an experience where you go off and see your work produced.' At the time the pair were less than thrilled. "For two people who just moved from New York it was like 'You can rewrite us—rewrite us, *please*,'" Lippman says. Today she thinks Kelley was right and that not putting them on staff was "a fantastic gift. The best way to learn is to make your own mistakes." Instead the pair would learn some of their formative lessons at the short-lived *Eddie Dodd* and at the more enduring *Sisters*.

During a difficult but rewarding first season of *Party of Five*, Keyser and Lippman learned, among other things, how to play network politics and translate network notes into English—generally how to play the network TV game while also creating a show out of thin air on a weekly basis. It wasn't always easy. They have been with Fox through five different presidents—on the other hand they have also watched as a few executives put their careers on the line to save the show. At times this drama about TV's sexiest orphans had to come back from the dead itself. One day early on when Lippman was up with the cast shooting scenes in San Francisco, Keyser was given some bad news by the head of development at Columbia Tri-Star. "I've seen the board," Keyser was told, in reference to Fox's big scheduling board. "And you are *not* on the board anymore."

*Party of Five* struggled mightily but gradually hit a nerve. "I always say to Chris, where would we be right now if the show hadn't taken off? He always says, 'We'd be supervising producers on a medical drama.'" Five seasons later, however, the *Party* goes on with John Romano currently running the show under them. During recent seasons at least two of the show's cast members—Hewitt and Neve Campbell, who plays Julia Salinger—have even established themselves as box-office draws in their own right.

Even with *Party of Five* on what passes for solid ground in TV, there have been other dark moments for Keyser and Lippman, including the almost instant failure of another Fox series that appeared briefly mid-season in 1998, called *Significant Others*. On that critically challenged ensemble drama, the pair learned more lessons, none of the particularly pleasant variety. *Significant Others* would not elicit the same sort of support that helped save *Party of Five* from a dramatic crib death. "It's a blessing and a curse having your first show be a success," Lippman says. "You begin to think that's the way it works. And it's *really* not the way it works."

At the end of 1997–1998 season, Keyser and Lippman sat down together to assess where they were headed now that *Party of Five* was facing the September of its first-run years. The decision came down to whether they should simply move on or try to figure out some way to extend their franchise. Lippman admits she initially didn't believe there was a spin-off to be spun here. Soon, she concluded there was only one character who was spin-off-able, one *Party* fixture who they thought could carry the show, who had the chops for it, and whom they could in good faith take out of *Party of Five* without destroying the premise of the show. "We couldn't exactly say to Neve or Scott or Matthew, 'Leave *Party of Five* and do this,' right," she explains. "We thought we had a storyline with Love that gave the us the beginning of a series.

A woman feeling increasingly rootless, who could go to a new city in search of herself." Here was a story that has some of the same themes from *Party of Five* but from a different perspective. "Obviously it's somewhat less dark," Lippman says, "in that it's not starting from a tragic place."

Keyser and Lippman felt they had to tread carefully—they certainly didn't want to bring shame on their initial beloved creation. After some discussion, they concluded they could do a series about Sarah because she is only an honorary member of the Salinger family and if she did head off on her own, there was a story to tell. During her second season on *Party of Five*, Sarah discovered that she was adopted. This storyline raised issues of identity and family that are classic Keyser-Lippman themes. "Without any calculation on our part, we'd given her an issue that was substantial enough to become a series," Lippman explains.

"There's something about this idea of a young girl without any sense of who she is going to the big city that reminds us of a Dickens story," Keyser adds, "an *updated* Dickens story."

"I am terrified about how lofty and awful this sounds, but the Dickensian element is actually important to us," Lippman says. In her Harvard-educated mind, the New York that Sarah journeys to in the *Time of Your Life* pilot will be a magical world of amazing benefactors and people seeking to take advantage. "It's a highly romantic view of the city," she says. "That's interesting to us and it's not the world of *Party of Five*. That could sustain us, sustain our interest for a number of years of writing and producing." Now generally speaking, invoking a dead English literature great wouldn't be the quickest way onto a fall schedule. However, with a red-hot—in every sense of the word—young property like Hewitt, this sort of classy pitch is unlikely to scare the Dickens out of even a television executive.

Though *Time of Your Life* is clearly a Jennifer Love Hewitt vehicle, the pair are working to make sure she is surrounded by a strong ensemble who will be able to carry their own storylines. Still, on day seven of the shooting of the pilot, Hewitt turns to Lippman and points out that they are shooting the first scene she isn't in. The idea

is to keep Hewitt front and center but not put 100 percent of the
weight of the project on Love's slender shoulders.

First, Love had to sign on the dotted line. "We weren't sure that
she was going to say yes," Keyser recalls. "We thought we had a
good idea to bring to her and an interesting career opportunity. She
has a *lot* of opportunities. We were excited when she said yes."

Keyser explains they were particularly hopeful because recent
examples like Helen Hunt proved that an actress could maintain a
TV lead role and a major film career, in Hunt's case winning an
Academy Award for *As Good As It Gets*.

Hewitt came to her meeting with the pair with an entirely different concern. She was worried her *Party* hosts had decided they were
tired of Sarah. "I was scared to *death*," she recalls. "I was like crying
in my car on the way to the meeting because I thought, 'Okay,
they're going to fire me. Bailey is going to break up with me terribly,
or they're going to kill me off and good-bye Sarah forever.' I *totally*
thought I was going to be fired. They said, 'Well, we think we're
going to move off from the Bailey and Sarah situation a little bit.
And I went, 'I *knew* it, I *knew* it.'" Finally Keyser and Lippman
explained that while they wanted to ease off on Bailey, they wanted
to stay in the Sarah business in a *very* big way.

Before long, everyone agreed to move forward. Love—who these
days is involved in producing some of her own movie and TV projects—trusted the writing team to find something new in Sarah.

"The idea of the show, their vision of who Sarah was, comes from
them," Hewitt says of Keyser and Lippman. "I didn't really have any
specific ideas of my own about where she should go. I didn't really realize until we started that Sarah would be so different. She's definitely
like a new character to me because she is in a much different place.
She's away from Bailey and the Salingers and she's sort of off on her
now. I'll be honest with you, I didn't know anything about the show,
whether it would be picked up, what the contract was going to be. The
reason I said yes was because of Chris and Amy. I knew whether it was
just for a pilot or thirteen episodes or five or six years of my life, that it
would always be fine, always be good, always be quality."

*DAVID WILD*

The goal for *Time of Your Life*, according to Lippman, is to be respectful to the audience that has come along for all these years with *Party of Five* and at the same time give it something slightly different. She sees the Love project as one that "capitalizes on some *Party of Five* assets," yet with a slightly different tone.

As showrunners, Keyser and Lippman are closely linked, but that doesn't mean they are inseparable. Though they tend to break stories together, they often write and edit separately. During the making of *Time of Your Life*, in fact, they've worked independently enough so that at one point Keyser grew a fairly substantial beard without his partner Lippman noticing it.

In a few weeks, the *Time of Your Life* team heads to the real New York to shoot some exterior scenes for the pilot; then there's postproduction in March. If things go according to the current plan, the show will be on Fox's fall schedule—one rumor even has Love sharing a night with *Ally McBeal*.

At the same time, Keyser and Lippman both realize that can't-miss pilots miss all the time. As Keyser puts it, "If anyone tells us, 'Oh, Jennifer Love Hewitt, there's no *way* this is not going to go all the way,' we say, 'We'll wait and see.'" As if their plate weren't full enough, the pair are also in the middle of developing a pilot for CBS called *Partners*—which Keyser characterizes as "our version of a cop show, one that focuses principally on the personal relationships of cops with their families, with about a third of it about the work they do." Right now they are casting that show and expect to start shooting the *Partners* pilot right after *Time of Your Life*.

Love, meanwhile, appears confident she has made the right decision, even if she's committing to a potentially very long run.

"You have to go, 'Okay, I'm signing a piece of paper that could basically control the next six years of my life,'" Love says. "But I try not to think of things too far ahead like that. My schedule is *so* busy that if I do that, I just drive myself nuts. I just think I want to do the pilot, I like playing Sarah, and I know that Chris and Amy are not going to do something for six years if it's not a *great* something. Chris and Amy are *not* going to do it just for the sake of doing it. And I don't believe Fox would either."

Over the years, Hewitt says, she finds herself inspired by what Keyser and Lippman create for her. "Four years later I still know that every script that's written by them is going to be *amazing*," she says. "I think they have a great way of taking what's a very common language—the way people talk every day—and adding twists and turns to it. I just think they're really really brilliant and they care about their stuff and they care about me. I care about them deeply and it's just such a good relationship. It's just really *nice*."

All those intensely nice things said, the teen goddess remains uncertain that she has unraveled the secret of Keyser and Lippman's success. "I wish I knew," she says in her trailer as she prepares for another scene. I think most people wish that they knew because then they could steal it and they *too* could be brilliant. I know that they never stop thinking or working on making the show better. You can ask them a question like, 'What shoes did Sarah buy on Wednesday?'—just because it would help me in a scene. They know where and they have a receipt for it."

"Can we *not* talk about pilots?" Paul Simms asks.

It is midafternoon on a *NewsRadio* shoot night and Simms sits in his office, caught up in a Nintendo game called *Oddworlds 2: Abe's Exodus*. "I've always made enough time to play," he explains with a grin. Now that *OverSeas* is officially over and done, there should be no shortage of time for Simms to play. That's partly the reason that he recently rented a beach house in Malibu for the next few months from an older TV writer. Yet here he is spending a lovely potential beach day in distinctly noncoastal Hollywood, getting drawn back inland to be close to some outstanding *NewsRadio* matters. "It's actually been fun," Simms says, invoking an f-word not heard much from his mouth in recent months. "I got more involved in *NewsRadio* last week and rewrote the script like I used to."

*DAVID WILD*

*Used to*, that is, in a more carefree time before the death of Phil Hartman, and before Simms spent most of the past year falling victim to the sort of mishap that afflicts almost every showrunner somewhere down the career path—a dreaded pilot error.

Turning off the game and moving over to his desk, Simms pulls out a worn sketchbook that now serves as a sort of flight log of his aborted *OverSeas* mission. "This is a year ago," he says, turning to a page that shows his first rough sketches about how to shoot the show, about how the set should look. After that come more pages reflecting subsequent *OverSeas* meetings, as well as a few stray pages dedicated to *NewsRadio* ideas—including a *Titanic* parody that turned into a memorable episode.

"Here's one of my meetings with Don Ohlmeyer to discuss the pilot," Simms says, turning the page again. "This is all notes that came out of it." Paging through these notes, Simms still seems stung a bit by Ohlmeyer's failure to stay in his corner for the entire short life of *Over-Seas*. He recalls the veteran executive was seriously involved for a number of rewrites, and quite helpful at that. "Then after Littlefield left and Scott Sassa started, Don was less into it," he remembers. Simms was later told that Ohlmeyer felt Simms was not doing the work Ohlmeyer wanted from him. "*That's* the part that confuses me the most," Simms says. "I think the contacts with Ohlmeyer made the show better. He may not be a writer but he had good instincts, good ideas. But after doing four or five drafts he was like, 'It's good but it's not quite there yet.' After a certain point, I was like, 'I don't think it's *ever* going to be quite there for him.'"

In the end, Ohlmeyer didn't come to the *OverSeas* pilot taping, and he hasn't spoken with Simms between then and now. Somehow a man who found a way to stand by his friend O. J. Simpson has chosen to put some distance between himself and Simms's *OverSeas* team.

Joe Furey—part of that team—rushes into Simms's office to present a plausible explanation. "We don't have a Heisman Trophy," he explains, forgetting that at this point in legal history, neither does Ohlmeyer's infamous buddy.

Despite all the obvious cause for concern, Simms believed until late in the game that NBC would proceed with *OverSeas,* in large part because it had a vested interest in doing so, since it owned the show. That—along with protecting the continuing interests of *News-Radio*—was a large part of his reasoning in signing his overall deal with NBC Studios. "I thought the battle was going to be over whether they wanted to recast parts or get rid of a character or add a character—that kind of thing," he recalls. "I thought the battle would be over time slot. Then of course they sent it out for the audience testing."

During the week *OverSeas* was being tested, Simms finally spoke with NBC's Sassa. Simms recalls Sassa telling him the future of the show was not going to hinge on the testing. "He never really said if he liked or disliked it," says Simms. "On one hand that's good, because you're not getting inundated with *more* notes."

Around the time the *OverSeas* test results came back to the network, there was deafening, gut-twisting silence. "All of a sudden no one was talking to me," he says. "I'd even run into NBC people at *NewsRadio* run-throughs and they'd sort of be avoiding me."

Everybody at the network seemed concerned. "The guy at the NBC gate just thought the second act needed a little work," Simms jokes with a dark chuckle.

Finally, on a Monday, Simms called up the network's Karey Burke, who gave him the news that the testing results were indeed back and were—as she rather delicately put it—"not good." Indeed, the test audience's response to his show was nothing short of disastrous. Simms's supporters had hoped positive testing would provide Burke with ammunition to get the rest of the network enthusiastic about the show. Sadly, the numbers offered nothing but blanks.

A realistic sort, Simms had predicted that the testing report would be middling to weak—as had been the case with *NewsRadio.* He says Burke told him the network's research system had been revamped recently after the sitcom *Conrad Bloom* tested through the roof and got ratings down the toilet. Simms was worried at the prospect of *OverSeas* being a guinea pig for a new approach. In the end, he would have no shortage of reasons to balk.

*DAVID WILD*

Simms summarizes the bottom line: "The results were, they hated *every single thing about it*."

Sounds like helpful input.

"Yeah," says Simms, looking down. "Where do you go from *there?*"

"'The good news," Joe Furey adds, "is that they like *Gilligan's Island*."

Simms explains that someone in the focus group did feel *OverSeas* paled in comparison with "such seminal shows as M*A*S*H and *Gilligan's Island*." This afternoon Simms and Furey appear to have come to terms with being negatively compared with M*A*S*H, but the *Gilligan's Island* slight still hurts. There was an additional laundry list of complaints where that came from—one that might be longer than the twenty-two-minute pilot itself.

"Overall," Furey says, "their major note was 'more *Patch Adams*.'"

And—by clear implication—less goddamn *OverSeas*.

The test results are eventually put into percentiles, and Simms was told that the network likes to see their shows score in the 90s, embraces the 80s, accepts even the 70s. "The 60s is the lowest they'll go and still put it on," Simms says. "That's like a D. We got . . . a 5." In other words, *OverSeas* not only flunked—it was expelled.

A few days after getting this devastating research report which effectively killed whatever was left of *OverSeas*'s chances, Sassa called Simms.

By this point, the showrunner had a pretty good notion what was coming. He told the executive, "Okay, give me your rap." As Simms recalls, Sassa told him, "I liked it, it looks great, but I don't think it has enough of the elements we need to go forward with it. Then Sassa asked, 'Do you have another idea you want to come in and pitch?' I said, 'To you guys, *no!*' Then I stopped and we talked a little bit about how frustrating my time at NBC has been with *NewsRadio*. I was talking about how *NewsRadio* has had like eight moves and all that stuff. And he said, 'Yeah, but it's doing well now.'" Simms didn't even think until he hung up the phone that *NewsRadio* was at the time temporarily off the schedule to open up space for Al Franken's struggling *Lateline*.

After NBC passed on making any more episodes of *OverSeas* —despite a supposed "thirteen on air" commitment—Simms and Brillstein-Grey had a few conversations about trying to take the show to a different network. By now, however, Simms has discovered that most networks have their own irons in the TV fire. "Once that testing stuff happens, word spreads quickly," he explains. Simms ran into one former NBC executive who had gotten hold of a copy of the pilot. "He told me, 'Yeah it was *great*, I loved it.' Then I heard he was saying to people, 'It's a *colossal* disaster.'"

Throughout the entire grueling, stop-and-start *OverSeas* process, Simms would often say he was "just trying to keep the dream alive." The moment of truth came when Simms called Furey and told him, "The dream is over." Repeating that same phrase today, Simms lets out a curious yelp of existential pain followed by a visible wince. "It was really hard because there are so many people like Joe and Brian and all the production people who stuck with this for a long time," Simms says, looking down. "People like Brian and Joe who a year ago had other job offers. Brian was thinking of going to work on *Futurama* and I said, 'No, trust me, stick with me, this is going to go on the air, it's going to be great.'" The failure of the pilot is bad enough; now Simms also feels like he's let down some of those closest to him.

The final *OverSeas* indignity came about a week or so later. After some consideration of putting the *OverSeas* set in storage until the fall, Simms accepted that it was time to say good-bye. "Then they started loading that shit out of there," he says, pointing out his window at the now empty *OverSeas* stages. "That was fun," he says, his voice dripping sarcasm. "For about a week I was sitting here at my desk listening to 'Okay, just put those trees in the Dumpster.' And that was that."

*OverSeas* was over.

Just then Josh Lieb—who has been running *NewsRadio* for Simms in his absence, keeping the show alive under clearly difficult circumstances—walks into Simms's office.

"I want to talk to you about 'Super Heroes,'" Lieb says, referring to a new *NewsRadio* script.

"I'll give you the bad word now," Simms tells him. "It's not looking good."

"Oh yeah, it's looking good," Lieb says, willfully ignoring Simms.

"*No,*" Simms repeats more emphatically. "It's *not* looking good."

"No, it's looking good," Lieb repeats. "You're *so* wrong, man."

"It's *not* looking good," Simms repeats quietly but meaningfully as Lieb exits. "It's not looking good for this season."

At least for now, Simms still gets the last word here.

A week ago, Simms accepted an invitation for dinner with Scott Sassa. "I said, 'Fine, let's have dinner but I don't want to talk about *OverSeas,* it's over,'" he recalls. "The thing he said to me twice is 'I think we mishandled this as a project and you as a writer. There are two types of writers—the kind of writer who tells you an idea, then you help them rewrite every line. Then there's the kind of writer where they tell you the idea, then they go off and do it. *That's* what we should have done with you.' Well, that's fine, thank you, but the show is *still* not on the air."

Simms did have one request for Sassa: that if he was going to pick up *NewsRadio* for the 1999–2000 season, not to do it at the last minute. "Then I start losing writers who are worried about their jobs and this year—who knows—maybe even cast members who should be paid more," Simms explains. "He said he would." No early pickup has been forthcoming. As for Ohlmeyer, Simms was told he recently said to another NBC executive, "I like Paul, I want to be in the Paul Simms business. Ask Paul if he has any other ideas."

This coming Monday, Simms is planning on going to NBC to talk about an exciting new idea he has just hatched, not for a new show but for a favorite old one, *NewsRadio.* This idea's apparently so exciting that he whispers to Furey, "You haven't even heard this," as he closes his door for secrecy and goes into pitch mode. Simms explains he's been considering whether to move on or to do *NewsRadio* next year like he used to. Rewriting last week's script like in the old days has rekindled something in him. "The problem," Simms says, "is it's hard to come up with ideas after ninety-seven episodes—by the end of the season it will be ninety-nine. So here's what I want the next season of *NewsRadio* to be: Jimmy sells the station in New York and buys a little AM station and weekly newspaper in nowhere New Hampshire and asks everyone to move with him. What do you think, Joe?"

"Good idea," Furey says after pausing just a few seconds to consider this rather large twist.

"Then I can think of a *thousand* story ideas," Simms explains.

Rather than let *NewsRadio* die quietly, Simms suddenly sounds like a man trying to find a way to see his beloved creation become reborn.

Does he expect NBC will be receptive to such a radical idea?

"I have *no* idea, but it's a *great* idea," says Simms, sounding increasingly confident. "It gives us somewhere to go. Imagine Andy Dick interviewing some guy with a cow."

"Maybe it's not even a radio station anymore," Furey says, getting into the wide-open spirit of the conversation.

Suddenly, rather than rehashing the show's troubled past, the pair start riffing on each of the *NewsRadio* characters' motivations for moving away from the Big Apple, a brainstorm brewing.

Simms explains that he's not looking for any sort of new TV deal when his current one with NBC Studios runs out in June. The fact that NBC will not being putting thirteen episodes of *OverSeas* on the air means he might be able to get free even sooner were he in any sort of mood to strike another deal. "Theoretically, if I wanted to sue them I could say, 'You said you'd make thirteen episodes,' but Simms realizes that's not the way it usually works and that networks are not generally in the business of making shows they don't want to make. Money may in fact not be all that important to him—later this month it is reported that Simms was on the exclusive list of entertainment figures who contributed the maximum to the Clinton Legal Expense Trust in 1998. During the last six months of 1998, Simms donated $10,000, as did fellow FOBs like Universal chairman Lew Wasserman and Don Henley, while Robert DeNiro, Stephen King, and Tony Bennett each gave $5,000.

In the immediate wake of the *OverSeas* wipeout, Simms understandably felt little interest in developing other pilot ideas. During the making of *OverSeas* he would often say, "This is the last television show I want to do." Now he's not so sure. "Three years of *Larry Sanders* and four years of *NewsRadio*—I've been doing this pace for seven years," he points out. "For a week I was like I *never* want to do TV again, so now I've got to figure out what to do with the rest of my life."

A week and a half or so later, Simms had two or three ideas for other shows.

In retrospect, Simms sees that there were stop signs every step of the way for *OverSeas*. Perhaps they should have tossed in the TV towel early on.

"I don't think we should have given up," Furey says supportively.

"I guess if I'd known it was going to turn out this way I would have given NBC one of my more conventional ideas to fulfill my contract, and save this for someplace like the WB or Fox that's looking for something different. But they *always* say they're interested in something different."

Simms can't pinpoint the big lesson he's learned as a showrunner from his *OverSeas* episode. "I'm not so sure how much new stuff I learned," he says, "but there were things I knew all along that I kinda forgot as I got wrapped up in this." One point it illuminated goes back to something Simms realized back in his days writing for David Letterman. "Newer is *always* better," he says. "If Dave heard something more than three times, it became that old piece of crap. And next time I have an idea, I'm going to wait until it's the right time."

Has Simms considered the possibility that he was too collaborative with *OverSeas*, allowing too many cooks in his creative kitchen? The quick-witted Simms takes an uncharacteristically long pause before saying a word.

Writers are always told to write to please themselves first, Simms explains, but in reality, or in the TV business, it's not so simple. "You go back and forth," he adds. "You say maybe I shouldn't have taken any notes and stuck with the first draft but I believe the process was making it better. Plus if at any part of the process I said, 'Screw you,' they wouldn't have *made* the pilot. They would have said, 'Okay, here's your check.' The thing is I have *no* perspective on it, but the worst criticism for me is that a year from now I might look at it and think it's kind of bland. When it comes to sitcoms, the network people all have this sort of common language—it's all about 'Let's *care* about the characters,' 'Let's find the emotional beats.' It's very easy to get in that mind-set, but if I do a sitcom again, it's going to be *funny*. That's that. I've had four years of criticism from the network about *NewsRadio,* about how it's very funny but there's no warmth, it's too mean-spirited, none of which I really agree with. Ultimately when it comes back and you look at it you're just going, 'I should be *laughing* more.' *That's* a sitcom—that's what you're supposed to do—*laugh*."

Listening to his own painfully obvious yet unassailably true words, Simms lets out the tiniest of chuckles.

In the middle of the month, *Will & Grace* showrunners David Kohan and Max Mutchnick close an impressive $16–17 million deal with Warner Bros. Signing the youthful team is the first big move by the studio's incoming president Peter Roth, the former Fox chief who has taken over from Tony Jonas, who has been shown the door and given—you guessed it—a production deal. Under the terms of their new deal, which starts in June, the pair will continue to run *Will & Grace* next season, then move to Warner Bros. TV full-time for the 2001–2002 season. Roth tells the *Hollywood Reporter* that the pair "struck a chord among the viewing public with *Will & Grace* and securing their services for the future is a crowning achievement for this studio." The deal puts Kohan and Mutchnick in TV's big leagues. The deal is said to be the most the studio has ever paid anyone who hasn't already made Warner Bros. lots of money, like Bruce Helford with *The Drew Carey Show* or John Wells with *ER*. For the pair, it's tangible, bankable proof that they've come a long, profitable way from *Boston Common*.

*DAVID WILD*

Later in the month, after it is painfully clear that *Cupid* is dead, there is heartening news for the showrunners of that fallen series. Scott Winant remains busy—still in the works is *Anna Says*, the pilot starring Tracy Pollan he's executive-producing for ABC with Jill Davis, as well as another pilot for Fox created by Clyde Phillips, an irreverent family drama told from the point of view of three teens. Meanwhile, Winant's *Cupid* partner Rob Thomas signs a four-year, $8 million deal with 20th Century Fox Television to be showrunner for *Snoops*, the new ABC drama created by David E. Kelley about private investigators, expected to debut in the fall of 1999. Kelley—red-hot from *Ally McBeal* and the still-rising show *The Practice*—will create the drama pilot. Thomas, a man not deemed ready to run his own creation at the beginning of this season, is set to run the show. Making matters cozier, *Cupid*'s Paula Marshall has been picked to play one the leads of *Snoops* along with Gina Gershon.

In *Daily Variety*, Jenny Holtz reports that several studios were competing for the services of the thirty-three-year-old Thomas, "whose work on the canceled frosh drama *Cupid* was a critical favorite, despite the show's low ratings on ABC's black-hole Saturday and Thursday nights." As 20th Century Fox TV studio president Sandy Grushow tells the trade paper, "Hollywood is going to be talking about Rob Thomas for many years to come."

Kohan and Mutchnick, as well as Thomas, communicate that they are glad to speak about their new deals, but it might take a few days to get squeezed into their busy schedules. Apparently they first have some things to say to the people who are, after all, paying them millions of dollars for their increasingly pricey points of view.

*The Norm Show*—which won't debut until March 24—is shooting on Stage 12 at Warner Bros. This is the episode guest-starring Jack Warden, whose $50,000 fee has been supplemented in part by Macdonald. This episode also features the debut of *The Norm Show*'s new female character, formerly known as Tiffany La Boom Boom and now called Molly Carver and played by Amy Johnson.

Before show night begins, the now edited *Norm Show* pilot is screened for the studio audience, who readily eat it up. Afterward the actors take the stage to demonstrate their abilities in the art Macdonald calls "memorizing." Tonight, watching his cast of memorizers, Bruce Helford paces the floor a tad less manically than during the making of pilot. Receiving a quick network order will do that to a showrunner. Jack Warden makes his first big entrance, and soon after that the old pro slays the audience when his middle-aged macho-man character suddenly and leeringly praises Norm's "beautiful ass" and offhandedly adds that he'd like a "piece" of the aforementioned butt. Instantly it's obvious that Warden is worth every cent he got from Macdonald and Helford and then some. Sometimes, even in Hollywood, you get what you pay for.

If you're going to celebrate the miracle of childbirth, why not do it during a sweeps month?

W. C. Fields warned against working with children and dogs, but then again he's dead. On the other hand, *7th Heaven*—a show in which both figure prominently—is very much alive. In a season marked by a sense of retrenchment, this is one show that continues to grow, much like the population of the show's wholesome and fetching clan. Compared with the more teen-targeted WB offerings like *Buffy the Vampire Slayer* and *Felicity*, *7th Heaven* is an old-fashioned big-tent hit family series offering life lessons and eye candy for all ages as it tells the home truths of the Camdens: father Eric (Stephen Collins) and mother Annie (Catherine Hicks); their hunky, slightly brooding college-age son Matt (Barry Watson); the lovely, jock-ish sixteen-year-old daughter Mary (Jessica Biel); the adorable, boy-crazy fifteen-year-old Lucy (Beverly Mitchell); the wise-beyond-his-twelve-years Simon (David Gallagher); and the cutely precocious seven-year-old Ruthie (Mackenzie Rosman). That's not to mention *7th Heaven*'s two newest family additions, twins Sam and David, played by quadruplets and an unrelated pair of twins who all look pretty cute too.

On the February 8 episode of *7th Heaven*, Annie gives birth to twins and some God-given Nielsen ratings. This show—titled "In Praise of Woman"—takes the WB's Little Family Show That Could into the weekly top forty, a first for the network. The episode draws what is far and away the network's biggest audience ever—some 12.5 million viewers. As with other births, there is much rejoicing afterward. For May sweeps, Brenda Hampton jokes, "we're going to have Annie give birth to vampire slayers who drink and have sex."

"We're thinking of octuplets next," adds an overjoyed Aaron Spelling, who confesses that even he's been surprised by the show's slow but steady rise. "Surprised is a tiny word—*shocked*," Spelling says. "We were amazed because it's a sweet little family show. With what's going on in television—the sexuality and the outrageousness of it—there was a lot of hesitation."

This morning there is no hesitation but a growing sense of pride to be found on the *7th Heaven* set—a converted shower door factory in an industrial stretch of Santa Monica. The episode being filmed here today features not only all the Camden kids and Happy the Dog, but also a chimpanzee guest star. Within the extended *7th Heaven* family there is so much joy over these sweeps ratings that Brenda Hampton herself is making one of her rare "papal" visits here to congratulate the troops and, truth be told, to check out the chimp. Even before she arrives, the entire cast is quick to praise Hampton as far and away the biggest reason for the show's success. "Brenda *is* the show," says Catherine Hicks.

Actor Stephen Collins—whom Spelling calls "the quarterback" of *7th Heaven*—knows this show is far from an overnight sensation. "The one thing the WB has really done right is they've left us in place," Collins says in the trailer during a break from the action. "I think Jamie Kellner always understood it was going to take time for people to find a show like this. It's not high-concept. It's as *low*-concept as can be. The secret was that every time the show aired, ratings went up—even though they were barely showing up on the radar, they were going in the right direction."

*7th Heaven* is a show few expected to find such a foothold at century's end. Yet precisely because it doesn't fit in with the moral climate, it has touched a nerve with families in search of a little climate control. This may explain how it is now even defeating *Melrose Place*, a very different Spelling show that it's been running against. This month it's announced that 1998–1999 will be the last season for *Melrose Place*—suggesting that sexy good can triumph over sexy evil.

"We've always been treated as the dirty little secret, which is fine with me," says Hampton of the show. Only for once the dirty little secret is how damn—make that darn—clean *Heaven* is. How such a show became a hit remains somewhat of a mystery even to its own creator. "When someone finds out, I hope they call me and tell me, so I'll do it a second time," says Hampton, who's currently trying to do exactly that with her new WB drama pilot for the fall called *Safe Harbor*. As they celebrate the significant ratings bump for *7th Heaven*, Hampton and Spelling are hardly resting on their laurels—today they've been attending casting sessions for *Safe Harbor,* which concerns the life of a sheriff and—of course—his family. One supposes there will probably be cute animals too.

Though Hampton doesn't come around much, the set of *7th Heaven* seems a pleasant, even homey place to pass some time. Sure, Stephen Collins can be spotted kicking the nonliving heck out of Stuffy the Dog. Lest you worry, Stuffy is the stuffed stand-in for show's canine costar Happy. Truth be told, Collins appears to be administering these punishing blows to the inanimate beast purely for the benefit of a writer in desperate search of any wanton misbehavior on this hallowed TV ground.

To make things even more family-like, David Gallagher—a particular fave rave of Brenda Hampton's daughter, Zoe—has enjoyed a few sleepovers at Hampton's new Holmby Hills home, complete with a drive-by tour of Aaron Spelling's nearby house *and* the Playboy Mansion. Not that Hampton should worry much about corrupting young Gallagher. The kid, after all, has two *South Park* posters hanging on the wall of his personal school classroom on the *7th Heaven* set. "They're kind of the opposite of our show," the young actor says of the *South Park* gang. "They show death and violence—that sort of thing. I would be *so* honored if they would put me on there and kill me or something."

Ohmigod, they've got maggots in the *South Park* office!

While it is no real surprise to find maggots thriving in the greater Hollywood area, it still wasn't a pretty picture when Trey Parker and Matt Stone recently discovered that said pests were making themselves at home in their Casa Bonita office, which, it must be said, could use a good cleaning.

"Yeah, it's *really* fuckin' messy," Stone confesses with a hearty laugh. "We had to have it fumigated because there were a bunch of fuckin' maggots in here."

Other than those pesky maggots, things are going pretty well at the *South Park* office today. "We're just gearing up basically for what is the third season for us," explains Stone, who's here now while Parker's away grabbing a quick lunch.

These days the pair are dividing their time pretty equally between *South Park* the show and *South Park* the upcoming feature film.

"It's very schizophrenic," Stone admits. "But it's not as schizophrenic as when we did *South Park* and *BASEketball*, where it was hard to go from live action to our different kind of thing." What also makes this easier is that the *South Park* film is being put together in a facility only a quick drive away from the comforts of Casa Bonita, their preferred hang.

Though there will be synergy between *South Park* the TV show and *South Park* the feature film, Stone and Parker aren't planning on making the TV show build up plotwise to the *South Park* movie, unlike *The X-Files* feature film. Of their film, Stone proclaims with palpable pride, "It's *so* fucked up—I mean we're amazed with it sometimes. I think the movie is only going to get more fucked up. It really feels like a movie, not three episodes of the TV show strung out over ninety minutes." The movie, he promises, will earn its R rating, "which is the only way we were going to do it. There was *no* negotiation. This sounds really self-serving, but you wouldn't believe how much time we spend saying no to shit and really protecting what we think is our baby."

As proud parents of their *South Park* baby, they still remain a bit lax with deadlines. Parker and Stone continue to push episodes to virtually the last minute and even beyond. That's a testament to Parker and Stone's continuing passion for *South Park* and their always motivating fear of turning out an episode they hate. "It's not like we stress out every single detail of every show, but we do work pretty hard on it," Stone explains. "That's a constant."

Another constant is the seemingly unstoppable growth of cable. While the networks continue to battle things out, offering big-budget sweeps events like *The '60s* and *Storm of the Century* to compete, cable continues to flourish. In the thick of this month's sweeps, the *Hollywood Reporter* proclaims that *South Park* scored an additional 600,000 viewers weekly during the last half of 1998 and that it's passed wrestling to become the most-watched original series on cable among eighteen- to forty-nine-year-olds, while drawing an impressive 2.54 million viewers.

Today things appear fairly calm in Casa Bonita, but there have been some animator revolts in recent months. "It's a cyclical thing," Stone explains. "It's almost menstrual, like once every three-and-a-half weeks, but it's the men too."

Last month Stone and Parker spent a few more nights sleeping in the office, but lately they've been coming closer to having what Stone calls "a kind of a life." That may change in a few weeks when work on the movie goes into hyperdrive.

Lately, the pair have been struck by the rapidly escalating role of animation in prime time, a trend at least slightly attributable to *South Park*'s surprise impact, though Stone doesn't want to spend too much time pondering the big picture: "You realize, you can't pay any attention to any of that shit," he says. "We have to follow our own little guiding light, which still to this day is do Trey and I think it's funny." That much has already taken them further than they could have reasonably imagined.

Though *South Park* mania may be starting to wane, as manias tend to do, *South Park* merchandise continues to move. Released in time to capitalize on the true commercial spirit of Christmas, *Chef Aid: The South Park Album* went platinum. The album—which became an all-star affair featuring appearances from the likes of Elton John, Ozzy Osborne, and Master P, not to mention Rick James and Ike Turner—once again proved the pair's instincts were correct when the biggest hit off *Chef Aid* wasn't from the big-name acts the label wanted, but rather Chef's own tasty, Parker-penned "Chocolate Salty Balls (P.S. I Love You)."

This month Comedy Central finally announces its replacement for Doug Herzog—Larry Divney, fifty-five, who's the network's longtime executive vice president of ad sales. The network has good reason to be happy with Divney—ad revenues for Comedy Central climbed from $76 million in 1997 to $93.2 million last year. Projections for 1999 are well over $100 million. Not bad for a network whose biggest asset is a bunch of barely animated, trash-talking minors.

All the media reports that had Parker and Stone zealously pursuing the top Comedy Central job were, Stone insists, "total crap." To hear him tell it, this, like so many other of the pair's activities, was a lark, a semi-goof: "What we did was kind of a joke. We definitely wanted to meet with Tom Freston, because there was this vacuum with Doug Herzog gone," he explains. "We had some ideas about where the network should go and you know they *have* to listen to us basically. It was a we-could-get-a-meeting-so-why-not kind of thing. Tom wanted to meet with us and assure us that everything is fine at Comedy Central. But no way—we have another job, you know."

Because of Parker and Stone's overnight high profile, the story made good copy. Stone's parents heard about it on a Denver radio station and called, asking their son, "Are you going to be president of Comedy Central?" Of course, it could be argued that Stone and Parker are already way too busy to be bothered running a network. They have already done something far grander—they've established themselves as avenging angels of animation and the reigning kings of good bad taste. Indeed, during February sweeps the pair bring back the popular Mr. Hankey, that infamous Christmas Poo who returns in a very special episode of *South Park* in which the always bloated Cartman learns a very important lesson about the sweet smell of success. As the big guy himself puts it perfectly, "Being a sell-out is *sweet*."

*DAVID WILD*

# They Shoot Pilots, Don't They?

Success and failure are both difficult to endure. Along with success
come drugs, divorce, fornication, bullying, travel, medication,
meditation, depression, neurosis and suicide. With failure
comes failure.

Joseph Heller

*A* creeping sickness has overtaken the offices of *NewsRadio*, former base of operations for *OverSeas* and still home for a show
perennially on the brink of becoming network homeless. What ails
everyone here isn't some existential malaise but an eclectic and viru-
lent strain of the flu, which last week forced a rare delay in the shooting schedule. As a result, everyone here is attempting to squeeze in
two episodes this week—in part so *NewsRadio* can be done in time for
the wrap party scheduled for Saturday.

Only a half-hour before *NewsRadio*'s second-to-last episode of the
season is to go before the cameras, Paul Simms is still sleeping in his
office, having apparently pulled an all-nighter. Instead of taking it
easy at his rented house in Malibu, Simms has dragged himself right
back into the thick of his old show. And thick it is today—everybody
here seems to be running on mere fumes and Starbucks coffee.

195

Outside Simms's office his parents—visiting from San Diego—are waiting, as are writers Joe Furey and Brian Kelley, who scripted tonight's episode, called "Retirement"—the first of a two-parter that carries out Simms's vision of bringing his aging city series a new lease on prime-time life out in the country. "We tried to write it in two hours, and it shows," Kelly warns with a smile as Simms emerges and the entire group makes its way over to the nearby *NewsRadio* stage.

On the way, Simms's mother explains that she really enjoyed the *OverSeas* pilot. "I loved it," she says, with a mother's objectivity. It is pointed out that if *OverSeas* had become a profit center, Mrs. Simms might have had a pretty interesting lawsuit on her hands, since the show was based in part on the childhood she and Mr. Simms helped develop for her son.

"Yeah," Simms tells his mom, "you could get Shandling's lawyers."

Simms fills his folks in on the latest legal events involving the Garry Shandling suit and his own upcoming depositions. Earlier today Superior Court Judge Ralph W. Dau fined Shandling's law firm Howard, Smith & Levine for asking questions "calculated to harass" in depositions. The trial is currently set for June 30.

Simms has more than mere lawsuits to keep him busy. Standing backstage, near *NewsRadio* cast member Andy Dick's son Lucas, who is yo-yoing for the crew, Simms tries to marshal his ailing troops. Yet tonight Simms too seems to be growing sick—sick of waiting on word from a network he's come to see as pathologically afraid of commitment. A few weeks ago, he and Brad Grey went in to meet with NBC to plot the future—the now uncertain future—of *NewsRadio*.

Simms pitched his idea for reinventing the show in New Hampshire, then stated what he needed to make it work. If the network wanted him to carry on, it needed to pick up the show before the shooting of the last episode. He needed the same writers, writers who might have to take other gigs if *NewsRadio* remained too long "on the bubble," the series equivalent of purgatory. Simms also wanted a substantial raise for his cast of *NewsRadio* players. He had long felt bad that after all these years, the actors had never gotten significant raises. Because the show had never been a sizable hit, there had never been a chance for a renegotiation. Simms suggested that the right thing to do was give everyone a boost up to the same higher level.

The cast members appreciate the support. Standing near the bleachers, Dave Foley admits that "it would be nice to see NBC pony up this time." On the other hand, Joe Rogan—the *NewsRadio* cast member and briefly the closest *OverSeas* had to a leading man— admits he would gladly come back even with no raise. "Hell, yeah, don't tell NBC that, but it's the greatest job on the planet ever," he explains. "Even getting fucked over in this business means you're getting so much fuckin' money—like $30,000 an episode—which is more than what my mom got in a year."

Earlier today, the network called Brad Grey and informed him it wasn't going to make a decision by the deadline, in part because it was still waiting for departing WB chief Garth Ancier to join the network officially. NBC was cutting back on comedies but would like to keep *NewsRadio* alive if possible. According to Simms, Grey was displeased with the delay and relayed the possibility that Simms might have to let the cast know he was leaving the show. Furthermore, Grey told Simms he was asked about the possibility of continuing on without Simms—an idea he rejected.

Simms had tried to communicate to NBC that while it made more sense for him to move on, he had a sentimental interest in staying on *NewsRadio*. Certainly another season would almost have to be a relief compared with this one begun under such bizarre circumstances following the death of Phil Hartman. "Yeah, that's true," says Simms. "But who knows?"

Once the episode begins filming, Dave Foley is asked about Simms.

"Is Paul an inspiring leader? I'm not sure," Foley says. "He sort of motivates you to do well so he doesn't fall apart. He always looks like any second now this is all going to go. He's a great writer—and that's always the inspiring part."

One of Simms's strengths as a writer is the way he gracefully pours his own experience and emotions into the scenario of a sitcom. Early in today's episode, Jimmy James—the boss of the *NewsRadio* gang— addresses his staff in words that seem demonstrably apropos:

*DAVID WILD*

We are not going to be together like this forever, you know. I mean, eventually, we'll all move on with our lives.

Seconds later, the big guy—*NewsRadio*'s lovable embodiment of wacky capitalism—poses an increasingly timely question:

Anybody ever wonder what they're going to do when this is all over?

Two days later, the hour arrives to shoot the season—and perhaps series—finale. Simms has heard nothing new from NBC about *NewsRadio*'s prospects—this despite the fact that the network has seen fit to renew *3rd Rock from the Sun*, which also has struggled in the ratings, and just today, the less than smash psycho-drama *Profiler*. Beforehand, Simms, dressed all in black, tells the cast tonight's episode may well be their last. Then Simms heads up into the bleachers and jams with the house band on a funky version of "Low Rider," playing away like some soulful sitcom Nero.

Impressively, the episode titled "New Hampshire"—with story by Josh Lieb and Simms, and teleplay by Sam Johnson and Chris Marcil—works as either an ending or a bridge. Somehow the performances and the episode seem inspired, as if Simms and company are committed to going out with a bang, if they're going out at all. The mood on the stage floor seems an odd mix of buoyant optimism and premature nostalgia. "It's not over," Brad Grey offers hopefully. "We've been in tighter spots than this. Last season it took until two days before the upfronts to get the green light."

With everyone sick, tired, and underrehearsed, there are more blown lines than usual today.

"God, they are really out of it today," says Simms's mom with a smile after Jon Lovitz miss a cue.

"You're blowing my last shot at an Emmy," Dave Foley jokes to Vicki Lewis when she slips up in another scene.

As the filming draws to an end, Stephen Root—who plays Jimmy James—is asked how he's feeling on this possibly auspicious occasion.

"Like shit," Root explains. He couldn't rehearse today, has already done three hours of *King of the Hill* voice work, and is feeling feverish. "It's been a bit of a competition for who's feeling worst these days," he says. "I might have the crown today." As for the uncertain state of the show, he adds, "We'll wait and see, which is what we always end up doing."

Around five in the afternoon the episode is done and the audience sent home. When the studio is cleared, one last short scene is filmed on the soon to-be-disassembled main office set—a scene for potential use next season, assuming for the hell of it that there is one.

Afterward, champagne flows and the assembled cast and crew are called together for a group photo. Joe Rogan waits for a minute before heading over, and shakes his head at the indignity of the situation. If this turns out to be the final episode, it's safe to assume NBC isn't preparing for any *Seinfeld*-style send-off.

"The thing is we don't really know, so we're in this weird dormant stage," Rogan says, growing agitated. "Meanwhile the fuckin' *Profiler* gets picked up. If that doesn't give you fuckin' hate cancer, nothing will. It's a total lack of fuckin' closure."

As he fumes, Rogan stands near the set where a photo of Bill McNeal—and thus Phil Hartman—remains visible. By the nearest exit, the space on the wall for tomorrow's call sheet remains empty—fitting, since right now apart from the wrap party there is no tomorrow for *NewsRadio*.

At the wrap party—held at an elegant West Hollywood restaurant—there is still no obvious sense of closure but also no shortage of free food and beverage. Simms mingles a bit and seems in a decent mood, though he quickly confesses that generally this sort of party feels like work for him—ironic, since he often makes his work appear a lot like play. He's still awaiting news regarding the fate of *NewsRadio*. He says that Scott Sassa did call yesterday but it was on Simms's home machine during the taping of the season finale. "When he knew I wouldn't be there," Simms explains with a laugh.

Two nights after the party, Simms and the cast are reunited when *NewsRadio* is honored as part of the Museum of Television and Radio's

Sixteenth Annual William S. Paley Television Festival. The museum's Steven Bell begins the event at the Directors Guild of America Theatre by proclaiming, "Tonight we honor a true survivor."

Simms gets called out for a brief introduction. He explains that he has chosen two episodes to be shown tonight—one particularly surreal and creative episode from *NewsRadio*'s first season and another from this season. Of the latter episode, Simms explains that he has been around for only one quarter of the current season. "I was off doing a pilot that went absolutely nowhere," he says. "So this is the first time I've ever seen it."

When the credit "and Phil Hartman" appears on the giant screen during the playback of the first episode, there is tremendous applause. After the second show finishes, the members of the evening's panel—the cast, Simms, Josh Lieb, Joe Furey, and director Tom Cherones—are introduced. Simms is asked about the role of radio on *NewsRadio* and whether the medium has figured prominently in the show's storytelling. "We tried, but who cares about AM radio?" Simms asks, perhaps forgetting for the moment that this an event is being thrown by the Museum of Television and Radio. This begins a series of escalating put-downs of the radio industry. Soon the cast is letting the curses fly in distinctly nonmuseumlike lingo. When an attendee asks each actor to describe his respective character, a loose and extra-rambling Andy Dick responds by announcing, "Matthew is a retarded fag."

"Much like those of you who work for AM radio," Foley adds helpfully.

The mood turns more serious only toward the end, when a question is raised about Phil Hartman.

Simms refers to Jon Lovitz being "kind enough" to "fill the hole left by Phil's departure." Having made his profound respect for his old friend Hartman clear, Lovitz explains another reason he was brought in: "Josh Lieb said, 'Give me a Jew.' The show was good, but it was like the Boston Celtics."

"Jon was really our only choice," Simms says more seriously. "For us it's a way of sort of having Phil around still."

Simms tells the crowd about the move to New Hampshire and campaigns subtly for their support in encouraging NBC to grant these survivors another season.

"It's something the network's still considering, so we have the most positive feelings toward the network and know they're going to make the right decision whatever they do," Simms tells them, his tongue an indeterminate percentage in cheek.

Another audience member raises his hand. "*I* actually work in AM radio and you're right," this man begins good-naturedly. "But at least I have a job next year."

Thank heaven for little interns.

The last night of February sweeps falls this year on March 3, which not so coincidentally is the night ABC decides to air Barbara Walters's hotly anticipated interview with Monica Lewinsky, who has been the season's leading silent star. The pair's two-hour gabfest draws 74 million viewers for at least six minutes and almost single-handedly brings the network from having a weak sweeps into closely challenging Fox for second place in the hotly contested eighteen to forty-nine network battle. NBC still wins that title. Nonetheless, the world's most notorious intern reportedly helps bring in $31 million in ad revenue to ABC. That woman—Ms. Lewinsky—also helps Walters and ABC earn the second best TV ratings of the season, behind only the Super Bowl, a considerably more wholesome event.

Never before has a medium so visual been impacted so profoundly by an act so oral.

Larry Charles is dressed for his own sort of postmodern success today—a knit cap, a hooded sweatshirt, sweatpants, and sneakers, his hair about halfway down his back. His office looks messier than it did earlier in the season, and still not terribly like your average Dilbert-friendly corporate cubicle.

*Dilbert* is not exactly exploding in the ratings since its strong January debut, but another season of episodes has already been ordered by UPN. "I have reasonable expectations for how successful the show can be on UPN and that's okay with me," Charles says. For him, the important thing is to continue doing shows. He believes that eventually, as with *Seinfeld*, the audience will find the show. He remembers how *Seinfeld* was an abject failure for a couple of seasons—that for a time the sitcom of the nineties was getting roughed up in the ratings by *Jake and the Fatman*.

In the meantime, Charles finds himself an increasingly busy man. For one thing, running an animated show—unlike a live action show—means in essence doing two seasons at once. He's still overseeing the completion of the first thirteen episodes of *Dilbert* for this season. Today he will take a first look at show number ten, since the first animation has just come back from Korea. Tomorrow he's recording the voice tracks to go with next season's show number two. Overall, Charles isn't finding doing an animated series more difficult than he imagined. He calls his partnership with Scott Adams ideal and invigorating. "He and I just really mesh well," Charles says. "We complement each other. We don't have an ego problem or personal conflict. We do everything by phone and e-mail so we don't have to hang out together." All they share is ideas—Charles calls this "the perfect collaboration."

Not everything about making *Dilbert* work has proved quite so effortless. His biggest problem has been scheduling the show's voice cast to come in for the recording sessions. "For a live action show, you do the show on Friday, everybody has to be there or you don't have a show," Charles says. "Here there's a little more flexibility and people have gotten very lax about their schedules." Last Tuesday Charles wanted to record the actors for the first show of next season and couldn't get them together. "Getting the actors in the room—or some version of the actors—has been a nightmare of scheduling," he admits. This problem has a cascading effect on the rest of production: If you can't get voices, you can't animate their voices, and it slows down the entire already time-consuming process. "There is actually a coup d'état in Korea thanks to our chaos," Charles jokes.

While there has been no violence to date, there has also been an ongoing battle of sorts between *Dilbert* and *Suddenly Susan* because *Susan* costar Kathy Griffin is voice-cast in *Dilbert*, and both currently air Monday nights at eight. NBC won't let Griffin's name appear on the credits of *Dilbert*. "We've been talking about this for over a year," Charles says, "but they won't budge so far." Meanwhile, word comes that Charles is bringing an old friend to lend a voice to *Dilbert*—Jason Alexander will play Catbert, to whom Dilbert goes for Y2K help.

In addition to his considerable *Dilbert* work, Charles has been working on developing a number of different shows during the current pilot season. "Some of them have fallen by the wayside, some of them are still alive," Charles reports. A live-action, single-camera filmed comedy pilot that would find him collaborating with Daniel Stern—the voice of Dilbert—now ranks among the fallen. "I was calling it *Stone's Throw* but I pitched one idea, Danny saw something else, and CBS thought it was going to be something else," Charles explains. "We couldn't really synthesize those three visions of the show. I tried to make it work but it became too frustrating so I moved on."

Charles has also been helping Sarah Silverman—a talented young comedian/actress briefly seen on *Saturday Night Live*—with her own potential network project. Later today he'll be taking notes from CBS about the project. "Hopefully we'll get that together and shoot it for midseason," he says. "I think she's great."

He is also working on another project with actor and writer Jon Favreau, who made his name in the 1996 film *Swingers*. "That's still supposedly for fall, but we're in the middle of casting and figuring out how to do it on the money that we have," says Charles. The concept is a half-hour independent movie each week about a group of characters in Los Angeles who are a little more mature than the characters in *Swingers*. "That's for UPN as well, and the good thing about being a UPN project is that there's no creative interference whatsoever. They're letting us do exactly the show we want to do. With the Sarah Silverman thing, I think you're more beholden to network sort of standards. Our fear is they're going to try to take the edge away from the show." In that case, Charles says, they'll both walk.

With both the Silverman and the Favreau project, Charles is basically serving in a supportive function. "I'm helping them realize their visions because I like them very much and I can sort of help them through the maze, give them someone they can trust that's not going to bullshit them," says Charles. "In some of these other projects that I instigate myself I feel more emotionally involved. But those are more difficult—it's easier to be detached. Plus my own projects tend to be more eccentric and idiosyncratic and thus hard to sell to networks."

Then, closest to his creative heart, there is Charles's long-gestating project with James L. Brooks. "It occasionally crests or coalesces into something real, then it kind of evaporates again," Charles explains. "Right now we're in a cresting period—he seems to be excited about, I seem to be excited about it. We have a really interesting person to be the star of it and if all of those things coalesce we would have a great show. That could be for midseason too."

Charles wants things to coalesce a little bit more before he shares the name of that really interesting person with the world. "I don't think I should yet," he says. "He's a great TV star who hasn't been on TV for a while."

Could it be Larry Charles's old boss Jerry Seinfeld has been convinced to return to save the small screen?

Alas, Seinfeld hasn't been gone long enough to qualify—it just feels as if he has.

**THE SHOWRUNNERS**

As befits a young man who just signed a new $8 million, four-year TV deal, Rob Thomas is currently in the process of buying what he calls "this ridiculously big house" in the Hollywood Hills. The place can be found slightly northwest—and one giant step up the socio-economic ladder—from the more humble home where he held his premiere party for *Cupid* back in September. Though Thomas hasn't received his first check yet, he is looking forward to that day, since by any standard, it's going to be a big one. "They're giving me 20 percent of the overall deal on signing," Thomas says, still sounding a bit taken aback by his good fortune. "I'm so blown away, I just want to frame the check."

He has good reason, particularly since Thomas has been in Los Angeles only twenty-two months. "Before this I was making young adult novelist money—which is not a lot—so I don't think it all has sunk in yet," he admits.

"It all" for Thomas means more than simply being a hot TV property. These days, he's also a thriving screenwriter. Producer Robert Simonds, best known for his run of Adam Sandler smashes, is turning his novel *Slave Days* into a film for Universal. At the same time he has been adapting James Duncan's novel *The Brothers K* for Imagine Entertainment. "I got notes on that over the weekend," Thomas reports. "Hopefully it will be a one-week turnaround. I'm trying to do that from five till nine in the morning, then read spec scripts from nine till one, then go hang out on the set the rest of the day."

Clearly there is life after *Cupid*.

For the immediate future at least, Thomas won't have too much time to spend in his new house. Instead he'll be here in his temporary office inside David E. Kelley's headquarters at Raleigh Studios down in the Manhattan Beach area of Los Angeles. He has been here working on Kelley's new series *Snoops*, taking off a few moments to talk during day two of three during which the pilot will be shot in the studio—the other twelve days of the pilot shoot are being shot on assorted locations.

Thomas is only two weeks on the new job—time he has mostly spent reading scripts as he tries to assemble a writing staff. Already

*DAVID WILD*

he's finding there are pilots and then there are pilots. Working on a project with the red-hot Kelley imprimatur has an almost tangible impact. "It's such a different feeling than with *Cupid*, which was hoping and praying and wondering if you're going to get picked up," Thomas explains. "Here everyone sort of operates under the assumption you will."

As much as Thomas strove to keep *Cupid* alive, he wasn't unaware of other opportunities. After all, Thomas did take that meeting with David E. Kelley back in November. In retrospect, Thomas believes Kelley had a more realistic sense than he did of *Cupid*'s chances. "I think they knew over here," he says. "On the outside maybe people sensed it. Being involved in the show, things were less apparent."

Such an offer was ironic—here was a young TV writer considered too inexperienced to run his own show at the beginning of the season being approached to run one by perhaps the most famous TV creator of the era. Then there was the further irony that Thomas likely wouldn't have gotten nearly as profitable a deal if *Cupid* hadn't died a well-timed death, because he simply wouldn't have been at liberty to do so. The show's bitter end made him a free agent and thus a very wealthy young man.

Nonetheless, Thomas insists he never for a nanosecond rooted against *Cupid*.

"Oh, no, not on any level," Thomas says. "I had no idea there was going to be this much money thrown at me. Financially, I didn't really have incentive to root against *Cupid* at the time."

Besides the money and the chance to work with Kelley, another factor made *Snoops* attractive to Thomas—the fact that former *Cupid* star Paula Marshall would also be joining him on the *Snoops* case. The day after Marshall returned from Chicago, back to her home in Los Angeles and to her boyfriend Bruno Campos—a star of *Jesse*—she received a *Snoops* script. She soon auditioned and won the role. Thomas thinks the role will be great for her, since she's a fine comedic actress, and in *Cupid* she was so often in the thankless role of straight woman to Jeremy Piven. And now that the colleagues are in the same city, they're growing close. "We've bonded more in the last couple of weeks than we ever did at *Cupid* because it's like being two kids who come to a new school," Thomas explains. "We're each other's only friends."

Curiously, Kelley has never explained to Thomas what he liked about *Cupid* enough to import a significant amount of its creative talent to execute his own latest TV vision.

"Uh, no," Thomas answers with a chuckle. "Frankly it's funny, but the thing is I know he's seen the show. He's notoriously critical, but I don't think I'd be here if he didn't like it. On the other hand, I think what David was looking for was someone who could run a show, someone who can write a mix of comedy and drama, and someone who the ABC executives would sign off on because they know David isn't going to be very hands-on. Then there was the added factor that we had the same agent. I think it was the stars aligning for me."

Working with a writer of Kelley's stature must be an educational experience.

"David's not a real talker," Thomas reports with a small knowing laugh. "David sits in his office and writes. If there's an education I'm getting, it's not like David's saying, 'Spend more time on character arc here.' The lesson I'm getting is find great people, put 'em around you, delegate everything, and then you can just write the show."

On shows like *Ally McBeal* and *The Practice*, Kelley has tried to write many of the episodes himself—the idea with *Snoops* is for him to create a new series, then hand the showrunning baton over to Thomas.

"My sense is if I turned in the first two or three scripts to him and David thought I just missed it, I wouldn't be surprised if he rewrote me," says Thomas. "On the other hand, I think that's the last thing in the world he wants to do." That's why Thomas is getting the big bucks.

In Thomas's mind, Kelley would like to operate in essence as the studio in this situation, a setup that he imagines will make his own job easier. Rather than having to please many executives, Thomas really has to please one man—albeit one exceptionally powerful, famously demanding one. "In David's dreamworld," says Thomas, "*Snoops* will simply not be a headache for him."

In the meantime, Thomas will keep looking for a *Snoops* staff.

*D A V I D   W I L D*

Thomas doesn't enjoy this part of the process—being hawked by agents rather than actually writing the shows. Still, he understands how important laying this foundation is to the architecture of a show that he hopes will stand the test of prime time.

"David Kelley—and I don't mean this at all disparagingly—but I think he would rather rewrite and get exactly what he wants every time," Thomas explains. "I like working with writers and the slight variation in writer's voices. So I'm excited about hiring a new staff. I'd love it if *Cupid* had a second year and I wouldn't have had to do this, but that is neither here nor there."

The pressing issue now is what to make of the series. Thomas wants *Snoops* to become a detective show that's character-driven, in the tradition of *The Rockford Files*. He is looking forward to writing some intricate plots yet still having characters who are "funny and charming." Certainly there has been no shortage of "buddy cop" shows in TV history, but Thomas wants *Snoops* to offer something different. "What I want to get to is a buddy relationship based on an *Odd Couple* dynamic between two women on screen," he says. "It wouldn't be hard-boiled like *Cagney and Lacey*, it would be fun and goofy and charming. *Moonlighting* and *Cupid* did the male-female thing with underlying sexual tension. I think it will be fun to strip that away." Considering the sometimes racy oeuvre of Marshall's co-star, Gina Gershon (*Showgirls*, *Bound*), some viewers might be pulling for a little sexual tension between the leading ladies.

"Well, I think if you go on the Internet people will be talking about that," Thomas says with a smile.

Now it's time for Thomas to get back to the *Snoops* set. There he hangs out with Marshall, who says all this constant contact with her showrunner is a vivid improvement over their long-distance Chicago-to-L.A. relationship during *Cupid*, when they communicated primarily by phone and e-mail.

"The rare occasion when Rob and Scott Winant would show up, I'd be all over them," Marshall says. "I felt out of the loop. I would watch *Entertainment Tonight* just to find out what was going on back home." Now they can go out to dinner and discuss the new show.

This summer Marshall's already planning her trips to Thomas's new pool and Jacuzzi.

As much as she looks forward to *Snoops*, Marshall still sounds pained when recalling the end of *Cupid*. She reveals that word of the show's cancellation hit the Windy City toward the end of shooting what would be *Cupid*'s last episode—"Botched Makeover." Called into an office and given the bad news, Marshall remembers saying nothing, only crying. "The ending was bittersweet because I get to go home with my boyfriend and my friends, and be in my house, but it's also the end of a magical thing to me," she says. Still there was one more day to shoot—a swing dance scene. So it was that the last day of *Cupid* became an odd sort of party held at a Chicago nightclub—a TV wake of sorts. "We all drank and danced our butts off," Marshall recalls.

Now Marshall and Thomas find themselves moving back onto the TV dance floor together, hoping this time it's more of a marathon.

They shoot pilots, don't they?

Even in TV, a little real life has a way of sneaking in, for both the good and the bad. The good: Marta Kauffman of the Bright Kauffman Crane *Friends* triumvirate gives birth to her third child—a daughter—proof positive that even busy showrunners enjoy at least a modicum of free time.

Decidedly less welcome news comes a few weeks later, when Peter Boyle of *Everybody Loves Raymond* suffers a heart attack right on the set of the show. *Raymond* showrunner Phil Rosenthal first hears there is trouble while in his office discussing a scene on the phone with Ray Romano, who's on the set.

"By the way, Peter doesn't look so good," Romano told him.

"What do ya mean?" Rosenthal asked, concerned.

"He looks kinda pale—he's coughing and stuff," Romano said.

Rosenthal said to get a nurse down to the set. The nurse immediately called the paramedics. By the time Rosenthal got to the set from his office across the Warner Bros. lot, the paramedics had arrived and Boyle was in his trailer. Unfortunately, Boyle was refusing to go to the emergency room. "Peter kept saying he'd be fine," says Rosenthal. The paramedic asked if there was anybody around who might have some influence on this reluctant patient. "So I got the job of going in there and talking him into going to the hospital," says Rosenthal. "I made up some crap about how it was for insurance purposes and for the good of the show. Thank God we got him there in time."

Living and dying in prime time rarely have such high stakes. Yet one more pressing showrunning responsibility—lifesaving.

Christopher Crowe's time-traveling show *Seven Days* makes history, though not necessarily the sort for which anyone might wish. The March 17 episode of the show is reported to present the first virtual product placement in prime-time series history. Through a process from a company called Princeton Video Image, images were added in postproduction, apparently meant to spread the good word with Coca-Cola cans, a Wells-Fargo sign, Evian bottles, and Kenneth Cole shopping bags. Paramount seems to be seeking to find some way to boost revenues—not a bad idea in theory, considering the sort of season it's been for UPN.

For his part, Crowe simply refuses to share his own concerns about this groundbreaking and potentially horrifying strategy for economic survival, though his voice suggests he has no shortage of them. Crowe is more than happy to speak about his show, but about this new product placement phenomenon he immediately and unequivocally takes the showrunner's Fifth.

"I cannot talk about that," he says emphatically.

Crowe has always seemed an opinionated and easy speaker, rarely at a loss for words. Why the silence?

"I can't talk about that," he says simply.

Never?

"Maybe someday off the record. Maybe over a drink."

On March 24, *The Norm Show* and *It's like, you know . . .* both debut on ABC. Reviews for *Norm* are all over the adjectival map. The critics are generally warmer toward *It's like, you know . . .* but it's *Norm* that edges its way into the top twenty. The first time out *The Norm Show* draws 13.9 million viewers and hangs on to virtually all of its big *Drew Carey Show* lead-in. *It's like, you know . . .* brings in 12 million viewers, which seems particularly strong because its *Dharma & Greg* lead-in is preempted on the East Coast by President Clinton's address on the bombing that is just getting under way in the Balkans.

"That was the most bizarre day in the whole world because we're talking with the network about how exactly the bombing will affect our schedule," Bruce Helford recalls the next week. "It was completely something out of *Network*, man, really bizarre." Helford got word from ABC that the State Department had promised that it wouldn't do anything during prime time. "I swear to God," he says. "Then of course they did."

One always worries about bombing in prime time, but this was ridiculous.

"You'll notice they never start a war on Thursday night—I'm serious," Helford says. "I believe that the President or somebody says, 'You'll piss off a lot of people if they have to miss *Friends* or *Frasier*.'"

One might have guessed that social workers would be a forgiving lot, but the National Association of Social Workers wastes no time charging *The Norm Show* with ethical violations and declares its organization a "Norm Free Zone." The group's Josephine Nieves insists,

"Social workers have a great sense of humor," but nonetheless charges Norm Henderson with grievous violations of the professional Social Workers Code of Ethics, including misrepresentation, unprofessional and unethical conduct, violation of confidentiality agreement, and use of derogatory language. He is not charged with the crime of being entirely fictional.

Helford insists he actually got a call from Warner Bros. publicity asking, "Is there actually going to be a subpoena?" He found himself having to explain that Norm is not a real social worker, that it is only people acting or, as Macdonald would put it, memorizing.

At this early date Helford seems cautious about whether prime time will be a Norm Free Zone anytime soon.

"We'll see," he says. "All it really means at this point is that people would like to watch *Norm*. Now the question is how far they continue. The normal pattern is you have a drop-off the second week because some people who sample it don't stay. Then I'm hoping for the third and fourth week to either stay even or build—that'll be a really good sign."

Helford explains he was very happy that key reviews were generally positive, since he's already learned that Macdonald is not for all tastes. "I would love for every critic to love us—it's never going to happen," he says. "So I'll just hope that the audience loves it and go with that."

There are two more episodes of *The Norm Show* to be filmed, then Helford and Macdonald can relax a bit and see where things stand. "If ABC wants to pick us up early to help us add people to our writing staff, they could do it as early as like the fourth episode or something," Helford says. His best guess, however, is that ABC will wait until May. Still, he says, "you'll know by the third or fourth episode if we're going up or down."

With only one show aired and strong debut ratings, Helford is not acting cocky. Asked what *The Norm Show*'s chances are right now of making ABC's next fall schedule, Helford won't give himself better than a fifty-fifty shot. He knows the odds are always against anyone in TV who is foolish enough to believe the odds are with him.

What can you buy two young men in their thirties who've just signed a $17 million deal?

This being Los Angeles at the end of the twentieth century—sushi.

So it is that *Will & Grace* showrunners David Kohan and Max Mutchnick take a lunch break at Tera Sushi in Studio City near their office, where they're in postproduction for the last run of episodes before summer hiatus. Production on the successful first season of *Will & Grace* wrapped just a few nights ago, so this afternoon it's celebratory shrimp tempura hand rolls all around.

"Our deal with NBC was ending this year and we were debating whether we should make an overall deal," says Kohan. "When we went to NBC and said, 'What do ya think?' They said, 'Here.' The network's offer, he says, was essentially a continuation of their last pre–*Will & Grace* deal.

It was time to shop around.

"I can go on the record saying this—because I said it to Scott Sassa—it was disappointing," Mutchnick says. "We made it very clear we wanted to stay at NBC, but I don't think that they're really ready to become the studio that we need to handle the sort of business that David and I want to build."

"We had this notion that what we want to do is produce a number of shows under our aegis," Kohan adds. "NBC threw out a deal whereby they were basically saying, 'We'd like you for another two years on *Will & Grace* and maybe in the last year of your deal, write another pilot for us.' It was clear from what they offered us that's what their expectations were."

If *Will & Grace* was proving to be Kohan and Mutchnick's breakthrough show, they wanted the deal to go with it. The fact that they were being offered deals for twice as much at three other studios in town made it considerably easier to walk away from NBC and toward someone with deep pockets.

So when exactly did the process of making this deal really start?

"In the womb," Kohan ricochets back.

Ultimately it may have all been a matter of bad timing. Right as the new deal was to be negotiated, Warren Littlefield was out and the new regime arrived. "It couldn't have been more untimely for us," says Mutchnick between bites of his hand roll. "The guy who had taken us and brought us from our infancy to showrunners to this point left the network a month before we were going to go into negotiations. I would imagine Warren would have been a little more willing to open up his checkbook."

As for Sassa, Kohan says with no particular malice, "He hedges."

Despite rumors of unreasonable demands, Mutchnick insists that NBC Studios was never presented with a number it couldn't handle.

"They never heard a number that was inappropriate for what David and I had delivered over the past four years," Mutchnick said.

"We didn't ask a crazy number," Kohan adds. "They made an offer to us."

That offer was unacceptable. So next, in a move organized by their agent—"the delicious Scott Schwartz," Kohan calls him—the duo went to meet with three studios and in effect pitch not a specific show idea, but themselves.

The rules were such that the studio could not actually hear the young showrunners' series ideas.

"They're not allowed to ask," Mutchnick explains. "They have to just bank on it. I imagined there were things said at that meeting that enticed them, but an idea was never brought up."

When the pair ultimately made their deal with Warner Bros., Scott Sassa called them right away and said he hoped there were no hard feelings on their end, because there were none on his. "Scott said to me on the phone, 'We'll probably get along better this way.'" Mutchnick says. "But they still made a mistake."

Soon things started going the pair's way. *Will & Grace*, it was announced, would finally get its shot at eight-thirty on Thursday night, replacing *Jesse* for the last five weeks of the season. Soon after that the show got formally picked up for next season.

During February sweeps the show had retained virtually all of its *Just Shoot Me* lead-in, an encouraging sign. "That really told the network something," Mutchnick explains. "People weren't turning off the set at all, no one was having a problem with subject matter. People were simply liking the show."

News of the Thursday slot was met on the *Will & Grace* set with what Kohan calls "a very tentative kind of rejoicing." Everyone had begun to feel very comfortable on Tuesday nights.

Still, Mutchnick admits, "Nobody doesn't want Thursday night, but people were concerned—we're just like this at *Will & Grace*—we worry. We worried that Thursday would be a death knell—what if we didn't hit? What would it mean for our next year? Clearly they gave us the vote of confidence the next week, that it doesn't matter how we do on Thursday night, we're around for next season."

The move to Thursday means *Will & Grace* can also stop going up against and beating *Sports Night*, arguably the most critically acclaimed new show of the season. For Kohan, the satisfaction of beating a show on a different network was diminished by the fact that *Sports Night* is a program he genuinely likes. "At this point, I no longer think it's about kicking the ass of another network," he explains. "A good show on any network is good for all networks."

In giving *Will & Grace* the Thursday night nod, Sassa told the pair what sort of performance he was looking for—a drop of no more than four points from their *Friends* lead-in. "*Jesse* was dropping five and six points," Mutchnick explains. "There are a bunch of numbers the NBC brass looks at—the demo, the half-hour drop-off—that's really where Scott's eyes light up," Kohan says.

"That's what he's most comfortable talking about," Mutchnick adds.

Kohan and Mutchnick's deal with Warner Bros. was formally signed in their offices at one in the morning after a show night, with their lawyers and agent present. They were exhausted and unprepared for the big moment. "We didn't have anything for them,"

Kohan remembers. "We didn't even have hors d'oeuvres. Did we have crackers?"

"No," Mutchnick answers, "but we did drink scotch out of good crystal, and we opened a new Mont Blanc pen, and we signed away."

They had arrived, though Mutchnick hastens to add that they still worry as much as ever, if not more. They are, however, getting better compensated for such concern.

"It's almost like, but now we really have something to prove," Kohan adds. "Yes, we feel incredibly fortunate just to be in a business where something like this can happen, where you can win the Lotto. But to us it also represents an incredible amount of hard work to come."

Like hitting the jackpot in the lottery, signing a big overall deal offers plenty of immediate gratification—a signing bonus. "I'm not going to give numbers, but there was an extravagant check that was given to us at the signing that actually made that signing a phenomenal experience," Mutchnick admits. "There was something stunning about receiving a check that significant."

Kohan will never forget the time he worked for a director who kept a carbon copy of a check for approximately $5 million framed in his bathroom. Now Kohan has his very own suitable-for-framing (not to mention cashing) check.

Mutchnick calls theirs "a one-of-a-kind deal," one that is value-added in that it's an entirely "fresh-cash deal with no recouping from any of the money we make."

Perhaps it is better that the pair didn't make their deal with NBC, considering all the talk of huge layoffs at the network. "I actually thought about that—making some exorbitant deal while the people we work with are being laid off for budget cuts," Kohan says. "There's something a little . . . uncomfortable about that."

But, he adds, "There was a definite strike-while-the-iron-is-hot mentality," Kohan says. "First, this is a TV business constantly waiting for the other shoe to drop. Also, there's no real longevity to a television writing career unless you're really lucky," he says. "It's almost like an athlete—when the opportunity presents itself, you have to seize it for fear of what's going to be ten years from now, fifteen years from now. Also, ageism seems to be a fact of this business."

As Kohan speaks these words, he is fully thirty-four years old.

Having the fiscal details of their good fortune hit the trades was no thrill.

The night before, Kohan was out of the office when Mutchnick got a phone call informing him that the amount of the deal was going to appear in print. Mutchnick furiously worked the phones trying to stop this unwanted disclosure.

Why would anybody want to hide such good news?

"One, because David was in the middle of a divorce—that was my thinking for him," Mutchnick explains. "Two, I'm a guy who didn't always have money and when it finally comes your way it's not something you want to be . . ."

"Advertising," Kohan says, jumping into his good buddy's ellipses.

Mutchnick remembers having a rough day, taking no pleasure in getting a few dozen calls from friends and associates jokingly asking to borrow a million dollars. "Every single actor on the show knowing what you're making," he explains. "You can't make a deal like this without getting knocked around a little bit by people you've worked with."

Eric McCormack—who stars as Will Truman on *Will & Grace*—explains later that when your showrunners sign a huge new deal, "Your first reaction is fear—what does this mean? Are Mommy and Daddy leaving the nest? Who's the baby-sitter going to be? But then you realize they're not going to give this up. This is their baby. They want the freedom and the finance to do other things, but they're not fools."

To celebrate their deal, Kohan and Mutchnick had a dinner with their new Warner Bros. boss Peter Roth. "We had a fabulous dinner at Mr. Chow in Beverly Hills, where we sat next to Elizabeth Taylor," says Kohan. "She was wearing a white shock wig which struck me as redundant," Kohan recalls. To them, Peter Roth had a totally different style. "Scott Sassa seems like a corporate animal—I don't mean that in a disparaging way at all, but he's a real business head," Kohan says. "Peter Roth is an embracer of creativity and talent, that's what he loves."

"We kissed the first time we met," Mutchnick explains.

"No aversion to the man kiss for Peter Roth," Kohan adds.

With all that money coming in, these two have certainly had time for a few extravagant purchases between kisses.

"I guess the most lavish thing I got is some brand-new child support figures," says Kohan. Once postproduction is in, Kohan says he might splurge on a really high-end mountain bike, even though he could probably afford a few mountains to go with it.

Mutchnick, on the other hand, explains that he has already bought houses for his mother and his brother—something he calls "a very satisfying experience." Having revealed this act of generosity, he briefly debates whether it's proper to say so, then somewhat uncomfortably proceeds. "I didn't come from a lot of money to begin with and your fantasy in life—especially when you're a Jewish boy—is to take care of your mom." Oh, yes, he adds, he also bought himself a home.

Kohan, meanwhile, lives in a rented house with no immediate plans to buy. He is in no rush—first he wants the dust to settle from his divorce and from his newfound success.

"The equivalent of buying your family homes is a divorce," Mutchnick says with a dark laugh.

"It's true," Kohan says, shaking his head in agreement. "You get pretty good at fractions."

Now that their showrunning is coming to a temporary summer slowdown, Kohan and Mutchnick have a little time to fully consider what they've pulled off during *Will & Grace*'s first season. One impressive achievement has been making a sitcom that presents a gay character in a positive, nonclichéd way and yet does not have sexuality be much of an issue.

Mutchnick believes *Will & Grace* may be the first time a gay man has been fairly represented in television. "Sensational journalists like to say Will Truman is not gay enough," he says. "But the truth is he's gay enough. This success is sensational as an executive producer and as a gay man."

Kohan doesn't believe viewers ultimately care much about the show's gay themes. "People just like the characters," he says.

"I think they'll care if it becomes a monster hit," Mutchnick answers.

After they "lock" their last episode of the season, Kohan jokes that he's going to do some important Warner Bros. development from a ski lodge in Vail. "I'm taking my daughter to New York, and really gear up for next year," he says. "We have a couple of ideas for under the new deal that we've already discussed, but this next month and a half is about recharging. In the throes of it, it's painful knowing the mountain of work ahead of you. Look, I understand this is something everyone would love to do, and we're incredibly fortunate, but there is an incredible amount of anxiety."

Just then a fellow showrunner stops by the table—it's Drake Sather, who has worked with Paul Simms at *NewsRadio* and is now collaborating with David Spade on *Sammy*, an animated show based on Spade's less-than-idyllic childhood.

"Congratulations, you guys," Sather tell them.

Slightly embarrassed, Kohan confesses he once tried to hire Sather away from *NewsRadio* for *Boston Common* on the assumption—utterly mistaken—that the former sitcom would be canceled and the latter would go on to a second season.

Sather speaks of his current job overseeing "the Spade animation thing."

"I've got my own fish to fry—I've got my own nightmares now," Sather says. He tells the pair he's never been the boss before and he's shocked to find himself really enjoying telling people what to do. "I didn't know I had that in me," he says, "but I do."

Kohan and Mutchnick—brothers in arms when it comes to the pain and pleasure of showrunning—nod in unison.

Now it's time for all the young showrunning dudes to get back to work. Before lunch, Kohan and Mutchnick just finished working on their first Thursday night episode, but there are four more shows to go.

Have they rethought *Will & Grace* for Thursday night?

"Yeah," Mutchnick offers with a hearty laugh. "Will's not gay on Thursdays."

*DAVID WILD*

# Finales, Flame-Outs, and the Future Tense

Television is now so desperately hungry for material that they're
scraping the top of the barrel.

**Gore Vidal**

**W**ait, this can't be David—he's not circumcised," Kevin Bright
says with a tired laugh.

On the last day of Passover, Bright stands in front of a huge
replica of Michelangelo's *David* blocking a shot for the season's final
*Friends* episode entitled "The One in Vegas, Part 2," trying to make
one last masterpiece.

Bright explains to his cameramen his desired effect for this brief
establishing shot: "We think we're in Florence for a moment, then
we pull back and realize we're in the Caesars Palace gift shop."

Marta Kauffman stands nearby holding her one-month-old daughter while David Crane confers with fellow writers Adam Chase, Scott
Silvari, and Greg Malins. This is day four of five in the making of the
finale, which means Bright is in the thick of overseeing the camera
blocking of the most ambitious *Friends* episode since last season's high-

profile trip to England—a massive cross-continental success and a logistical nightmare to boot. For "The One in Vegas" episodes, a hundred extras are being used for the casino scenes—the sitcom equivalent of a cast of thousands.

Briefly there was talk of actually going to Las Vegas, but the decision was made to render Caesars unto *Friends*. The *Friends* production team has re-created Caesars brilliantly right here in fashionable Burbank— with some help from the staff at the actual casino, who wisely were thrilled at the prospect of a prime-time plug. And as things work out, a TV soundstage makes for a pretty natural faux casino, what with its lack of windows and its cavernous space, not to mention all the big money trading hands and the long odds against success.

The Bright Kauffman Crane triumvirate has survived the 1998–1999 season with the position of *Friends* strengthened. Post-*Seinfeld*, it's consistently the most popular comedy on television and arguably the best. Currently their other shows are in somewhat shakier condition. *Veronica's Closet*, while still highly rated, and *Jesse* are both "on the bubble" at NBC, meaning they could return next season or not. Tonight *Will & Grace* gets its first shot in the *Jesse* eight-thirty P.M. slot, with a *Just Shoot Me* repeat substituting for *Veronica's Closet*. Furthermore, there's word that Ira Ungerleider, who created *Jesse*, is leaving the show to develop under his own deal, and Amy Palladino, who ran *Veronica's Closet* this season, is departing.

Still, there's no sense of panic inside Stage 24. Rather, there's an aura of relief to be so close to the end of a long, demanding, and, in the case of *Friends* at least, extremely successful season. Jess Cagle of *Entertainment Weekly* stops by to do interviews for the magazine's "TV Winners & Losers" issue. *Friends* will take its rightful place in the winner's circle, having almost single-handedly kept the very concept of must-see-worthiness alive. The cast, meanwhile, continues to pop up in the strangest places. Last night Jennifer Aniston appeared on *South Park* as a music teacher who takes the boys on a trip to the Central American rain forest in the third season premiere, titled "Rainforest Schmainforest."

The *Friends* wrap party is at a rented mansion in the Hollywood

Hills, but before the celebration of this season can get under way there's the matter of ending on another hilarious high note. After Monday's table read, the *Friends* writers were working until five A.M. Greg Malins—who joined the show in the second season and who is now an executive producer with Adam Chase and Michael Curtis—recalls times when the writers worked straight through Monday night until the cast arrived at nine A.M. on Tuesday. "Some of our best episodes are totally rewritten Monday night," he says.

"The One in Vegas, Part 2" offers a typically amusing series of storylines. Ross and Rachel play pranks on each other, Monica and Chandler feud, Phoebe copes with a casino "lurker," and Joey meets his identical "hand double." As these scenes are blocked, the high-flying Steadicam gets some serious use this episode—Bright screened the film *Casino* as part of his preparation, and in some shots, he's bringing a Scorsesean ambition to this amiable sitcom.

Tomorrow "The One in Vegas, Part 2" will be shot in front of a live audience. At least most of it will be. The crowd will see Monica and Chandler impulsively head off to a Vegas wedding chapel. After that the bleachers will be cleared so Scene AA can then be shot. Scene AA is the soon to be heavily promoted cliffhanger ending in which Monica and Chandler discover that the couple coming out ahead of them is none other than a totally bombed Ross and Rachel.

"How's it going?" Matt LeBlanc asks Bright.

"Good, but this last one's a little . . . complicated," Bright warns with a grin.

Along the way there are the usual hassles. A veiled Siegfried and Roy gag doesn't clear legal. The music publisher for the Woody Guthrie estate may stop Joey Tribbiani from singing "This Land Is Your Land" to his hand double as "This Hand Is Your Hand." Few denials are taken lying down. Producer Todd Stevens argues his case all the way to Guthrie's daughter Nora. For the first part of the episode, Bright worked hard for his money as he fought to use Donna Summer's ultra-sexy disco anthem "Love to Love You Baby" during a prime-time near-nude scene by Aniston, despite initial objections from the Summer camp.

*DAVID WILD*

The next afternoon, time pressure claims its first casualty—the annual cast and crew photo is blown out. As the clock ticks, Bright debates absurdly small details, such as the proper water level in the wedding chapel fountain. Some on the set predict this episode could go until four in the morning.

When things get under way, nobody in the audience seems to mind the pace. It may help that there's an actual star, Sporty Spice of the Spice Girls, sitting in the crowd tonight. In the end, they are ushered out at about two in the morning—well ahead of most estimates—and the secret kicker is shot. A half-hour later, it's a wrap for the *Friends* fifth season.

David Crane isn't proud of the long hours, yet he feels *Friends* doesn't suffer for such perfectionism. "They're young and have energy and they manage to rise to the occasion," he says of the cast. "It's sort of a factor for us on *Veronica's Closet*—Kirstie tends to do her better work early in the evening rather than later. Still, nobody likes to work that late. Every season we determine we'll do it differently and we're not going to work as late. But, of course, we do."

A few days later at home, a more rested David Crane is thinking back to the August morning when he and his partners finished their first episode of the season with only sixty-seven to go. "It was a sinking feeling," Crane recalls. "I once ran a marathon—and only once—but I remember that in New York you go to the Library on Forty-second Street and they pick you up on a bus and take you to the start of the race in Staten Island. I remember this feeling of riding in this bus, it's still dark, and we're going through Brooklyn, and I'm thinking, 'Holy shit, I've got to run back?'"

Now at the other end of the race, besides exhaustion, there's a sense of accomplishment and relief. "As with the marathon, when I reached the end it wasn't even a clear emotional response, I just couldn't believe it was over, that we actually did it," he says. "That was the feeling I had this year. *Friends* had one of the strongest seasons it's ever had and that's a tremendous feeling. For my money, we haven't had a weak one. People thinking well of us makes me happy, but I never thought we went anywhere. And if you look at ratings, the viewers never thought we went anywhere either. The fade is an invention of the media as much as anything else. Also, I felt *Veronica's* was a stronger show than it had been the year before. I don't think it's everything it can be but certainly we got closer. *Jesse* . . . it's the first year and we're learning a lot. So, yeah, I felt very good about the season."

Crane believes the Monica-Chandler relationship helped this year of *Friends*, but that "each season has had its new areas, its new ways to approach these characters as they gradually grow up before our eyes."

One might think that, as the leader of the writers' room, Crane would already know how the gang will grow next season. "Not a clue," Crane confesses. "We have an eight-week preproduction period starting the middle of June. From the beginning of June to the beginning of August, we figure out 75 percent of it." What Crane has already figured out is that he doesn't want to focus on developing new shows for a while. "If I have my way I don't want to do any development until *Friends* is over," Crane says. "More is not better. Personally, creatively, emotionally. More is just more."

At the same time, Crane openly covets the prospect of more *Friends*, like the potential seventh season that is still being negotiated. "Nothing would make me happier," he says. "I want to do this until they make me stop. I know there are shows that writers get tired of. Not me. I'm loving this." So he's more than ready to write dialogue for the children of *Friends*? "Truly," Crane says, savoring the prospect. *Old Friends*.

Marta Kauffman shares Crane's desire for a seventh season and beyond. "I want this show to never end," she explains. "I sort of feel like this will be the high point of my career. I will never do anything in television after *Friends* that will come close to the creative satisfaction, the sheer joy of doing it. This show is something really special and when it's over it's going to change our lives enormously." Kauffman also has no interest in more development for the time being. *Jesse* was the first time the trio worked on a show they didn't create: "When David and Kevin and I originally formed the company we said, 'Yeah, we're going to do that. We can step back and be more like executives.'

*DAVID WILD*

I think this year we realized that's not really for us. It's too frustrating. We're control freaks."

Crane says that he and his partners are happier now that *Friends* has reached a more mature stage in its popularity. "I do think to a degree the kind of insane heat has died down, which is nice," he says. He finds the show's current temperature incredibly comfortable. "Yeah, now we're just a regular good TV show instead of this event. I think that's what prompted so much of the backlash. I don't think it's so much that the quality of the shows changed but people really resented the event of them—they looked at the cast and said they're too young, too hot, too pretty."

Don't forget too rich.

"Which is ironic because they weren't making nearly what other people were making in television," Crane points out. "A few months later the *Seinfeld* cast was negotiating for ten times what they were getting. It's like, come on, folks, lay off."

"We're not a phenomenal success anymore," Lisa Kudrow adds the next day. "We're a success but now everyone is not trying to pick it apart and figure out why. We've been around for well over one hundred episodes and it's just accepted that *Friends* is a good show, *that's why.*"

For Kauffman, "the glorious backlash" that once hit *Friends* was resentment that the show got too big too fast. To her "the storm" of popularity didn't really affect the day-to-day work. Yet in other ways, she feels, a price continues to be paid. "There are times when we feel like we're the unpopular kids in the class in terms of Emmys, Golden Globes," she admits. "I mean this show can't get an award no matter what it does. I think that's a shame because the work is really good—the writing, directing, cast, across the board. So I don't think we've come through it and everything's all peaches and cream now."

Still, Kauffman's proud of the season—"I'm proud we didn't kill ourselves," she says—and thankful her partners took up the slack when she was busy giving birth. "The shows look good," she says. "They're just happy I had my tubes tied."

Finally, does Crane feel proud he and his partners have helped prove network TV can still work big-time in a season that's often suggested otherwise?

"I certainly wouldn't want that burden," Crane says. "I'm just trying to do a good show every week. Speaking for network television? God forbid."

A month after NATO begins bombing, *It's like, you know . . .* is still alive. At home the morning before his critically acclaimed sitcom airs its fourth episode, the show's creator, Peter Mehlman, takes time out from his "not too taxing schedule" to ponder the absurdity of his show's premiere night as he awaits news whether his show is like, you know . . . picked up.

"I was sitting on my bed watching Clinton's speech and it started at five o'clock, which would be eight o'clock Eastern time," he remembers. "I was told that if it went past 8:36 that the show would be canceled on the East Coast and hence canceled all over the country. Which after everything we'd been through seemed kind of funny."

"Everything" has been an extended home version of the waiting game for everybody at *It's like, you know . . .* For Mehlman, it was already surreal enough doing the initial order of the show essentially in a vacuum, with a studio audience of a few hundred viewing the episodes instead of an entire grateful nation. Eleven months elapsed between the filming of the pilot and the airing.

Then things got truly strange. "There's all this hype and then there was this huge possibility that it wouldn't air," Mehlman recalls. "I'm thinking I can't believe the country's going to war, there's this virtual genocide, and all I'm wondering is, 'Will the show air?'"

Despite the unusual competition, the pilot still did well, thanks in part to an exceptional amount of early publicity and good press. Helping the show along in this regard was the novelty value of having Jennifer Grey playing and poking fun at herself, particularly at her nose job heard 'round the world. "The amazing thing is every-body knows there are a million actors and actresses who have had plastic surgery," Mehlman points out. "It became a big hook into the show even though it was such a nonstory really. Jennifer and I laugh about it now because the *Seinfeld* comparisons go on and on. I say to Jennifer, *Seinfeld* is my nose job."

Indeed, *Seinfeld* has become a touchstone in most reviews of the show, which was, after all, heavily promoted as coming from a pro-ducer of *Seinfeld*. But most favorably noted that the sitcom is graced by some of the same uncompromising wit. While much of the credit for all the press must go to the show itself, Mehlman's quick to share: "I guess this is the same at all networks—the very top people are hesitant to be superenthusiastic about a show. On the other hand, the people in the promo and publicity department have been unequivocally so."

It is all well and good that the boiler room came through for *It's like, you know . . .* but what about those captains steering things at the top of the network—the ones who have to renew it?

"There were certain executives who seemed to be with the show the whole time," Mehlman answers. "I think Stu [Bloomberg] always liked it—I believe he had some doubts whether it would really catch on, and that was a very legitimate point of view. I was never really exactly clear on how Jamie [Tarses] felt about it."

Mehlman doesn't expect to know anything definitive about the show's future until May, but he's gotten every indication from ABC that he should be thinking about putting together a writing staff for another season. Assembling one, however, isn't an easy mission. As *Seinfeld* is his only credit, he can't really afford any of his old collabo-rators. "It's hard for me to get people who I've worked with before—they all have deals and are committed elsewhere," he says. He also doesn't want to read scripts from other sitcoms. "I won't read some-body's *Friends* script because I don't really follow these other shows, and the fact is most are very 'gang written.' So I don't know what they've really done," he explains.

Mehlman views the prospect of returning for another season of the show with a mixture of excitement and anxiety. "It's a fifty-fifty split," he estimates. What if *It's like, you know* ... were to be canceled? "It would be 75 percent outrage and 25 percent relief." Recently, though, he realized that deep down he wants the show to continue.

Potentially, some of the leftover episodes of *It's like, you know* ... could air during the summer to help build momentum, but Mehlman would be happy to keep them in reserve for next season. "In theory, I'd like the seven episodes to air, do very well, and then sprinkle the other six in next season," he says. "Everything in sitcoms works against you. You're doing too many shows, one on top of the other. You finish one, the next one's right in your face." All the delays, however, have worked out. "Your regrets are tempered because the show is not firmly established as what it is," he explains. "So I have all this time to think about it."

Trying to turn that advantage to his creative benefit, Mehlman's planning on pushing the envelope further. "The more experimental and more unconventional the episodes, the better it's been for the show," Mehlman explains. "To be perfectly frank I was involved in *Seinfeld* for a long time and I'm creatively restless as far as just doing sitcoms and episodes and I feel like doing something different."

Along these lines, Mehlman's particularly interested to see what the reaction is to the seventh and final episode to air this season in early May. "Because there is truly nothing going on in that episode," he says. Most of the episode, entitled "The Conversation," is simply the characters of Robbie and Arthur talking about relationships and marriage—a willfully talky experiment in sitcom minimalism.

These days, with the future of the show still up in the air, Mehlman goes to the office in Studio City only once or twice a week, usually in the afternoon after he's gone to the gym. "All I do is hang out, bullshit with Berg and Shaffer," he admits, referring to two other former *Seinfeld* scribes, Alec Berg and Jeff Schaffer, who also have a deal with DreamWorks TV.

Thus far Mehlman has found his partnership with his fellow executive producer Ted Harbert pleasant and profitable, even though, or perhaps because, they look at everything from a different angle. It should come as no surprise that as a recovering executive who once ran a network—indeed the network that's now running *It's like, you know* ... —Harbert has shown considerably more interest in and understanding of the weekly ratings. Every Thursday morning Mehlman comes back from walking his dog at a quarter to eight and hears the phone ring. He says, "Hello, Ted" before he even hears Harbert's voice. "Ted runs down all the numbers," he says. "But first he says, 'Good news' and then basically everything he says after that is gibberish."

It's just after noon in Malibu, but Paul Simms is already preparing to get out of bed and head off to the local record store to pick up the new Tom Petty album.

He's heard "absolutely nothing" lately about the fate of *NewsRadio* and doesn't expect to until "whenever the last minute is." The other day Simms went to the first table read for his friend Drake Sather's pilot for *Sammy*, the animated David Spade show, and ran into NBC's Scott Sassa and Karey Burke. "They're very cordial, friendly," Simms reports, "but they seem to avoid the topic altogether of whether the show's picked up or not."

Now as Simms unwinds from his trying season amid clearing skies and ocean breezes, he seems almost mellow, but only almost. "For some reason, maybe it's because I'm on vacation, I just don't care," he confesses. "They picked up *Suddenly Susan* yesterday, and it's like, great. I'd like to do one more season, but, right now, I'm not in a frame of mind to fight for it."

Simms enjoyed completing the last few *NewsRadio* episodes, but since then he's not written a single word. "I keep thinking of things to write and I keep telling myself, 'no, don't write' because I've been working at this pace for eight years or whatever it is," he explains. "I'm trying to teach myself not to work for a while."

At the *NewsRadio* wrap party, Simms had seemed a little cozy with one of the actresses in the *OverSeas* pilot. Are they dating? "Shut up. That doesn't belong in your book," he insists. Apparently something nice did come of the pilot after all. "It actually is very nice," he admits. "It's been a long time since I've had a girlfriend I actually like." So is that the real reason he did the pilot? "No, I did the pilot to get a show on TV and do another good show for five years, I'll be honest with you," Simms says.

It was bizarre for Simms to watch *Suddenly Susan* renewed right around the time there was a death in the cast—the suicide of David Strickland. "Maybe it's a sympathy renewal for the guy who died," Simms says. "Andy Dick was with him that day, and partying with him. Andy is like the fucking black widow; I don't know what to do about him. I put him in rehab last year and he was fine all this season. Then at the end of the season he went off the wagon again. Then he's with that Strickland guy."

Having already coped with the death of Phil Hartman this season, Simms sounds sickened as he recalls watching the news coverage of Strickland's suicide and having to see *NewsRadio* footage, not just of Andy Dick but also of Maura Tierney, with whom Strickland costarred in *Forces of Nature*. "Andy gets himself in bad situations with bad people," Simms says, suddenly seeming less relaxed.

His voice brightens, interestingly, when talk turns to his recent deposition in the Garry Shandling case. "It was good," Simms offers. What, you might ask, makes for a good deposition? "It means it's over with," Simms explains. "It was ten hours long and it was the first time I've seen Garry since the night I went to his house and told him I was leaving." The estranged collaborators spoke briefly outside the lawyer's office. "It was fine, sort of cordial," Simms says of the legally inspired reunion. "It was just weird, very strange."

The case is now expected to go to trial in June. This could cut into Simms's beach time, but still the case sounds fascinating.

"Maybe to you," Simms says, laughing slightly. "For me, it's a pain in the ass." (The pain ends—the case settles.)

In two months Paramount will release the film *South Park: Bigger, Longer & Uncut* into American malls, but *Entertainment Weekly* dubs *South Park* "Loser of the Week," noting that the audience of this year's first two new episodes of the show was down 43 percent from the same period last season. Soon after this dubious honor, J.C. Penney announces it is going to stop selling *South Park* merchandise—its reason for the decision: complaints from customers. All this bad news arrives in the same month that sees the video release of such pivotal *South Park* episodes as "Cartman's Mom Is a Dirty Slut," "Cartman's Mom Is Still a Dirty Slut," and "Conjoined Fetus Lady."

Ohmigod, the glorious backlash has hit cable's punky poster boys!

Everyone, very much including executive producer and creator Phil Rosenthal, is loving Peter Boyle today on the set of *Everybody Loves Raymond*. The actor who plays Raymond's father, Frank Barone, is back to film his part in this penultimate episode of the season. In the end, Boyle missed only a couple of episodes as the result of his heart attack. This evening he'll film one key scene, then head back East to further recuperate during the hiatus.

Boyle—looking pale but sounding upbeat—makes his way onto the set, stopping for an interview with *Entertainment Tonight* to mark his return. Boyle tells the interviewer that everyone's being "so warm and well-wishing" and that he's okay, though he still gets a little out of breath.

Timing has helped *Raymond* stay on schedule despite recent setbacks. "The truth is that it just worked out that the episodes in which Peter played the biggest role took place when Patty was so pregnant we couldn't use her that much," Rosenthal explains. "Now that Patty has had her baby we're using her a lot more, so Peter had a lighter load in these last few episodes."

As a result, there's been remarkably little rewriting to do. Yet Rosenthal insists such issues were secondary—when Boyle was sick, he says he worried not about the show, only about his ailing friend. "To hell with the show, I could care less about that day's work or anything," he says. "That's kind of how it's been on the show. The show's about families, for families, and now it's being done by a family, I feel—we're very close."

Rosenthal's enjoying his time with the extended clan of *Raymond*— now an established hit around which CBS has built a successful night— so much so that he doesn't want to leave. By now he was supposed to be turning his attention to his deal with Disney and creating something new for them. "I've been stalling and stalling because I really want to stay on *Raymond* as long as possible," he admits. "Who knew that *Raymond* would take off and be a big success? I had no idea. It's something I always hoped for and always thought was warranted but I never thought it would happen."

In truth, Rosenthal is trying to postpone his Disney deal. Negotiations are ongoing. "CBS obviously wants me to stay with the show longer and Disney is very understanding of my feelings," he says. "It actually says that I'm loyal and if I created a show for them I'd be loyal to that show. Disney just wants to know. There's a lot of money at stake so they're looking to be compensated for this delay."

Rosenthal finds himself encountering separation anxiety without even separating.

"Yeah, I want to stay as long as possible here," he says. "I love the show and I love the people very much and I'm not stupid. This kind of thing doesn't come around very often."

For his part, Ray Romano is in no rush to let Rosenthal go either. "Phil is my first showrunner, so I can't gauge him against other showrunners," Romano says. "But I ask around. I'm amazed at what he does. Apart from writing, and running the room and the creative part, he amazes me with what he does on the floor with the actors. That is where I have the most anxiety about his leaving—picturing who's going to fill that spot. Handling the actors, there's a lot of egos involved. If you watch our show, the punch lines don't live and die on their own, it's all execution, a look, a tone. Sometimes we do a scene and it totally flops and I know Phil is going to come down and get it out of us."

Before the filming starts, the studio audience sees a playback of "Working Girl," which airs in two weeks. It's an especially funny episode in which Ray's wife, Debra, has a bumpy reentry into the professional world. As it plays, Rosenthal and Romano sit side by side offstage watching on a monitor. Phil laughs appreciatively; Ray laughs only once or twice, grudgingly. "Phil's a great laugher," Romano says later. "Aside from everything we're going to miss, we're going to miss that laughter."

Backstage is very much a family affair today. Romano's kids are here, as is Rosenthal's wife, Monica Horan, who is playing her returning character Amy, the girlfriend of Robert Barone, who's played by Brad Garrett. Rosenthal first glimpsed his future wife when she was onstage and he remains a big fan. "Whatever wife I had I'd have to put on the show, so thank God she's good," he says. "Otherwise, people might wonder."

At showtime, Romano takes to the stage to work the crowd. "This is the next to last show—we have one more next week and that's it," he tells the studio audience. "Tonight's a very funny episode called 'Robert Moves Back.'" Romano announces who wrote the episode but gets it wrong. "They all look the same to me, those writers," Romano jokes before correcting himself. "There are ten or eleven great writers headed by Phil Rosenthal, there's Phil Rosenthal, yeah." Romano then announces his own kids are here and brings them out. Possibly for his little ones' entertainment pleasure, Romano spontaneously leads the assembled in a spirited chant of "Phil Rosenthal is a doody-head."

After the first scene, Rosenthal migrates over to the catering table, sampling the pasta, the chips and guacamole, the hummus and pita. There are also healthy selections tonight—fruit and carrots. "It's going to be a clean set," Rosenthal promises. "A man had a heart attack here. Before the food just had to be great. Now it's gotta be healthy and great."

Tonight Boyle appears only in Scene H—a complex, uproarious scene that died a mysterious death during an earlier run-through. Writer Tom Coltapiano—an old standup buddy of Romano's—believes any other showrunner might have ordered the scene rewritten. "Phil knew it could work," the writer says. "He rechoreographed everything and it kills."

"You hear a lot of horror stories of shows where the writers are there until three in the morning the night before, rewriting scenes," Romano explains. "Part of it is they'll have a scene that is funny, will perform it in a run-through and not get any laughs, so they go and rewrite it. When in reality, everything has to be right: the timing, the blocking. And I don't know if other people have the ability to see it and get it—that's what Phil is great at."

As the evening goes on, Rosenthal discusses his plans for the break, which include going to New York for the May network upfronts, when the networks formally present their new schedules to the advertising community. "I'm going to help Les," he says, referring to CBS president Leslie Moonves.

Things move quickly tonight. Around eight-thirty, with only two scenes left to film, pizza and bottled water are served to the studio audience. Unfortunately, filming Scene H—Boyle's scene—is held up by an unexpected lighting problem. The generally amiable Rosenthal is suddenly and visibly pissed. "I never heard of a show where you can't make the lights go on and off," he declares angrily. This delay gives Romano a little more time to worry—"This doesn't track," he rushes over to tell Rosenthal about one line of dialogue.

Soon things calm down. "You get mad because you want the audience to be fresh, you want the energy from the audience, then something like *that* happens," Romano explains. "Phil's got a little temper on the floor but nothing . . . nothing to write in your book."

Eventually work resumes and a berobed Peter Boyle makes a grand entrance and sits down in a chair in Ray's kitchen in front of a big lasagna. Soon Boyle delivers a distinctive, hardy cry of "Holy crap" and it's clear that Frank's back and all is well with *Raymond*.

"Is Norm here?"

It's a little after ten A.M. on Stage 12 at Warner Bros. and the time has come for the last table read of the season for *The Norm Show*. Executive producer and cocreator Bruce Helford has expertly pinpointed the pressing problem—no Norm.

"We're waiting for Norm?" cast member Ian Gomez wonders aloud in mock surprise.

Seconds later Macdonald ambles in and takes his assigned place between Laurie Metcalf and Gomez at a table set up on the stage floor with the appropriate scripts and bottled water. Metcalf has a Wine Country travel guide right alongside her script, suggesting that she's already looking forward to the hiatus. Helford sits at one end of the table with the episode's director Steve Zuckerman, while seated around the table are a couple dozen other observers, writers on the show, and production crew, as well as representatives of the network and studio here to give their feedback.

"Welcome back to the tenth show of *Norm*," Helford tell the assembled group. He explains that this is the last week of production and the show has not been officially picked up for next season. "I just want to prepare those of you who haven't experienced this before for the weirdness ahead," he says. "Since we don't have our pickup yet, there's some anxiety. It's a very strange state, as some of us can testify, a sort of roller-coaster feeling—it's going to be interesting." In a warm, almost fatherly tone of voice, Helford reminds his cast and crew that *The Norm Show*'s numbers have been encouraging so far, but warns them that there will probably be no ultimate decision until May.

*Daily Variety* has reported that *The Norm Show* "cooled significantly" in its second episode, but it's still performing well and retaining a healthy percentage of its significant *Drew Carey Show* lead-in. Not that everyone's convinced—representatives of the National Association of Social Workers have already picketed outside ABC's New York headquarters, chanting "No degree, no show." Degree or not, Macdonald has continued to be unusually honest as he meets the press on his show's behalf, even confiding to *USA Today*'s Gary Levin, "I would like to do the minimum amount of shows to get into syndication and then quit."

With ninety episodes left to go, it's time to read this season's last, titled "Denby's Kid." Denby is Norm's new boss, played by veteran character actor Max Wright, familiar from his work on *ALF*. As of *The Norm Show*'s fifth episode, Wright has replaced Bruce Jarchow, who played Norm Henderson's first boss. In this episode, Norm encourages Denby's young son to follow his dream and attend the Culinary Institute rather than the Virginia Military Institute as his father insists.

True to the spirit of *Norm*, there's a slightly deviant twist—the kid's dream is to open a restaurant in which every recipe includes a very special seasoning, marijuana. On first hearing, the result's a veritable stoned-soul comic picnic. Macdonald mumbles distractedly through his first lines, but gradually grows more engaged once his character gets accidentally high.

After the table read, Helford heads upstairs to an office above the stage to receive network and studio notes. Usually Macdonald would sit in on the notes session, then accompany Helford back into the writers' room, but today he must grab a quick shave in preparation for a joint appearance with Metcalf on their old boss Roseanne's struggling talk show.

On the way over to the production office's men's room, Macdonald chats for a second with Max Wright, who is asked if he's found any similarity in working with Norm and ALF.

"Well, yes," Wright says dryly, "They're both juvenile."

During his shave, Macdonald addresses the wildly mixed critical reaction to the show. "I think some people really hate me," Macdonald says. "Some of them really hate my guts so they'll take shots at me they wouldn't on a regular sitcom. What I hate about reviewers is what bad writers they are. Sometimes they'll put little jokes in their reviews that suck, you know. Like 'This guy's funny . . . compared to an earthquake.' And they're criticizing the writing."

Once shaved, Macdonald heads to the stage for makeup, running right into Helford, who's just coming down the stairs from the notes session.

"Very few concerns, Norm," Helford reports. Everybody loves the script, apart from what they see as a slow start.

"Well, that's true," says Macdonald sardonically as he sits in a makeup chair next to Metcalf. Helford shares a couple more notes. The boy's lines are a bit "expo-y"—too full of overt plot exposition—and the character of Denby's son has to be clarified further, hashed out if you will. Helford cheerily adds that the network seems to support the episode's stoner humor.

"Is it all right for the kid to say, 'People love pot'?" Norm asks.

"We'll see," says Helford. He explains that when it comes to such controversial material the writers and the network each have their own responsibilities. "Ours is to be funny," he says. "Theirs is to be party poopers."

Helford only has time for a brief visit to the writers' room before he is due to oversee editing last week's episode of *The Norm Show*, then on to casting for this week's kid. After the *Norm* run-through tonight, Helford will be checking out the editing of *The Drew Carey Show*. Tomorrow he'll follow much the same process—but with the two shows reversed.

For a few minutes, ideas are tossed around the room about how to fix the show's first half, as the writers' assistant types away. The room will keep working until about one in the morning. Helford's trying to get all his shows edited before April 20, when he's going on vacation. As the nonflying Helford did that summer when Roseanne summoned him back to Los Angeles, he's taking a long cruise to Europe before beginning another season.

Before he sails off, Helford is asked if the odds of *Norm* coming back next season are better than fifty-fifty now.

"Just fifty-fifty," Helford insists. He says he doesn't want to say more than that, partly out of superstition. "The truth is they're very happy with the numbers. They love the characters and the stories. So everything's very positive right now, but a couple of weeks of bad numbers would take care of that real good."

The next week's ratings for both *The Norm Show* and *It's like, you know . . .* fall for a reason not hard to figure—many prospective sitcom viewers are otherwise engaged watching the breaking, not remotely funny news coming from Columbine High School.

Erstwhile *Cupid* executive producer Scott Winant is on the road again.

"I'm on the 101," says Winant, who's near the Coldwater Canyon freeway exit on his way from home in Santa Monica for postproduction work on the *Get Real* pilot in Burbank. The show will be turned over to Fox tomorrow and Winant is happy with the end product of what he hopes will be a new beginning. "It's excellent," Winant says. "I think it's some of the best work I've ever done, but if excellence were the criterion for getting on the air, things would be a lot different. As usual I'm doing aberrant material which isn't easily categorized, so somebody's going to have to step up and be courageous."

Whether or not anyone steps up, Winant—who has executive-produced and directed the pilot—has found the collaboration with creator Clyde Phillips (*Parker Lewis Can't Lose*) to be very stimulating. "Clyde and I, I will confess, do work differently," he says, "but he's very talented and I think we brought out the best in each other." Assuming *Get Real* gets picked up for fall, Winant would like to stay on with the show while also developing other projects with his partner Kelly McCarthy.

Already in the can is *Anna Says*, the pilot for ABC starring Tracy Pollan. "We've been holding it and we're going to submit it with the other fall pilots," Winant says, his phone cutting out momentarily in the canyons. "It was originally designed for midseason but we went late so we're going to hold it and submit it with everyone else." Winant is proud of the *Anna Says* pilot, though he understands it may be a hard sell.

All this work has meant that Winant hasn't had much time to catch up with his *Cupid* collaborator Rob Thomas. "We've talked but not a lot," he explains. "We're both sort of fulfilling our obligations right now." Winant confirms that the fact that he and Thomas are both set up at Fox is not a total coincidence. "We really do want to do another project together," he says.

Even though it's gone the way of all network flesh, *Cupid* lives on months after its cancellation in the hearts and minds of the few, the hardy. "Yeah, it's amazing, the twenty or thirty people who saw that show, I seem to keep running into them," Winant says with a chuckle. "I get a lot of compliments and a lot of sad looks, like they can't believe that it's canceled. I keep coming across one of two groups—either they've never seen it or they saw it and loved it." Winant has no delusions about which is the larger group.

Winant hasn't had time yet to stop by the *Snoops* set to visit Thomas, former *Cupid* star Paula Marshall, or two of the ex-*Cupid* writers now signed on for new duty with Thomas. "It sounds like it's old home week over there," Winant says.

As if his hands weren't already full, Winant has two or three other projects that he's trying to do with Kelly McCarthy under his Twilight Time production banner. "I'm excited about that and maybe doing some co-ventures, probably my highest priority being wanting to work with Rob again."

In the meantime, he will see what happens with *Get Real* and *Anna Says*, the latter of which puts him back in touch with some of the same ABC executives who killed *Cupid*.

"I have no hard feelings because I accept—I understand—the nature of the business I work in," he says philosophically. "Although I may not like it, there's nothing I can do other than dust myself off and do it again. I do have faith that one day my work and my time slot will all sort of jibe and I will be rewarded. That might be foolish to think, but I still have hope."

Speaking of hope—or perhaps Hope—Winant's former *thirtysomething* collaborators Marshall Hershkovitz and Ed Zwick have their own much talked about new pilot called *Once and Again,* starring Sela Ward. The buzz is the new drama will be a sort of *fortysomething* winner.

"I saw Ed about two days ago," Winant says. "Knowing those two, it has to be good. Ed told me he's frightened that they're going to be picked up."

It's an inside gag only a showrunner really gets—what's the only thing more painful than a pilot that doesn't get picked up?

One that does.

*Seven Days* is seeming to go on forever.

"This may be the most delayed episode in the history of the medium," says Christopher Crowe, with a tired laugh, of the season finale. There was no way around it. Cast member Norman Lloyd got double viral pneumonia—no small matter for a man in his eighties— and then the father of star Jonathan LaPaglia had a massive heart attack, which meant the show's lead had to take an unexpected trip to Brisbane, Australia. "We were down for eight or nine days," Crowe says, "hellish stuff."

That hasn't been the only real-life drama. As with other series, including *Buffy the Vampire Slayer* and *Promised Land,* an episode of *Seven Days* had to be pulled from the UPN schedule because of the tragedy at Columbine High School. Crowe was home watching the horrific news unfold when he realized there was trouble for the upcoming episode called "Save the Children," in which a group of young people are killed en masse by a terrorist attack. Though proud of "Save the Children," Crowe recognized that the episode was "suddenly tasteless," and he wanted his name pulled from the credits if it ran in the midst of the tragedy.

After a long, bumpy first season for *Seven Days* on UPN, Crowe has reason to feel a little like the leader of a really good band booked to play on the *Titanic*. The show is, however, expected to return in the fall.

First, Crowe needs to decompress, which is why he's heading to Hawaii this weekend. "Damn it all, I'm so goddamn tired," he says. The best news recently is some research Crowe received from Paramount which suggested that the show is connecting with its viewers despite all the hurdles. "This was from marketing guys—really dry, cold, miserable souls who only read numbers—and yet they were enthused," Crowe explains.

"Enthused" isn't quite the word to describe Crowe's attitude about a second season of *Seven Days*. "It's been a very difficult year," Crowe says. "Do I look forward to next year? Yeah, if we can make it less draining." For a reformed hard-liver like Crowe, however, the drain may actually have been healthy. "You know what this show has caused?" Crowe asks. "Sobriety. It's required it."

At the *Seven Days* wrap party at a Hollywood billiards club, Crowe stands alone for a moment in front of Sticky Fingers—a Rolling Stones tribute band who are providing the night's entertainment. As his cast and crew and staff eat, drink, and look merry, Crowe bops to the sound of faux rock gods with a funny new look on his face—something very much like satisfaction.

Jennifer Love Hewitt is in the men's bathroom trying to strike up a conversation with a middle-aged gentleman.

In reality, America's cutest cottage industry is off playing Audrey Hepburn for a TV movie during her summer hiatus, but Love's pretty oversized image still looms large this morning on the giant screen at the front of a dub stage on the Sony lot. On a couch in the back of the room, Amy Lippman oversees this final stage in completing *Time of Your Life*, the *Party of Five* spin-off pilot she has been cocreating and executive-producing with her longtime creative partner Chris Keyser. This key scene—which ends the third of the episode's four acts—finds Hewitt's character Sarah Reeves barging into an elegant men's bathroom to confront a distinguished theater impresario she's come to believe is her biological father. This is a big moment in *Time of Your Life*'s make-or-break pilot, and Lippman is taking her time to make sure every nuance is right.

"This is it," Lippman explains. "We'll get the sound right—levels, cues, sound effects, and we'll marry it to the pictures, then ship it." Soon the pilot will be "locked" and then "delivered" to Fox. This last part of the postproduction process can be crucial, yet even for a showrunner with Lippman's experience, such technical details can prove a bit elusive. "The funny thing is I don't know what a single button does in here except the ones on the phone," Lippman says with a laugh.

It is only a few long weeks until the mid-May upfronts when the networks announce their new lineups—the public proclamation of which pilots will fly. Before then, Fox must decide the fate of *Time of Your Life*, while CBS will determine whether Lippman and Keyser's other pilot *Partners* makes its fall team. Already these pilots are being sized up, an intense, only partly scientific process that will continue as they are quickly tested on focus groups and closely scrutinized. A combination of research data, politics, and pure instinct will influence which pilots will make the new fall schedules that are only now taking shape in the tortured minds of network executives.

One might think a show like *Time of Your Life*—with proven showrunners and a major youth star like Hewitt—couldn't miss, but Lippman knows otherwise, which is why she and Keyser have kept trying to get things right. A few weeks after production wrapped, for instance, they took the time to shoot the small, seemingly innocuous moment now on screen in the dub stage in which Sarah stands outside the men's room deep in thought. "We felt we needed to see Sarah debate going into the restroom to approach him," Lippman explains.

With the future of their series—or lack thereof—hanging in the balance, every frame counts. "I don't assume anything," says Lippman. "I absolutely think it could go either way. There aren't any guarantees with this stuff." Certain factors work in their favor—"I think Love's a huge star and she's committed to the series," Lippman says. "There's tremendous interest in the show, but I've stopped thinking there are sure things."

With *Partners*—in which Keyser and Lippman attempt to merge the cop genre with an intimate family drama—there is also reason for optimism. The duo's one-off deal with CBS for the show—which stars Marg Helgenberger (*China Beach*) and Johnathon Schaech (*That Thing You Do!*)—included significant penalties for early withdrawal. The network will pay a high price if *Partners* doesn't make its fall schedule. Like everything else in show business, however, such contractual commitments can become disadvantageous to enforce from a political and practical perspective. Lippman says she can understand the network's predicament in such situations. "Do you give people carte blanche if the show is no good?" she wonders. On the other hand, not picking up a show has serious implications. The future of *Time of Your Life* will likely shape Keyser and Lippman's relationship with Fox's new chief Doug Herzog—the fifth Fox president during their *Party* run. "Obviously our relationship with Fox would change if they don't pick up the spin-off," she admits.

Lippman finds talk of commitments and deals less interesting than the creative process. That's why God made agents. No matter what happens during this pilot season, Lippman—a showrunning vet at thirty-five—knows she and her partner won't likely go begging for work anytime soon. "There is so much need for product and there aren't that many tried-and-tested showrunners," she says. "If you've produced a show that's critically acclaimed or well produced, you'll dine out on it forever."

Leaving the dub stage, Lippman heads over to the nearby editing rooms, where she's checking on the main title sequences for the two pilots. The *Time of Your Life* sequence seems perfect—a gorgeously shot, instantly inviting audio-visual introduction into the show itself. We see Hewitt looking fetching in assorted Big Apple–flavored settings: getting in a taxi and swinging on a subway pole, all to a haunting song by British singer Beth Orton.

The *Partners* title sequence still needs a little work. The network rightly pointed out that while the drama is a relationship show set in a cop genre, the original main title sequence made it look more like a cop show with relationships. "It was a good note," Lippman says. "We all want the sequence to more accurately reflect the subject matter of the show." Unfortunately, finding the ideal images to convey such crucial information to the viewer can be difficult with only one episode's worth of visuals from which to draw.

Creating a pilot offers showrunners at least two overwhelming challenges. First they must deliver something that seduces a network into putting their show on the schedule. That oft impossible mission accomplished, they must figure out how to make an entire series out of the first offering. With *Time of Your Life*, Fox's questions were indicative of the fact that the show wasn't starting from scratch. The network wanted to know where the show would go from there. "It's like the question we got with *Party of Five*," Lippman says. "They said, 'When can the family move past the tragedy which defines them?' We said 'Eventually.' You have to establish the premise of the show before you're able to move past it." What Keyser and Lippman desire—like any creators—is that crucial time to discover exactly what their new show can become, time they weren't given for *Significant Others*.

Sometimes it comes down to luck. After initial filming in Los Angeles, *Time of Your Life* shot four additional days in New York. The plan was to fake March in New York for September in New York— easily done. The only problem was that the script also called for a freak September snowstorm as a major story point—a dramatic moment of chilly kismet for Sarah in the big city. A special effects house was hired to create the faux snow effect, but in the end such high-tech help wasn't needed. Lippman remembers it raining as cast and crew drove from a subway scene on Forty-second Street, uptown for the next setup. "On Fiftieth Street, it was still raining. On Sixty-third Street where we shot the scene, it was snowing. You look at the shot and you can't believe it's real. It was like a blizzard, beautiful and perfect and we saved a lot of money."

As Keyser and Lippman have worked hard creating not one but two new pilots, dividing and conquering all the jobs involved, *Party of Five* continues to make news. Recently there's been a big buildup to a lesbian kiss Julia Salinger (Neve Campbell) will be sharing during May sweeps as well as Campbell's own comments to *Jane* magazine that make it clear she's not the happiest of *Party* goers.

Lippman makes no apologies for Julia's brush with prime-time lesbianism—hot on the heels of the same character being beaten by her college boyfriend. "We thought it was the right story to tell when we told it," she says. "We didn't do it for titillation value. It's not why we told the story, although we'll take what we can get. It's not done in a gratuitous, let's-get-ratings kind of way."

As for Campbell's public complaint, Lippman seems more frustrated with the media. "It's irritating when they excerpt things she says and make it appear worse," Lippman says. "There was a story that said she was tired of the show. The quote actually was, 'It's exhausting doing a series.' And it is absolutely exhausting doing a series."

Of course, Keyser and Lippman could potentially have an exhausting three series going next fall. Not that they won't have plenty of help, especially when they finish staffing up. *Party of Five* will be looked over by Ken Topolsky—who's long run the physical production of the show—and a new showrunner, P. K. Simonds, who's replacing John Romano, who held that post this past season. Still, Keyser and Lippman won't abandon their first success. "The spin-off would be one thing that would keep us involved because it would require synergy with *Party of Five*," Lippman says. "We'd hope Sarah could go back and forth."

Do we smell heavily promoted sweeps visits between shows?

"I think there could be sweeps visits," Lippman agrees with a little grin.

First, there has to be a new show from which Love can come calling. The spin-off must be spun.

# All-You-Can-Eat Shrimp in Spin City

We shall stand or fall by television—of that I am quite sure.

E. B. White, 1938

*I*n a few hours NBC airs the season finale of *NewsRadio* on the West Coast. Back East, the show's remaining fans have already viewed what could be their last first-run transmission of Paul Simms's comic creation. Simms is spending this auspicious night at his rented Malibu beach house. In recent days, he's enjoyed all sorts of ultra-Malibu experiences—spotting neighbors Goldie and Kurt on the beach and stopping one of his dogs from attacking the pet of Steve and Eydie, all neighbors on this lovely, pricey stretch of sand.

Tonight Simms finds himself busy with less glitzy pursuits, splitting time between his two favorite Nintendo games—*Super Bomber Man* and *Star Wars Rogue Squadron*. Such diversions relax and entertain him, certainly more so than the less clear-cut, tougher-to-win games he's been playing lately with NBC.

May is a month of drawn-out, high-profile departures—*Mad About You*, *Melrose Place*, and *Home Improvement* are among the most publicized departing prime-time shows. For tonight's *NewsRadio*, there has been no such hype. NBC, for whatever reasons, seems to be on the verge of letting one of its best shows die an oddly quiet death.

"Well, NBC has about an hour and a half left, so we'll see what happens," Simms says with a chuckle. "Tonight is probably the last episode, and I guess I should figure out some way to celebrate. I hate to admit it, but the way I'll probably celebrate is by watching *Futurama*. I really like it."

Having thrown himself back into *NewsRadio* after the failure of the *OverSeas* pilot, Simms now seems ready to put it all behind him. The other day, Scott Sassa finally called, the first time he and Simms had spoken since *NewsRadio* wrapped. It was small talk, Simms says. They spoke about life at the beach and the difficulties of commuting. Finally, Simms broached the talked-around topic: "I said, 'What's going on with your network and my show?'" Sassa put Simms off a little more, telling him NBC was still reviewing the pilots. "So keep checking in," he added. Simms, resigned, said, "Okay."

"It's hard," Simms says, "after five seasons, to still be getting a 'We're still waiting to see what our pilots are like' phone call, which basically means 'We hope we get a pilot that's better than your show. If we don't, you're in luck.'"

Simms laughs at the indignity but his weary voice suggests the increasingly uphill trajectory of his battle is beginning to wear down his resolve to keep *NewsRadio* on the air. He confides quietly, "I'm sort of leaning toward wanting just to let it end now. I don't even know if I want to keep doing this. I think I want to retire for a year."

Certainly retirement would seem premature at Simms's age, but with each new offer to his writing staff, any future for *NewsRadio* looks less and less likely. "Brian Kelly went and he's working with another guy at Disney on the animated *Clerks* show," Simms reports. Writers have gone to *Just Shoot Me*; others are talking to *Frasier* and *Futurama*. "They're starting to all scatter," he says with no malice.

Recently, Simms has discussed these issues with two *NewsRadio* cast members—Maura Tierney and Andy Dick. "And I think Andy was drunk at the time so that doesn't count," Simms says. "I guess the right thing for me to do is call them and ask them what they think, but I've been putting that off."

Simms is heading to Manhattan in a couple of days, not for the network upfront presentations, but instead for a publication party for *Turn of the Century*, the new novel by his onetime *Spy* boss Kurt Anderson. Simms actually had a hand in helping Anderson's dead-on send-up of the TV business. He has no regrets about not sticking around for the network hoopla. "I'm not gonna be there for that upfront bullshit," Simms explains. "I hate it."

The upfronts—the annual presentations of the fall schedules for the advertising community—are arguably the year's most important TV extravaganzas. It's a process that keeps the entire enterprise of network television afloat.

Before the new schedules are even set, however, the networks go through an intense, largely secretive week of decision-making that varies slightly from network to network. It's the time of the season, Simms explains, when every day is "wall-to-wall bullshit." Pilots go from manna to muck in a flash. "This is when the network people feel like it's their time," Simms says. "Everyone's spinning everything."

As Simms speaks, NBC has just completed its second day of formal pilot discussions. Members of the network's various departments gather in groups of ten to watch and evaluate pilots. Learning of NBC's relatively open-door policy in this regard scares one showrunner from a competing network. "The fact that someone from business affairs could be deciding the fate of a show is the most fuckin' frightening thing I've ever heard," he says, shuddering at the thought.

Fifteen pilots are being considered by NBC. There are also opportunities to judge episodes of four current shows now considered up in the air or, in industry terms, "on the bubble"—*Veronica's Closet*, *Jesse*, *Homicide*, and *NewsRadio*. This process goes on for four days, and then a group leader communicates the consensus to the higher-ups. These TV juries constitute only part of the decision-making process. Hard research is carried out in the form of cable tests, in which the shows are piped into Middle America and participants fill out long forms, as well as old-fashioned focus groups. At the end of each day, the groups are presented with the data on the shows they have just dissected. Finally, the powers-that-be—this year a troika of the departing Don Ohlmeyer, Scott Sassa, and the newly incoming Garth Ancier—get together and make the life-or-death calls.

Inside the biz, the buzzing escalates to a din. Agents call, desperately looking for an inside word from anyone—middle managers or loose-lipped secretaries. Eventually, the schedules will come into focus—or what passes for focus in this myopic business. The decisions are made, the actors and often showrunners are called, frequently at the last minute, and informed whether they need to head to New York or not bother.

Simms isn't planning on showing up either way. He's asked if there's anything at all he's liked about the upfronts. "Yeah, lots of free shrimp," he says after a moment's thought. "You can get a little Coca-Coca with a miniature straw and a napkin, but after a while, the whole thing makes me nauseous."

A couple of years back—when he was perched atop the ABC Entertainment food chain—Ted Harbert was one of those behind closed doors in these early days of May, playing programming god as he sought to fashion a winning fall schedule. Today, as others tackle the future of prime time, Harbert finds himself waiting like so many other mere mortals to see if his show, *It's like, you know . . .* , will survive the cut.

Harbert, wearing shorts and a T-shirt, sits in the third floor of his recently completed new house in the canyons. There's no chance of his donning a suit today. "If I put on long pants, it will be a big deal." At ABC, he explains, the scheduling process takes place inside a screening room big enough for forty-eight. The seats are filled by everyone from Disney chairman Michael Eisner down to the directors of development and employees at lower levels.

ABC's Stu Bloomberg and Jamie Tarses, he says, will have put some time into selecting the order of the pilot presentations. After each one is screened, the lights come up and the head of comedy development or drama development nervously waits to hear the collective wisdom. These screenings will continue at ABC; then the process falls to a small group of key decision-makers. In such an inherently political business, the lobbying can become intense. "I was a big believer in giving everybody their shot, but you have to limit it," Harbert says. "You'd give the studio head a shot to make his case, the executive producer, and an agent here and there."

For TV executives, this is the most exciting and draining time of the year. "It's the Olympics," says Harbert. "It is exciting but it's also a very flawed system. You look upon it with no small amount of dread."

The biggest glitch, Harbert believes, is the dependence on research. "I am so bored with how long networks have been talking about how ineffective the research system is," he says. "There's so much proof that it's just so wrong. Yet there it is every year. Management is afraid to get rid of it and save millions of dollars. The truth is most shows that test miserably fail, so you can usually be right by keeping off a show that tested badly. *It's like, you know . . .* tested badly. There were those who tried to keep it off because it tested badly—that would have been a mistake."

As Harbert sees it, the reason for this dependence is the false sense of security such data gives upper management. "They use numbers as a crutch," he says. "That's buying into the whole idea that this research really represents what America thinks—and that's demonstrably false. What is demonstrably true is that giants like William Paley, General Sarnoff, and Leonard Goldenson looked at the research, threw it in the wastepaper basket, and put on what they wanted."

Having picked a schedule, the network must then sell it to the advertising world, as well as some media and affiliates. "That's where network people deserve their high salaries, because the scheduling process alone is enervating," Harbert reports. "You'd go from this intense, internal boot camp of putting together a fall schedule; then you've got to turn into a showman, a totally different skill than scheduling." Some network chiefs call upon proven comic talent, such as CBS's Les Moonves, who gets help from *Everybody Loves Raymond* creator Phil Rosenthal. Harbert enjoyed writing his own material, with mixed results. "I wasn't that smart," he says. "Sometime I bombed; sometimes it worked."

Having looked at ABC from both sides now, Harbert thinks the odds for a second season of *It's like, you know . . .* are good. "I don't put much faith in rumor or the conventional wisdom—that we're a shoo-in to get picked up," Harbert says. "Anything can happen and often has." When he gets the telegram saying the show's picked up, he'll believe it.

The irony is that even if *It's like, you know . . .* is renewed, Harbert may be gone. Rumors have it he could be returning to the executive life—possibly as president of Columbia TriStar TV. "I'm so torn," Harbert admits. Harbert has loved working with Mehlman— the forced marriage arranged by DreamWorks has been a surprisingly happy one. At the same time, opportunities are knocking that may require taking his suits out of mothballs.

If Harbert were still running ABC, he says he would keep *It's like, you know . . .* on the air. As he sees it, what's strangling television is its homogenization. "More-of-the-same isn't working," he says. "Now it's killing the business. It's no longer profitable. Time's up."

Earlier today President Clinton held his youth summit at the White House, where he was joined by gun manufacturers, gun control advocates, clergy, network executives, Mothers Against Violence, Maya Angelou, former *Melrose Place* star Andrew Shue, and Gloria Estefan. Inspired by recent tragic events at Columbine High School in Littleton, Colorado, Clinton, from the comfy pulpit of the Rose Garden, made quite a show of criticizing what he perceives as "a coarsening of the culture."

Two of America's favorite cultural coarseners, Trey Parker and Matt Stone, are otherwise engaged, trying to finish up work on *South Park: Bigger, Longer & Uncut*—the big-screen version of their small-screen phenomenon. Making the movie has not been easy. "It was a clash," Parker admits. "We had our system for doing things, the studio has their system. They're like, 'This is how you do a movie.' And we're like, 'Well, this is how you make *South Park*.' It was a constant battle."

Surrounding the pair are cards with evocative descriptions of the movie's scenes, for example, "Saddam's Detachable Penis." The film looks to be your average R-rated animated musical movie about censorship, war, and sodomy between Saddam Hussein and Satan. (When it is finally released, *South Park: Bigger, Longer & Uncut* will earn some of the most positive reviews of the year—stronger than the late great Stanley Kubrick receives for *Eyes Wide Shut*.)

With some critics suggesting that *South Park* is past its peak and others reaching to link the show to the problems of our youth culture, it has been a chaotic, largely sleep-deprived few weeks for the pair. "As soon as we came out with *South Park*, the media was saying, 'This is trite stuff. It won't have any impact,'" Parker points out. "Now they bring us up when they talk about America's youth, and how we're to blame. It's like, I thought we were trite and we would have no impact."

*South Park* has thus pulled off the neat trick of being viewed as both insignificant and influential. Parker remembers watching a journalist ask in a press conference about a young man questioned in the Columbine murders who was wearing a *South Park* T-shirt. Parker was relieved when the sheriff pointed out that lots of the kids running out of the school that day were also wearing *South Park* shirts.

Neither Parker nor Stone regrets a thing they've done on *South Park*. They don't believe they're part of the problem.

"Not at all," Parker says. "Not for a second. We grew up with *Monty Python*, as fucked up as that all was, and *Dirty Harry* and Charles Bronson and ultraviolence. People seem to forget that the world's been ultraviolent for a long time. Both of us—and all our friends—grew up in that culture and we're fine. There's nothing

*DAVID WILD*

about Marilyn Manson that says, 'Pick up a gun and kill people.' And there's nothing about *South Park* that says that either."

Stone—who coincidentally took his SATs in the Columbine cafeteria—explains that like anyone else, he watched the news footage and felt confused and saddened, struggling for some sort of explanation. "The explanation is that some people are fucked up. That's a scary answer—but it is the answer," Stone says. "When someone older does something sick, it's like, 'What a psychopath, what a perverted sociopath, what a nut.' When someone under the age of eighteen does something, then we have a huge problem with youth culture."

This month Parker gives the commencement speech at his own old high school. His opening line: "What the hell am I supposed to tell you?" Predictably, the speech goes over well. The kids love it. Some of the teachers even hand Parker résumés.

The show has become emblematic of the success of cable and the sort of edgier programming it offers. Perhaps some of the negativity is the empire striking back. If ever two people were perverse enough to wallow in their own backlash, it would be Parker and Stone. But the pair confess that they've found these outbreaks of negativity frustrating, even though they've seen it coming with the help of a friend who's been there. As Parker says, "Mike Judge—who did *Beavis & Butthead*—told us, 'This is how it's going to happen.' He gave us an exact map of how our popularity would go, how we'd peak and then it would drop and then level out. He warned us people would start calling us 'sellouts' just for doing the same thing they called us 'geniuses' for before."

For Stone, it is all proof that there's a formula to the way everyone gets chewed up in the gears of pop culture.

"What's so funny is that everybody who's dissing *South Park* thinks they're being so rebellious," Parker points out, "but it's all actually going according to the fame handbook." Whatever happens to the *South Park* movie, the pair say they are happy they still have the TV show. Last night, they had to leave work on the film to rush back and—as Parker charmingly puts it—"shit out a new script." Both are thrilled with the result and declare themselves "psyched" to return to the small screen.

**THE SHOWRUNNERS**

"Because making this movie is such a fuckin' pain," Parker explains. "It made me realize how much I like doing the TV show."

"In our setup, because we just barf it out, it's great and very creatively satisfying," Stone adds.

There is some buzz in the industry that the sitcom as a form is in decline—a turn of events that thrills both Parker and Stone.

"We hate sitcoms even more now," Parker says.

"I don't think the sitcom will die," Stone says, "but God, I wish."

If sitcoms are becoming less dominant on the networks, perhaps that will help the increase the niche-value of Comedy Central, *South Park*'s cable home.

"I hope so," Parker says. "I hope they're not counting on us. If I was the president of some company and we were, like, laying the golden egg, I'd be pretty fuckin' scared."

To the shock of no one in attendance, the upfronts turn out to be less about being upfront than about spinning. That and—as Paul Simms correctly suggested—all the free shrimp.

NBC goes first with its presentation at Lincoln Center's Avery Fisher Hall on Monday afternoon. Word has already leaked out that *NewsRadio* has been canceled, along with *Homicide* and *Caroline in the City*. For weeks, these shows shared space "on the bubble," but now the bubble has burst.

To make matters worse, on the morning of the NBC event, the papers carry further discouraging news for *NewsRadio* fans—Andy Dick has been arrested after driving a car into a utility pole in Hollywood and attempting to run away. Cocaine and marijuana, it's said, were found in his car. Dick's show isn't on the fall schedule, but his name will soon be on the court dockets.

For others, there is better news. In the entrance foyer of Avery Fisher Hall, Kevin Bright checks in. He is representing his partners here. After wide speculation that either *Veronica's Closet* or *Jesse* wouldn't make it back for fall, it turns out that Bright Kauffman Crane again will have three shows on the air.

"It was very last-minute," Bright admits with a grin. He and his partners figured they would have only two shows on the fall schedule, but "the miracle of three has returned." Bright Kauffman Crane knew *Veronica's Closet* was coming back two weeks ago. *Jesse* got the pickup only this past Thursday. Had NBC opted to let the latter show go, there was already interest from the WB. "I think NBC maybe would have liked their development to turn out a little better," Bright says. "The main thing with *Jesse* is the network has total belief in Christina as somebody who could make a show work," he says. "Everybody believed in that and while the show needs some retooling, everybody was ready to wait till midseason." Instead it's on for fall. *Friends* alumni will run each of Bright Kauffman Crane's other two shows. Wil Calhoun will reinvent *Jesse* while Jeffrey Astrof and Mike Sikowitz try to tidy up *Veronica's Closet*. "We robbed Peter a little bit to pay Paul," Bright explains as he heads off to find his seat.

Inside the great hall a giant screen reads:

**NBC**
**PRIMETIME**
**PREVIEW**

The *Saturday Night Live* band warms up the crowd with songs like "Hot Fun in the Summertime" and "Kiss and Say Goodbye." The NBC presentation has been created in the style of a *SNL* episode, with members of that show's cast kicking things off and popping up throughout the proceedings. Soon our "host" Scott Sassa is introduced. His monologue isn't hilarious but it seems heartfelt. "Standing up here today is a real dream come true for me," he says. He speaks of NBC's programming legacy—where some of the greatest leaders in TV stood before him—Fred Silverman, Grant Tinker, Brandon Tartikoff, and Don Ohlmeyer. He publicly thanks Ohlmeyer as a partner and mentor. "Don will be remembered for taking the network from being number three to number one, and he did that when there were six networks," Sassa says. Sassa mentions some of the notable shows that hit on Ohlmeyer's watch, among them *Friends* and *Will & Grace*.

*Will & Grace*'s David Kohan and Max Mutchnick take seats together right at the front as Sassa speaks. The buzz is that *Will & Grace* lost a Thursday night slot at the last minute. Instead the show has landed back on Tuesday night with *Just Shoot Me*.

A veteran of cable, Sassa takes some time to defend the networks. "Many critics believe there is nothing good on broadcast television," he says. "We strongly disagree with this. The reality is this is a fantastic time to be a network TV viewer. You've got shows like *The Simpsons, The X-Files, Touched by an Angel, The Practice, Ally McBeal, Everybody Loves Raymond, Home Improvement, King of the Hill, Sports Night, 7th Heaven, Dawson's Creek, NYPD Blue, Star Trek: Voyager,* and I'm sure I'm missing some other shows."

"*Will & Grace*," Mutchnick whispers to Kohan.

Sassa continues, explaining that he wasn't mentioning any NBC shows "because I didn't want you to think I was being biased." He tells the crowd that the highest-rated comedy show in cable is *South Park*, yet *Friends* delivers ten times as many adults. Having defended networks in general, he moves on to defending his own network.

"The perception is NBC is down and not in first place," Sassa tells them. "The reality is we're on the upswing and we're firmly in first place. . . . Later this week CBS is going to tell you that they've made significant gains in households, and they have. But you as advertisers, you as our affiliates, you don't buy and you don't sell households. The currency we trade in is demos. CBS is in fourth place in demos." No mention is made that NBC is down 14 percent in total viewers, 18 percent in the key eighteen to forty-nine demographic.

Sassa brings out Garth Ancier, and the former WB boss confirms his current view that NBC is indeed "poised for growth."

To break things up, stars are brought out for brief appearances. "Nice to see y'all," David Spade says when he comes out to speak briefly about his animated show *Sammy*, which is now scheduled to premiere in midseason. "It's good to be here for this three-hour day of information. I think most of us realize this day could have been covered in a fax."

By the time Sassa announces the new Thursday schedule, Kohan and Mutchnick exit to the NBC tent outside, where they hang a bit with the *Providence* team.

The presentation's high comic moment comes during an appearance by Conan O'Brien. "Thank you, Warren," he tells Sassa, before blaming his slip-up on some old cue cards. "I'm sorry that Warren retired," O'Brien says. "I wish he could have been here tonight—but apparently he's busy. He's working on an off-Broadway production of *Conrad Bloom*. Don't you like the new slogan for NBC—'Let Us Entertain You'? Isn't that a great slogan? I think it's much better than last year's slogan—'Let Us Squander an Incredible Lead.'"

Also good for a laugh is Matthew Perry's Letterman-esque list of the Top Ten Things to Expect Next Year on *Friends*.

10. Charles Manson joins the cast and the following week there are only three of us.

9. The gang starts hanging out at a bar because that's what people our age actually do.

8. They change the name of the show to *Chandler and Some of the People He Tends to Hang Out With*.

7. We all get even bigger apartments just to piss off the critics.

6. We stop dancing in a fountain because nobody does that.

5. Matthew Perry is currently shooting a movie opposite Bruce Willis. (How did that get in there?)

4. Chandler, Phoebe, and Rachel have a threesome.

3. Chandler and Monica go on a cruise. The ship hits an iceberg. Chandler chooses to save everyone but Celine Dion. (That's a one-hour.)

2. They change the name of the show to *Dateline* so they can officially announce that *Dateline* is on NBC twenty-four hours a day.

1. Once again, Chandler, Phoebe, and Rachel have a threesome.

**THE SHOWRUNNERS**

After the presentation, the crowd moves quickly to a nearby party tent set up with an impressive spread. As the tent fills up, Kevin Bright takes a shrimp off a server's platter and explains that after Perry wrote his top ten list, he called to make sure nothing would offend the sensibilities of Bright Kauffman Crane. "I only gave him one note: His original number ten began 'O. J. gets added to the cast.' I said, 'I know Don Ohlmeyer isn't going to be there, but why put salt in old wounds? Matthew said, 'I need another serial killer.' So I gave him Charlie Manson."

As for negotiations regarding the future of the show past next season, Bright allows, "There have been active discussions that have been very pleasant and very unpublicized, which is a good thing. It's complicated." (By July, it's reported that NBC was close to a deal that would pay Warner Bros. Television approximately $5 million for each episode of *Friends* through the 2001–2002 season.)

Toward the back of the tent, photo booths have been set up so partygoers can line up and pose with cast members of shows both old and new. A line builds for Brooke Shields, who is here and looking lovely despite a few rough months, what with the death of her *Suddenly Susan* cast mate and friend, David Strickland, and the breakup of her marriage to Andre Agassi. Still there's a show to be promoted. Midway through her picture session, a tipsy-looking affiliate from the Midwest hands an NBC employee his drink and takes his turn beside the star. "So you're single again," he barks. The NBC representative looks horrified, yet Shields keeps her composure and smiles until the man can be ushered away.

A big crowd also gathers to take pictures with the cast of *Will & Grace*. Debra Messing—who plays Grace—is off in Morocco playing Mary Magdalene in a TV movie. Eric McCormack, however, is here, having flown in this morning from L.A., where he's just finished acting opposite Jennifer Love Hewitt in the Audrey Hepburn TV bio flick. McCormack has already come to terms with the non-Thursday time slot. "It's a glass half-empty or half-full thing," McCormack says. "We know on Tuesday we can be a bigger fish in a slightly smaller pond, but it was sure nice being a top ten show for a while."

*D A V I D   W I L D*

Later Kohan and Mutchnick admit to being disappointed though not dejected. Tuesday's been good to them. Still, Mutchnick confesses, "When you go and rent a Fifth Avenue apartment and you stay there for a while, you can get used to it. So when you have to move, it bumps your perspective a little. I still think we're in good shape."

Despite any letdown, the pair are having fun this week, staying at the St. Regis on the network dime and doing the party scene.

"It's been fantastic," Mutchnick says grandly. "Who wouldn't love a week at the St. Regis and Kathie Lee, all expenses paid by the National Broadcasting Company?"

"Kids who are getting away with something," Kohan adds. "That's what we feel like."

Mutchnick also points out he is happy to see that Will was allowed to come way out of the closet in this year's upfront presentation, a long leap from last year when NBC was "basically—one could say—hiding the fact that Will was gay."

As he leaves the NBC party, Scott Sassa is asked if he has spoken to Paul Simms about the cancellation of *NewsRadio*.

"Not yet," he says.

Tuesday morning kicks off with the presentation by perhaps the only network that can really be said to be growing—the WB. While total viewership held steady during 1998–1999, the network was actually up 2.2 million in the key demo. Outside the Sheraton New York Towers, the Dubba Bus, the network's promotional vehicle bearing the image of the network's frog mascot, is parked. Inside the hotel, the advertising crowd sucks down the free coffee and pastries. Apparently, nine A.M. is too early for shrimp.

Inside the ballroom, an overflow crowd take their seats, while all around an impressive slide show flashes images of the network's mostly young and hunky cast members. Stars of *Buffy the Vampire Slayer, Felicity,* and *7th Heaven* pop up in a series of ever-changing images.

The real audience today isn't the WB-ready kids, or the media, but people like Julie Friedlander, senior partner, director of national broadcast negotiations for the advertising firm Ogilvy & Mather, who's saved a bunch of prime seats up front for her blue-chip clients.

Friedlander started attending these events back in 1976, and she's seen it all. Whatever the networks are selling for next season, people like Friedlander and her clients are the buyers. Indications are that despite network TV's problems, they'll be buying big and for record prices.

These presentations used to be far more intimate, Friedlander recalls. "There were probably a hundred of us in the beginning," she says. "The buying departments have grown because we're buying sixty, seventy channels." Today, she is accompanied by representatives of companies like Hershey, IBM, and Kimberly-Clark—big shots who control the purse strings. Afterward, she and her colleagues will review the upfronts for their clients and offer predictions of future performance. They are looking not only to see what's going to be a hit, but also what shows look suitable for specific products. Her client from Kimberly-Clark happily advertises on WB shows—Huggies, for example, on *7th Heaven*; and Light Days, a feminine hygiene product, on *Dawson's Creek.*

As the lights dim, Friedlander is asked about the best and worst presentations she's ever seen. The best proves elusive. "The worst was Fox's first," she recalls. "It was in Central Park, it started to rain, the tent collapsed, and there was a bird flying around. They had to call it off. Then they gave out umbrellas a few months later saying, 'I survived the Fox new season presentation' or something like that. It was an absolute disaster, but they've clearly gone on to greater success."

Jamie Kellner, a former Fox executive, explains that in television, the real Y2K problem isn't about computer malfunction. It's the decreasing audience the Big Three offer advertisers. "Fortunately," he points out, "there have been companies like Fox and the WB who have come along to try to drive new viewers into entertainment programming in prime time." It's pointed out the WB's median age is 26.6, while CBS is at the other extreme, with a median age of 52.5.

Jed Petrick, the executive VP of sales, speaks of wanting to build the network of choice for "future adults—also known as teens." Young adults, he reminds, are highly receptive to advertising. In announcing the schedule, Susanne Daniels, president of entertainment, and Jordan Levin, executive vice president of programming, stress that the WB's emphasis on drama over sitcoms has been vindicated, since dramas have been losing less ground.

If the WB was ever a bit shy about trumpeting its biggest show, *7th Heaven*, it is not so today. Unfortunately, Brenda Hampton isn't here to enjoy the show of support. Her invitation arrived too late, and she's just returned to Los Angeles after taking her daughter and new husband to New York. "I think you have to have three shows on to be invited a full week in advance," Hampton explains.

Daniels says, "1995 was also the year we introduced talented comedy writer Brenda Hampton to Aaron Spelling. The result of course was *7th Heaven*, the fastest growing show in television. *TV Guide* called *7th Heaven* the best program you're not watching. Well, that was then, and this is now. Not only is *7th Heaven* the WB's highest-rated show, but on February 10, 1999, the night the twins were born, more viewers watched *7th Heaven* than any of its competitors in the eight P.M. hour. . . . Most of you in this room are strong supporters of *7th Heaven* and you've been rewarded."

Daniels speaks of the difficulty in finding the perfect companion piece on Monday nights. "We finally wised up and asked Brenda and Aaron to create a program which will naturally flow out of *7th Heaven*," she says. "They responded with *Safe Harbor*, a show that once again matches the warmth of Brenda's writing with Aaron Spelling's unparalleled expertise."

"On the coast of Florida, in a little town called Magic Beach, in an unusual home lives an unconventional family," a voice-over proclaims as the clip teases the story of a sheriff and his four sons. "Protecting an entire town isn't easy, but John Loring is about to learn that fatherhood is the toughest job of all."

After the clip is over, *7th Heaven*'s Stephen Collins and *Safe Harbor*'s Gregory Harrison address the crowd.

Collins speaks eloquently about the show and its impact. "Wherever I go in the world now, kids come up to me on the street and tell me they wish they could become part of the Camden family," he says. "It's a family, they tell me, that is so uncool, it's cool."

"We want to build on what *7th Heaven* has established in the eight o'clock hour," Harrison adds. "I think you'll find that *Safe Harbor* has the same family values as *7th Heaven*, but of course we're wrapped in a totally different package. For one thing, I'll be carrying a badge instead of a Bible."

Even though *Safe Harbor* was developed specifically for its time slot, Hampton admits the process hasn't been easy. "The network doesn't get the concept of the all-male show they told me to write," she says. The pilot will be reworked, and some recasting done. "It was much easier when I did *7th Heaven*," she says. "I was writing what I wanted to write and no one was paying any attention. I have no idea whether a show designed for a specific audience will work or not. The network seems to have every confidence, so I'm very happy to have a second show on the air."

Elsewhere the WB is offering hour after hour filled with every sort of sexy young "future adult"—from alien (*Roswell*) to vampire (*Angel*—a *Buffy* spin-off) and, what the hell, even human (*Popular*).

Whatever the WB's message may be, it appears to be connecting with an audience. There's something curiously hopeful about all the talk of "future adults," perhaps because the phrase itself at least implies that there is a future.

Later in the day, ABC takes its turn; its total viewership and key demo numbers are both down 4 percent. The show begins with a little song and dance from *The Drew Carey Show*, a preview of a production number of "Brotherhood of Man" from *How to Succeed in Business Without Really Trying* that will be seen in the *Carey* season finale.

Bruce Helford's still cruising along on vacation, but Carey himself does fine putting this big moment in perspective. "It's so great to be here—isn't it amazing how every year the world gets saved by a prime-time network schedule?" Carey tells the audience. "You're gonna have so much smoke blown up your ass, you're gonna get cancer." Referencing Michael Eisner's recent legal battles, Carey offers this: "I saw Jeffrey Katzenberg at the *Star Wars* premiere in Los Angeles and he is short."

On a more serious note, ABC's Stu Bloomberg stresses the network's "reach," and he says he is thrilled to state that for the first time in two years "ABC now reaches more viewers per week than any other network."

Jamie Tarses emphasizes that the network is finally operating from a position of stability, with only six new programs on the fall schedule—the fewest new series ABC has had on a fall schedule in ten years. She starts off with Sunday night, which allows her to quickly sing the praises of the man who seems like the biggest star in TV, David E. Kelley, whose ABC show *The Practice* continues to grow into a critical and ratings hit.

"I don't know what is left to say about the remarkable talent of David Kelley, although every single word of praise is earned," she offers effusively. "It seems everything he touches turns to gold so we've asked him to lay his hands on Sundays at nine. What better lead-in for David Kelley than David Kelley? *Snoops* is best described as the private detective show for the new millennium. David has twisted this traditional genre as only he can."

The clip begins as a deep-voiced narrator declares, "He's raised the bar for lawyers on television. He's also raised their skirts. What will David do next?"

Interestingly with all this intense name-of-David-dropping, Rob Thomas's name doesn't come up. That's odd, since it is Thomas who's expected to be running the program on a day-to-day basis. Thomas is here, and he's not surprised. "To me that would be the last thing they'd want to say: 'Hired to run David's show is the executive producer of last year's failed show *Cupid*.'"

Low-key though his attendance is, Thomas feels appreciated. "Last year the *Cupid* people were in the Hilton, which in New York is sort of a glorified Motel Six," he says. "This year I'm in the Four Season with the best seats for everything." Those who do spot Thomas offer him congratulations for a *Snoops* pilot he has precious little to do with. Of course, not everyone's offering congratulations. In *New York* magazine Nikki Finke writes that the show "looks like *Charlie's Angels* as Pentium chippies."

Thomas says he is still not having as much contact with Kelley as he feels he needs, "but probably as much as I expect. David's a really busy guy and I'm prepared for that."

Right now Thomas also needs a new home. That house in the hills he was supposed to buy back in April never closed because of multiple liens against the property. His old house is already sold. Unless Thomas hurries, he could become one of the best-paid homeless people in America. (In July, it's announced that Thomas will leave *Snoops*.)

Finding a lovely abode on the ABC schedule is *It's like, you know . . .* , a cozy Tuesday time slot nestled between *Spin City* and *Dharma & Greg*.

Peter Mehlman, like Ted Harbert, is here and finding the pickup thrilling. "I was kinda shocked by how exhilarated and euphoric I felt," he admits. "It was almost physical. We did the shows in a vacuum," he explains later. "Everybody on the show—the actors and I feel incredibly validated."

In addition to hanging with the cast members until around midnight at the post–ABC upfront bash, Mehlman spoke with a lot of the top brass. He says he had "a somewhat brief but really kind of nice conversation with Jamie. That was pretty gratifying because we've been in the getting-to-know-ya process for a long time."

The night before the ABC upfront, Mehlman had a wonderful dinner with an older friend, his former boss Jerry Seinfeld. The pair spent much of the evening reminiscing. At one point Seinfeld suggested a writer Mehlman should hire; Mehlman insisted he wanted Seinfeld himself to take a job on *It's like, you know . . .* even offering him a retroactive cocreator credit. Though Seinfeld declined, it was a great night. "There I was focused on the past," he says, "and the next night I'm right into the present and hopefully the future."

*DAVID WILD*

Part of what has moved Mehlman this week is the realization there really is life after *Seinfeld*. "It is nice to know," he says. "And to tell you the truth, this is probably the first week I'm really convinced of it." Mehlman is also supportive of Ted Harbert whether he chooses to leave or stay. "Whatever's best for him," Mehlman says. "I'm a rugged individualist, except for the rugged part."

*The Norm Show* also gets picked up, though the name will be changed to *Norm* because of a legal issue with a cable show called *The Norm*. Helford receives the news on a ship-to-shore phone call.

When Tarses gets to Wednesday nights, she says, "At eight-thirty, Don Ohlmeyer's loss has been our gain." She touts the show's strong ratings, then praises "the incredible talents of *Saturday Night Live* alum Norm Macdonald and Emmy award–winning actress Laurie Metcalf in a truly hysterical half-hour of television." At nine o'clock, she says, "God bless 'im, *Drew Carey* is back." Tarses notes that the success of both *Drew Carey* and *Norm* is due not only to the comedic skills of their stars, but also to "a true collaboration with the man who's created both these shows, producer Bruce Helford. Bruce has a knack for taking personalities just left of center and making them accessible, relatable, and most important of all, funny."

The praise is almost warm enough to make one forget that both shows will be on a night that begins with *Two Guys, a Girl & a Pizza Place*, though the buzz is the *Pizza Place* part may be cut.

"Your husband's gonna do great, plus he's number one."

Backstage at Carnegie Hall, minutes before CBS's upfront presentation begins, *Everybody Loves Raymond*'s Phil Rosenthal assures Les Moonves's wife she has no reason to worry. As befits an event taking place in historic Carnegie Hall, this is a big show, and already there's been practice, practice, practice.

This is a production in its own right, Rosenthal explains, and there are many factors to be considered: the graphics that come up on the big screen, the sound, the music, the clips to be shown from each series. "It all has to be integrated," Rosenthal says. "There are comedians who come out and do bits, and with Les we want to have ad libs that sound off-the-cuff. We want to make his tone conversational so that he's not just some suit up there going, 'We're up 42 percent in demographics.' That's boring. The advertisers who come to these are one of the more jaded audiences you'll ever play to."

Just last Friday, Rosenthal finished editing the season's final *Raymond*. After taking a few days off with his wife's family in Pennsylvania, he came to Manhattan to help Moonves out. By early June, Rosenthal is planning to be back to work on *Raymond*. This tight schedule means he won't have the time to rush across town to see how things are going at P. J. Bernstein's, the deli on the East Side he once ran. "No," he says. "But tell me how the pastrami is."

Though there was never any doubt about whether *Raymond* would return in the fall, this upfront job offers its own sort of pressure for Rosenthal. "They bring me in every year to do this and I'm happy to do it," he says. "I feel so lucky to have my job and my show. This is a little payback I can give them." Rosenthal explains that Moonves has a professional speechwriter who structures his speech and ensures that all the pertinent information from research is included. "My job—in conjunction with some of the other people who work at CBS—is to humanize it," he says.

One of Rosenthal's biggest messages to Les Moonves is that less is more. "This will be under two hours. If I do one job, it's to get them to cut."

The presentation hits an early high when Joseph D. Abruzzese, CBS Television's president of sales, introduces "a very special exclusive preview." The lights dim and what appears to be the new *Star Wars* movie fills the screen, only there's a curious new name in the title:

### LES MOONWALKER—

The parody—timely, since this is the film's opening day—blends actual clips and hysterical newly shot footage. The film shows Moonves as Les Moonwalker, our hero who has defeated the masters of the Dark Side, represented by the likes of Darth Littlefield and E Roth D2. There are sly references to an evil Emperor Murdoch, Sassa the Hut, and a Princess Tarses.

Yoda tells Moonwalker, "It is not just demos, but households you must seek."

MOONWALKER: What makes you so wise?
YODA: I am one thousand years old
MOONWALKER: Oh, a *Diagnosis Murder* fan.

Moonves comes out strong and unforgiving. "Today is indeed a celebration for CBS, a very different upfront," he says. "When we first booked this hall several years ago, it was because we needed a place where our presentation to you would at least sound good."

He recalls NBC's promises that *Frasier* would equal *Seinfeld*'s numbers and that fast-fading shows like *Encore! Encore!* and *Wind on the Water* would be must-see TV. Later, during new CBS Entertainment president Nancy Tellem's presentation, the provocative phrase "must flee TV" appears onscreen to a mix of laughs and groans.

"With one week left," Moonves says. "We can now officially declare that CBS has won the 1998–1999 season." This statement, while true when it comes to households, sounds significantly better than saying, "We're down 7 percent in total viewers, 9 percent in viewers eighteen to forty-nine."

Ray Romano is introduced as "Les's special friend."

"For those of you who don't know TV talk," Romano explains from the stage, "that means I win my time slot."

"Just about everyone thought we were crazy to put *Everybody Loves Raymond* up against *Ally McBeal* and *Monday Night Football*, including *Raymond*," Moonves tells the audience. "Well, *Everybody Loves Raymond* is now the top-rated series on Monday night and I truly believe this show is TV's best comedy." Of course, it's not just Moonves who loves Raymond either; the show has now been sold in syndication for more than $3 million per episode.

The CBS presentation runs smoothly, though things take a turn for the surreal when returning *Chicago Hope* star Mandy Patinkin breaks into a bizarre comic riff in which he ends up stripping to his boxers and requesting stool samples from the audience.

Far sharper is the turn by CBS's new host of *The Late, Late Show* Craig Kilborn, who gets a big laugh with his pants on. "You may be the sexiest group of media and advertising executives I've ever seen," he tells them. "I've never seen so many different shades of gray suits." Kilborn thanks Tellem and "The King," Les Moonves. "They've been very supportive and I'll never forget the first time they came down and watched the show," Kilborn tells the crowd dryly. "They were stunned by what they saw— not the comedy, they have never seen an audience of eighteen to thirty-four men before."

Afterward, buses line up outside Carnegie Hall to transport the audiences through the pouring rain to CBS's big party at Tavern on the Green in Central Park. The party quickly becomes jammed as a steady stream of attendees moves inside for shelter and, of course, free shrimp.

On the way out, a few partygoers can be heard discussing the unusually high number of shows returning next fall, a surprising outcome for a season with relatively few outright new hits.

"People don't know the bottom anymore," one TV industry veteran explains. "They prefer the devil they know with a twelve share to the devil they don't know with an eight share."

To its credit—assuming it has any credit left—nobody at UPN suggests it is number one during its event inside the Manhattan Center Studio on Thursday morning. The network has ended its season with a 31 percent decline in both total viewers and the key demos— a nauseating drop from an already nonstratospheric height.

The network's top men Dean Valentine and Tom Nunan put the best face possible on the situation during a pre-upfront press briefing.

*Dilbert* and *Seven Days* remain two of the brighter spots in a season of blinding darkness. The pair end the season tied for 135th place among all shows, UPN's best showings besides *Star Trek: Voyager*.

Still, the executives stress that while they see *Seven Days* as being on "an uptrend," they still have ideas about how to improve the show for its sophomore year. They want to see more comedy, less apocalyptic plotlines, and hipper music. Afterward, Valentine calls Crowe "a good friend and a really cool guy." He adds that the showrunner is "just a terrific writer." Valentine then offers what must now be the ultimate UPN compliment: "He really knows how to write for guys."

That quality makes Crowe ever more valuable now that UPN is dedicating itself to the "guy-friendly programming" niche. The key to this new direction is the network's addition of *WWF Smackdown!,* a weekly presentation of professional wrestling. If you can barely beat cable, the thinking appears to go, why not co-opt its leading franchise?

Not on the UPN fall schedule is *Smog*, the pilot that Larry Charles collaborated on with Jon Favreau. "Nobody called me," Charles says a week later. "Actually yesterday was the first time somebody called me from UPN to tell me what I already knew—that it wasn't picked up." There's been some mumbling about *Smog* having a shot at midseason, but Charles isn't waiting by the phone.

The buzz is that the *Smog* pilot was smart, accomplished, and original, and that it's been developed for absolutely the wrong network. "Yeah, I think if you look at the UPN schedule it's clear there was no place for it," Charles admits. "What do you put it between, *Star Trek* and wrestling?"

Technically, UPN has a few months to decide whether to do anything with the pilot. "The network that commissioned the pilot basically has the rights to it until it's dead," Charles explains. "No one wants to be in the position they were in a few years ago when *3rd Rock from the Sun* went from ABC to NBC and became a hit. Nobody wants to look like an idiot, so they'd rather smother a show than let it live somewhere else."

Instead, UPN will offer something called *Shasta McNasty*—a title with a certain *Desmond Pfeiffer*–like ring to it, not to mention the network return of TV's Urkel, Jaleel White from *Family Matters,* in *Grown Ups.*

"There's tremendous madness as these networks get close to picking those fall schedules," Charles says. "There's some sort of fever that takes over like a virus. It would be a good David Cronenberg movie called *The Upfronts.* Even the semantics of their claims are funny. One network says, 'We're the number one network.' The other says, 'We're the most watched network.' That's a very Clinton-esque distinction."

Speaking of presidents, Fox's still relatively new one, Doug Herzog, meets the press this same morning at the Millennium hotel. Beforehand, Herzog explains that he stays in touch with his old Comedy Central charges, *South Park*'s Trey Parker and Matt Stone. He spoke with them in the past few weeks, and he is unmoved by talk of their show declining. "It's still the biggest series in cable," he says. "It's still a huge, huge hit."

Herzog would gladly accept some new huge hits of his own for Fox, though the network actually ended the season up 1 percent in total viewers, and stayed even in the key demo. "For the second year, Fox was the number two network for adults eighteen to forty-nine," Herzog tells the media crowd. "For the first time we were number one with adults eighteen to thirty-four. For the first time we were number one with men eighteen to forty-nine, and for the first time we were number one with men twenty-five to fifty-four. For the first time we were number one with women eighteen to fifty-four, tied with NBC." He proclaims that Fox has "the most distinctive brand in network television."

The first series Herzog speaks of is *Time of Your Life*, which he has given the hour preceding *Ally McBeal* on Mondays. Herzog calls Hewitt "America's It Girl" and expresses his belief that the spin-off can take the *Party of Five* base to a new level. After showing a highlight clip—one that ends with Hewitt screaming "I love you, New York"—Herzog speaks of *Ally McBeal*, calling it "maybe the best show on television, period," and judges the combination of Hewitt and *Ally McBeal* "very promotable. We get to talk about, arguably, two of the biggest stars in television in Calista [Flockhart] and Jennifer."

Next Herzog explains a move already making news in the morning paper. Fox will offer a second weekly dose of *Ally McBeal* on Tuesdays, a half-hour version of an earlier hour episode, called *Ally*, with previously unused footage mixed in. "A disco remix," the executive calls this unusual idea for a show. Herzog confides that when he got an urgent car phone call from Kelley's agent saying Kelley wanted a half-hour *Ally McBeal*, he was horrified at the thought of losing thirty minutes of such a key show. Then he realized Kelley was offering an extra half-hour, and all was well.

The media challenges Herzog about the soundness of the move. He reminds them of the WB's successful experiment with double servings of *7th Heaven* and suggests, like it or not, a change is gonna come.

"I came over from cable, and this is a really tough business," Herzog says. "We're the only guys out there that are showing things once a week. There's only four or five of us that are doing it. The rest of the world is running *South Park* all week, and wrestling all week, and their original movies over and over all week. That's the way America watches television now. Let's get used to it. We're no longer in charge anymore—the viewer is in control. At the end of the day, I can stand up here and talk about all these great creative things we're doing—we've got to make some money, guys."

The Salingers on *Party of Five*, meanwhile, are moving to Tuesday nights, which means they will be sharing their evenings with *Ally*. Herzog explains that the network is expecting *Party of Five* to be a slightly more intimate affair next season, with the family spending more time together.

Herzog speaks of other promising series including *Get Real*. The pilot for the dramedy—with two *My So-Called Life* references and a *South Park* homage—has been wonderfully directed by former *Cupid* boss Scott Winant, who also served as an executive producer, along with series creator Clyde Phillips. However, just days before the upfronts, Winant discovered he won't be part of the team trying to make good on the show's promise. Creative and personal differences with Phillips have proved insurmountable. "I am graciously bowing out so that Clyde can, well, clobber it in the way he wants to. It's one of those 'Life's too short' scenarios," says Winant. "Now I'm thinking of opening a gift basket business for other showrunners," jokes Winant, who also saw *Anna Says* not get picked up by ABC. In fact, the calls are already coming from others seeking his showrunning help, including his old *thirtysomething* pals who've made the ABC schedule with *Once and Again* and the team at *Felicity*.

Later in the day, Herzog's presentation is repeated on a grander scale at Fox's upfront presentation at the Beacon Theater. These are, as Fox's David Hill declares, "the final moments of the 1999 upfront hostage crisis." Hill introduces "the lovely and talented Herzog," who finds the advertisers somewhat less receptive to his self-deprecating humor than the media this morning. "This is a very tough room, by the way," he jokes at one point. "I don't even hear my staff laughing."

Still, Fox offers a star-studded show. For the opening number, a stage full of network stars including Jennifer Love Hewitt and Calista Flockhart—form a circle on the Beacon stage, while Jennifer Holliday sings "And I Am Telling You I'm Not Going" a diva-esque declaration of network intent to live long and prosper.

The after-party takes place inside a tent at Lincoln Center with the festivities overflowing outside, where Jennifer Love Hewitt and the cast of *Ally McBeal* pose with advertisers. Between shots, Love explains that she heard about the time slot while in her hotel room in New York. "I'm thrilled," she says convincingly.

Amy Lippman is not feeling well, and didn't make the trip East— thus missing what she has dubbed "the big shrimp-fest," but Christopher Keyser is here. He was sitting having lunch with his two kids when Doug Herzog called—having conferenced in Lippman—and gave the pair the good word about *Time of Your Life*. They had gotten the time slot they coveted—a sweet victory, though in the weeks to come it gradually is decided that the pilot will be reworked substantially to make it more *Ally*-ready and perhaps a bit less Dickensian.

*DAVID WILD*

As for the fate of *Partners*—which didn't turn up on the CBS fall schedule—Keyser says only, "I'll keep my fingers crossed. We were disappointed that it wasn't on for the fall. No one has said a word to us one way or the other. We're just sitting and waiting. The CBS decision was obviously disappointing, but we're not giving up hope." By month's end, the show's future remains unclear. Still, Keyser and Lippman understand that having two out of three shows on the air ain't bad. In fact, creating anything from thin air—one fair definition of the creative process—is pretty damn good.

As the last upfront party of the twentieth century hits its peak, Buddy Hackett—the self-proclaimed oldest man in prime time as a regular on a new Hollywood satire called *Action*—sits in the VIP area, taking in the scene. "I am having the time of my life with all these young people," he says. "I feel like a young man again just hanging around. And I'm looking at all these young beautiful girls with breasts that are trying to puncture their dress, with asses that are so firm you'd think they were sealed in cement. And if my wife is lucky she will reap the benefits."

A few yards away, Jennifer Love Hewitt hits the dance floor with a member of the *That '70s Show* cast. The DJ blasts "September," a classic Earth, Wind & Fire tune.

> *Love was changing the mind's pretenders*
> *While chasing the clouds away*

To the dancers' right, a middle-aged ad man grabs a few last free shrimp.

> *Our hearts were ringing*
> *In the key that our souls were singing*
> *As we danced in the night*
> *Remember how the stars stole the night away*

Love smiles, and her star power appears to draw a bigger, young crowd to the dance floor.

> *Ba de ya—say, do you remember?*
> *Ba de ya—dancing in September*
> *Ba de ya—never was a cloudy day*

This is what becomes of the winners in the prime-time game each May—they dance the night away, at least until September.

A year ago today Phil Hartman was killed.

This evening Paul Simms is at the beach, explaining what it was like when he got word that *NewsRadio* was over. The main emotion that hit him was the dread of having to call the cast and others who worked on the show to tell them the show wasn't coming back. Simms had pretty much settled things in his mind. In some ways, the cancellation order brought a sense of relief. "It's like knowing someone with a terminal illness," Simms explains. "You don't want them to die, but you know it's coming. When it comes, you're sad but at the same time a little relieved."

In this sense, every TV shows suffers from a terminal disease, with syndication acting as a tubular equivalent of cryogenic preservation.

"That's true," Simms says. "Except *60 Minutes*."

The cast members, he reports, were all saddened, although they too had seen this coming. Simms is uncertain what big lessons he has learned from all he has been through, though it seems a safe bet they weren't ones taught even at Harvard.

"That's going to take me another five years to figure out," he says.

Does Simms intend to spend those five years on the beach?

"At the beach," he says without committing. "Maybe out of the country."

Overseas?

"Perhaps," he says. Simms does not sound bitter today, but philosophical. "As with almost everything, one out of ten network people are good," he says. "It's a matter of timing and luck whether you're around for the good ones."

*DAVID WILD*

Simms hasn't spoken to Scott Sassa about the cancellation, nor has he heard from Don Ohlmeyer since the *OverSeas* network run-through. It fell to Garth Ancier—whom Simms didn't know—to make the call.

"Garth called me up and said, 'Nice to meet you.' I said, 'Nice to meet you too.' Then the first thing he said was 'I just want to thank you for all the years of good work on the show.' I said, 'Does that mean it's canceled?'"

According to Simms, Andy Dick's recent accident had nothing to do with the show's demise. "Oy, no," Simms says, sounding pissed off and concerned at the same time. "Andy's accident happened two days later. And let's not call it an accident—that's a little too . . . gracious." If this was an accident, apparently it's one that has been waiting to happen.

With everything he's been through this season, Simms remains proud that the *NewsRadio* team somehow managed to work past the human tragedy that immediately preceded the season. "Definitely," he says without hesitating. "As hard as it was moving past the Phil stuff, I'm glad we did."

These days Simms is glad for a number of things—that *News-Radio* lives on in almost constant syndication, that there are nearly a hundred episodes still there to be enjoyed. He is also relieved that in a tough time for sitcoms, virtually everyone associated with the show is already gainfully employed elsewhere.

Basically, the only one unemployed is Paul Simms himself.

"Pretty much," he says. And Simms can afford it. "For now," he adds.

The next afternoon, Simms uses a little of his showrunner money to throw a last-minute Memorial Day weekend barbecue at his beach house. The local weather condition known as "June gloom" has arrived early, making for a mostly overcast day. Still, the sun peeks out a bit as a small crowd gathers at Simms's Spanish villa–style rental. He and his three dogs mingle warmly with friends, former colleagues, and their children. Kids from the neighborhood are glued to his Nintendo. "Yeah, today I have to share with some actual children," Simms says with a grin. Impressively, the trade papers on a table in the living room are more than a month old.

It is a lovely party. Sure, the pilot crashed, *NewsRadio* ended, and Andy Dick is rehabbing. On the other hand, the kids all look happy; the hamburgers and hot dogs smell delicious. Simms may be taking a seaside breather from the prime-time life after his longest, most death-defying season, but he's still here. That counts for something in a game where survival is one true measure of victory. For now Simms is busy. There are people—some of them even in the key demo—expecting to be fed and made welcome.

In the real world—even in Malibu—it turns out there are other things to be run besides TV shows.

DAVID WILD